MANAGING ELECTRONIC RECORDS

William Saffady

ARMA International

Lenexa, Kansas

Consulting Editor: Mary Lea Ginn, Ph.D.
Designer/Compositor: Rebecca Gray Design
Cover Art: Jason Vannatta

ARMA International
13725 West 109th Street, Suite 101
Lenexa, KS 66215
913.341.3808

ISBN: 1-931786-05-4

Printed in the United States of America.

TABLE OF CONTENTS

Introduction vii

CHAPTER ONE: Concepts and Issues 1
    Growth of Electronic Records 2
    Importance of Electronic Records 7
    Issues and Concerns 8
        Inadequate Controls 9
        Information Redundancy 10
        System Dependence 11
        Media Stability 12
        Transparent Arrangement 12
        Remote Access 12
        General Concerns 13
    Program Components 13
    Summary 16

CHAPTER TWO: Storage Media for Electronic Recordkeeping 19
    Magnetic Media 20
        Hard Disks 21
        Removable Hard Disks 23
        Floppy Disks 25
        Nine-Track Computer Tapes 28
        Half-Inch Data Cartridges 29
        Digital Linear Tape 31
        Linear Tape–Open Technology 31
        Quarter-Inch Cartridges 32
        Eight-Millimeter Data Cartridges 34
        Digital Audio Tape 36
        Other Computer Tape Formats 37
        Audio Tapes 37
        Video Tapes 39
        Obsolete Magnetic Media 42
    Optical Disks 43
        Magneto-Optical Disks 44
        Compact Disks 45
        DVD Media 46
        Obsolete Optical Disk Formats 48

Optical Cards and Tape 49
Paper-Based Electronic Media 50
Summary 51

CHAPTER THREE: File Formats for Electronic Records 53
Text Files 54
Coding Schemes 54
Word Processing Files 56
Formats for Compound Documents 57
ASCII Text Files 59
Spreadsheet Files 59
Databases 60
Image Files 61
File Compression 65
Video Recording Standards 67
Audio File Formats 68
Summary 70

CHAPTER FOUR: Inventorying Electronic Records 71
Inventory Strategy 72
Inventory Methodology 77
The Survey Instrument 79
Series Title 80
Summary Description 81
Copy Type(s) 81
File Type 81
Dates Covered 82
Arrangement 82
Quantity 83
Estimated Growth 83
Physical Storage Requirements 84
Storage Location(s) 85
Media Characteristics 85
Media Manufacturing Date 85
Hardware Environment 86
Software Environment 86
Reference Activity 87
Retention Requirements 88
Relationship to Human-Readable Records 88
Supporting Files 88
Vital Record Status 88
Inventory Follow-up 89
Summary 89

CHAPTER FIVE: Retention Schedules for Electronic Records 91
   Retention Concepts 93
      Retention Criteria 94
      Electronic Records as Official Copies 95
   Legally Mandated Retention Periods 96
   Legal Status of Document Images 101
   Admissibility into Evidence 103
   Legal Status of Electronic Signatures 110
   Administrative Retention Requirements 112
   Media Stability and System Dependence 115
   Summary 119

CHAPTER SIX: Managing Vital Electronic Records 121
   Establishing the Program 123
   Identifying Vital Records 127
   Risk Analysis 129
      Identifying Risks 130
      Qualitative Risk Assessment 131
      Quantitative Risk Assessment 132
   Risk Control 134
      Preventive Measures 135
      Protective Measures 139
      Auditing for Compliance 144
   Summary 144

CHAPTER SEVEN: Managing Files and Media 147
   Labels and Names 148
   Records Management Application (RMA) Software 153
   Media Filing Equipment 155
   Autochangers and Hierarchical Storage Management (HSM) 159
   Media Management 161
      Selecting Blank Media 162
      Storage Copies 165
      Media Handling 171
   Summary 173

APPENDIX A: Glossary 177
APPENDIX B: Suggestions for Further Study and Research 187
Index 189
About the Author 197
About ARMA International 198

INTRODUCTION

The amount and variety of recorded information created and maintained in electronic formats has increased dramatically over the past two decades, and significant continued growth can be expected. The amount of electronic information was growing in 1992, when the first edition of *Managing Electronic Records* was published, and it remains the case today. Given the already widespread and rapidly expanding use of computers, audio recorders, video systems, and other information-processing devices, the proliferation of electronic records can only intensify in the twenty-first century. Historically, records managers in government agencies, corporations, and other organizations have directed the majority of their professional efforts toward control of paper documents. Since the late 1980s, however, they have received growing pressure to address records management problems associated with electronically stored information. A number of organizations have initiated systematic programs for the storage, retrieval, and control of electronic records. Others can be expected to do so as the growing accumulation of such records demands active professional management. Many records managers view problems posed by electronic records as the most important challenge facing our profession.

The third edition of *Managing Electronic Records* provides a comprehensive discussion of records management concepts and methods as they apply to electronic records; that is, to records that contain machine-readable as opposed to human-readable information. This book is intended for professional records managers, computer systems professionals, office systems analysts, archivists, administrative system specialists, data center managers, librarians, and others responsible for the creation, maintenance, management, control, and use of electronic records created by computer, audio, and video systems. The treatment is practical rather than theoretical. On completion of the book, the reader should understand the following:

- Special records management issues and problems associated with electronic records;
- Physical and application characteristics of electronic records encountered in offices and other work environments;
- Principles and procedures for inventorying and scheduling electronic records;
- Factors that influence the stability and durability of electronic records;
- Methods of protecting vital electronic records against damage and destruction;
- Guidelines for the daily management of electronic records as working information resources.

Like its predecessors, this edition is organized into seven chapters. Chapter One defines electronic records and discusses their importance in present and future information systems, their relationship to conventional records, and special issues and concerns associated with their management. Chapter Two presents a detailed survey of the physical and application characteristics of electronic storage media employed by computer, audio, and video systems. It emphasizes magnetic and optical storage media but also includes descriptions of paper-based media. Obsolete media that may be encountered when inventorying electronic records are also covered. Chapter Three discusses file format concepts that records managers must understand in order to deal effectively with computer-processible information. It also includes a discussion of video recording formats. Chapters Four and Five address the critical issues of conducting inventories of electronic records and preparing retention schedules based on the inventories. Chapter Six discusses vital electronic records. Chapter Seven presents guidelines for the storage, care, handling, and labeling of electronic media.

Although terms and concepts are defined in the text, a glossary—located in Appendix A—summarizes important definitions in one location. Previous editions of this book provided listed books, articles, and other publications for additional reading on specific topics, but those bibliographies were necessarily incomplete and quickly became out of date. They have been omitted from this third edition. In their place, Appendix B provides suggestions for finding additional information about electronic records.

CHAPTER ONE

CONCEPTS AND ISSUES

As their defining characteristic, **electronic records** contain machine-readable, as opposed to human-readable, information. Electronic records may contain any type of information. The possibilities include, but are not necessarily limited to, quantitative data of the type contained in databases and spreadsheet files; character-coded text of the type contained in word processing files and electronic mail (e-mail) messages; images, including electronic document images as well as video images, and computer-generated graphics; and sound, including voice and music recordings. Regardless of content, the information contained in electronic records originates as an electronic signal, hence the name. Further, the information is electronically encoded for storage and processing by computers, video devices, audio equipment, or other machines described in this chapter. Coding methods vary. Electronic records created by computers and computer-like devices usually contain digitally coded information. **Digital coding** is a coding scheme that represents information by predetermined sequences of bits. Video and audio devices have historically relied on **analog coding** methods, although systems that record digitally encoded video images and audio signals are increasingly available and may ultimately supplant their analog counterparts.

> ### Sources of Electronic Records
> - Computers and computer-like devices
> - Scientific and medical instrumentation
> - Communications equipment
> - Video recorders
> - Audio recorders

Whatever coding scheme is employed, electronic records can only be read (retrieved) or otherwise processed by designated machines; for computer records, software is required as well. By contrast, office documents, engineering drawings, and other

1

paper records contain information that is human-readable; no special equipment or software is required to access such information. Microfilm records likewise contain human-readable information. Although microfilm images are highly miniaturized, their contents are not machine-encoded. Information contained in microfilm images may not be eye-legible, but it is nonetheless human-readable. Once magnified, decoding is not required for reading or printing microfilmed documents.

For purposes of this discussion, the ability to distinguish electronic records from human-readable paper documents or computer-output microfilm (COM) images that are generated from electronic sources is important. Thus, a business letter created with a word processing program and stored as a computer file is an electronic record; a printed copy of that letter is not. Similarly, a database that contains information about customer orders is an electronic record; a computer-generated list of customer orders printed on paper or microfiche is not. Electronic messages created or received with e-mail programs are electronic records; printed copies of those messages are not. Faxes are not considered electronic records unless they are stored electronically rather than printed on receipt.

Computers of all types and sizes are the best-known devices that create, store, and process electronic records, but such records may be produced and maintained by other machines as well. Examples include scientific and medical instruments employed in diagnostic imaging, petroleum engineering, remote sensing, and other applications; videotape machines and other video recording and playback devices; and voice dictation equipment, telephone answering machines, and other audio-tape recorders. Electronic records have also been generated by special-purpose business machines that no longer exist. Examples include the electromechanical accounting equipment that automated financial applications during the 1960s and early 1970s, dedicated word processors that were widely utilized in office applications from the late 1960s through the early 1980s, and TWX and telex terminals used through the 1980s for electronic message transmission. Although computer systems have rendered such devices obsolete, electronic records created by them in the past continue to be stored by many corporations, government agencies, and other organizations. Like their newer counterparts, such obsolete electronic records require records management attention.

As discussed more fully in Chapter Two, electronic records exist in a variety of physical formats. Magnetic disks and tapes have dominated computer, video, and audio recording since the 1950s. Optical media, which use lasers to record and retrieve information, were introduced in the 1980s. With their high recording densities, they are particularly useful for electronic document imaging, digital video recording, multimedia presentations, and other applications that involve large quantities of machine-readable information. Punched cards and punched paper tapes are the best-known examples of paper-based electronic records. They were utilized widely during the 1950s and 1960s by computer systems and certain pre-computer products such as tabulating machines; but they are now obsolete media. Occasional attempts to revive the use of paper for machine-readable information have not been successful. Microfilm, which provides compact, stable storage for human-readable document images and computer-generated reports, can also store machine-readable information, but it has never been widely accepted for that purpose. Other forms of electronic records, encountered principally in consumer rather than business applications, include vinyl phonograph records, which have been supplanted by newer technologies, and nonoptical video disks, which were marketed during the 1980s but are no longer available.

GROWTH OF ELECTRONIC RECORDS

Paper has been the most widely utilized recordkeeping media for centuries. In many, if not most, work environments, paper documents remain the dominant records format in quantity, if not in importance. Given the huge accumulations of older paper records in offices and off-site storage locations, decades will pass before electronic records outnumber them. In fact, the existence of electronic records contributes to the growth of paper files because much computer-processible information is printed for reference or filing. Word processing documents are typically printed, for example, as are many e-mail messages, Web pages, spreadsheets, and graphic images. Databases are designed for on-line access to information; however, some database applications generate printed reports or other documents.

Since the 1970s, however, computer, video, and audio records created and maintained by corporations, government agencies, and other organizations have increased dramatically in both quantity and importance. In some work environments, these electronic records outnumber paper documents for newly created information. Their business value has similarly increased. For most organizations, electronic records are indispensable information resources for daily operations, as well as for long-term planning and decision making.

The growing quantity of electronic records is largely attributable to the proliferation of information processing equipment and software capable of producing such records, especially with computer-generated records. Over the past three decades, the number of installed computers of all types and sizes has increased significantly. According to the *Computer Industry Almanac*, 625 million computers, from personal computers (PCs) to mainframes, were in use worldwide in late 2001. The United States, with an estimated 182 million computers, has the largest installed base, followed by Japan, Germany, the United Kingdom, France, China, and Canada, each of which have at least 17 million computers installed.

Although the impending demise of mainframe (enterprise-scale) computers has been predicted for more than a decade, a study by the Meta Group, cited in the October 31, 2000, issue of *Computerworld*, estimated that installed mainframe capacity increased by 19 percent in 2000. In recent years, mainframe sales have benefited from a combination of innovative technology, falling hardware prices, lower operating costs, compatibility with popular operating systems, improved networking functionality, and new recordkeeping applications, such as data warehousing and electronic commerce, that require mainframe-class processing power, reliability, and storage capacity. Further, mainframes remain the dominant computing devices for many financial and transaction processing applications, some of which date from the 1960s and 1970s. Rather than replacing these mainframe-based legacy programs, many Y2K initiatives repaired and enhanced them, thereby extending their life spans. Some industry analysts estimate that, in large corporations and government agencies, as much as 75 percent of mission-critical electronic information resides on mainframe computers.

In multinational corporations, federal and state government agencies, research universities, and other large organizations, mainframe computers have historically operated as centralized, enterprise-wide information processing resources. They are timeshared devices that serve the computing requirements of multiple departments or other organizational units, each running its own applications. Departmental access is typically obtained through on-line terminals (or desktop computers functioning as terminals) linked to a central computer site by wide area networks, local area networks, or other data communication arrangements. That centralized approach to computing dates from the inception of business data processing and was well established by the late 1960s.

During the 1970s, however, many mainframe users began complaining about the difficulties of dealing with seemingly unresponsive computer center personnel. They wanted more direct control over computer resources that became increasingly indispensable to their business operations. Responding to this need, hardware manufacturers introduced smaller computers for departmental installations. Such smaller devices, so-called minicomputers, had been utilized in specialized aerospace and industrial applications since the late 1950s. In the early 1970s, many organizations began using minicomputers to decentralize, or distribute, their computing resources and electronic records. Distributed processing concepts gained popularity quickly. According to a report by the Business Equipment Manufacturers Association cited in the April 1991 issue of *Appliance* magazine, U.S. minicomputer shipments increased from less than 17,000 units per year in the mid-1970s to more than 150,000 units per year by 1990.

Today, minicomputers, also known as *midrange processors,* are installed at millions of sites. As an example, the June 29, 2000, issue of *Computing* cited an installed base of over 650,000 systems for the IBM AS/400, a popular series of midrange computers. A report by International Data Corporation, cited in the March 26, 2001, issue of *Network World*, estimated annual shipments of IBM RS/6000 systems at 608,000 units. In many medium-size businesses, government agencies, schools, colleges, and other organizations, minicomputers are implemented as enterprise-wide information processing devices; in effect, they function as mainframes for organizations that cannot afford or do not need larger computers. In large corporations and government agencies, however, minicomputers and their associated electronic records are typically decentralized at the department or division level, where they serve multiple users connected by on-line terminals. In such cases, minicomputers supplement or complement, rather than replace, mainframe installations. They provide another layer of computing and electronic recordkeeping capability in closer physical and organizational proximity to end-users.

The introduction of business-oriented personal computers in the mid-1970s, and their rapid and dramatic refinement during the 1980s and 1990s, permitted a further decentralization of computing power at the office or desk level. As cited in the April 17, 2000, issue of *Newsweek*, annual shipments of personal computers in the United States increased from 9 million units in 1990 to 43 million units by 1999.

The *Computer Industry Almanac* estimates that 600 million personal computers were installed worldwide in 2001. Various industry sources estimate that world-wide shipments of personal computers now exceed 100 million units per year, including both office and home installations of desktop and notebook models. This estimate excludes personal digital assistants, Web-enabled cell phones, set-top boxes for televisions, and other computer-related information appliances.

Since the mid-1980s, local area networks of increasing size and complexity have been implemented in organizations of all types and sizes. More recently, the Internet has provided convenient wide area network linkages of unlimited geo-graphic span. According to the *Computer Industry Almanac*, the Internet had 400 million users worldwide in 2000. A study by Angus Reid Group, cited in the March 24, 2000, issue of *ACM TechNews*, forecasts that one billion people will be using the Internet by 2005. With the advent of client/server technology and concepts, a growing number of information processing applications have moved to networked personal computers and servers as an alternative to historically dominant time-shared installations of centralized mainframes and minicomputers. That approach to computer utilization is variously termed *downsizing* or, more optimistically, *right sizing* by its proponents. The May 1, 2000, issue of *VAR Business* estimated that four million Windows NT servers are installed worldwide. A study by International Data Corporation, cited in the January 2000 issue of *Appliance* magazine, predicted that annual shipments of PC-based servers will increase from 1.16 million units in 2001 to 1.52 million units by 2005.

Installations of data storage peripherals and media, which provide the space necessary to accommodate electronic records, have likewise increased dra-matically. The April 10, 2000, issue of *Business Week* estimates annual revenues for the computer storage industry at $34 billion. As cited in the February 28, 2000, issue of *Computer Reseller News*, TrendFocus, a market research firm that covers the computer storage industry, reported that annual shipments of hard disk drives approached 200 million units at the end of the twentieth century. A study by Forward Concepts cited in the March 20, 2000, issue of *Electronic Buyers News* pre-dicted that worldwide annual shipments of magnetic disk drives would increase from 228 million units in 2001 to 345 million units by 2004. Various studies con-firm that annual shipments of CD-ROM drives exceed 100 million units. As cited in the May 15, 2000, issue of *Computer Reseller News*, Freeman Associates reported that annual shipments of magnetic tape drives for midrange computers and net-work servers exceed four million units.

Comparably impressive increases can be cited for computer software and services that generate electronic records. Corporations, government agencies, and other organizations have purchased hundreds of millions of copies of word process-ing, spreadsheet, and database management software packages. The November 25, 1996, issue of *Business Week* estimated that Microsoft® Office, a popular suite of pro-grams for business applications, was installed on 20 million personal computers. Today, industry analysts estimate the installed base at closer to 150 million. A report by Kinetic Information, cited in the September 1, 1996, issue of *Reseller Management*, estimated that business installations of Lotus Notes, Microsoft Exchange, and other groupware programs would increase from 19 million users in 1994 to 78 million users in 1997. In 2000, Ferris Research estimated the worldwide installed base of Lotus Notes and Microsoft Exchange at 77 million and 45 million users, respectively. According to the March 21, 1996, issue of *Data Communications*, worldwide users of electronic mail increased from 420,000 in 1980 to 45 million in 1996. The March 4, 1996, issue of *Computer Reseller News* estimated that 91 million electronic mail addresses were associated with computers of all types and sizes. According to the January 31, 2000, issue of *Network World*, over 440 million corporate personnel and individuals worldwide use e-mail.

By confirming the dramatic proliferation of technology that generates computer-processible information, the statistics and projections previously cited support the business case for systematic management of electronic records, but, like many business statistics, they quantify the obvious. Anyone who works in a business, government agency, or other organization knows that computer technology is pervasive and essential. For example:

- In many organizations, computers outnumber employees; seeing personal computers installed in empty offices that were formerly occupied by retrenched or retired employees is not unusual.

- Most office documents are produced by word processing software; conventional typewriters, where they remain in use at all, are reserved for special tasks such as completing forms or addressing an envelope.

- Desktop publishing programs permit in-house production of newsletters and other highly formatted documents that formerly required professional typesetting and printing services.

- Accounting, payroll, and other financial applications have been computerized for decades; manual bookkeeping is limited to the smallest businesses.

- Four-function calculators are commonplace, but programmable scientific and business models have been supplanted by spreadsheet programs and software for statistical analysis.

- Significant information is extracted from paper records for entry into computer databases, while electronic document imaging systems, text retrieval programs, and document management software maintain computer-processible file copies.

- A substantial part of each workday is spent reading electronic mail.

- Web pages on corporate intranets are replacing printed forms and procedures manuals.

Similarly dramatic growth can be cited for installations of video equipment, audio recorders, scientific and medical instrumentation, and other machines that create electronic records. The availability, variety, and functionality of video recording devices, for example, have increased dramatically since the early 1980s. Corporations, government agencies, and other organizations increasingly use video technology to create visual records of building inspections, laboratory experiments, meetings and conferences, and other activities where full-motion images are required to capture valuable information or occurrences. Videotape recorders, particularly video cassette recorders, are commonly used information storage devices. Video cameras, once encountered only in sophisticated television studios, are compact, easy to operate, and inexpensive. Although the use of word processing software by managerial and professional employees, combined with reorganization of the administrative workforce, has decreased the use of voice dictation equipment, voice mail systems and telephone answering machines are widely installed in organizations of all types and sizes. In medical specialties, such as radiology, CT scanners, MRI devices, and other computer-controlled instruments that generate electronic records are increasingly replacing conventional diagnostic equipment and methods.

IMPORTANCE OF ELECTRONIC RECORDS

In addition to being numerous, electronic records are important information resources, principally because many of them support mission-critical business operations. Corporations, government agencies, and other organizations rely on computers and other electronic technologies to automate their most important activities and store their most valuable information. Since the 1960s, the most significant information has received the highest priority for automation as organizations seek timely transaction processing, retrieval speed, remote accessibility, and other advantages of automated systems. Reflecting the perceived importance of electronic records, most organizations devote far more personnel and economic resources to their creation and maintenance than they do to human-readable paper and microfilm records. Information technology departments are well staffed; file rooms, records centers, and microfilming operations are small by comparison, while office filing is usually done by administrative personnel who have many other responsibilities.

> ### Importance of Electronic Records
>
> - Support mission-critical operations
> - Rapidly increasing volume in most organizations
> - Often more complete than nonelectronic counterparts
> - May contain unique information unavailable elsewhere

Accounting, payroll, and related financial activities were among the first business operations to be automated. Financial records have been widely computerized for decades. Electronic recordkeeping systems are likewise widely implemented for order fulfillment, invoicing, purchasing, reviewing insurance claims, loan management, and other transaction processing applications. Personnel records, which contain information about an organization's human resources, are similarly computerized, as are inventory management and property records that contain information about physical assets. Electronic records are also widely utilized to store critical information associated with specific industries or business activities. Examples include experimental data maintained by research laboratories, student records maintained by schools and colleges, quality control records maintained by manufacturing facilities, medical records maintained by hospitals and clinics, and drawings, site plans, and other records pertaining to architectural and construction projects.

During the 1960s and 1970s, automated information systems often stored small amounts of data extracted from **source documents** for specific purposes such as the preparation of invoices or the posting of credits or debits to specific accounts. Rather than being rendered superfluous by such automated recordkeeping systems, source documents typically retained their utility for reference operations; in many cases, they contained information not included in automated records. As automated systems have proliferated and gained acceptance, however, the records they create and maintain are increasingly viewed as the most valuable and authoritative sources of information pertaining to particular operations or activities.

Computer-based electronic records often contain more complete information and provide greater functionality than printed copies produced from them. Computer printouts provide a necessarily static and limited view of database records; on-line examination of the database may provide additional or more up-to-date information as well as more flexible retrieval functionality. Word processing files may include drafts, back-up copies, or alternate versions of documents that are never printed; in some applications, such as the preparation of legal contracts, printed documents may be assembled from prewritten paragraphs stored in multiple word processing files.

Information extracted from source documents is subject to calculations or other computer processing that generates new content for inclusion into databases, spreadsheet files, or other electronic records. With the proliferation of on-line information systems and centralized databases that can be accessed from desktop workstations, electronic records increasingly contain unique information that is captured in machine-readable form at its source. Such information may never have existed in paper form, and much of it will never be printed. Web pages, for example, may contain information extracted from paper documents, but their distinctive formats have no printed counterparts. **Electronic data interchange (EDI)** and other electronic commerce initiatives minimize paper records by transmitting computer-processible purchase orders, invoices, and other transaction-oriented information between organizations. Some scientists record results, observations, and other information pertaining to experimental research in electronic laboratory notebooks. Such research increasingly relies on machine-readable data generated by scientific or medical instruments. With video recordings, individual visual images can be printed, but the resulting paper copies are often inadequate substitutes for information contained in full-motion recordings. Many voice recordings will never be transcribed due to time and labor constraints; where audio recordings contain nonverbal information, such as music, transcription is impossible.

ISSUES AND CONCERNS

As outlined in the preceding section, electronic records—and the technologies that create and maintain them—are increasingly numerous and important information resources in corporations, government agencies, and other organizations. Although they are designed to address one or more problems encountered in specific information processing applications, electronic records can themselves pose problems that complicate their effective management. These problems are surveyed briefly in this section and examined more fully in subsequent chapters. They are not new to this book; the issues and concerns discussed here are widely acknowledged by records managers, as well as by computer systems analysts, office automation specialists, archivists, and others responsible for processing, storing, retrieving, safeguarding, or otherwise dealing with electronic records. In particular, significant differences between electronic and nonelectronic records necessitate the modification of certain well-established records management methodologies, many of which were developed for paper-based recordkeeping systems prior to the widespread implementation of computers and other electronic technologies.

Inadequate Controls

Through the mid-1970s, direct access to information processing technology was limited to a relatively small percentage of most organizations' employees. Many computer applications were implemented in the batch-processing mode, and their operation was closely monitored by well-staffed data processing centers that assumed full responsibility for program implementation and execution. Computer software was usually custom-developed for specific applications by in-house personnel or contract programmers; a laborious process that greatly increased the implementation time for computer applications and limited the progress of automation. Prewritten software and tools for rapid application development were seldom encountered before the 1980s. Prior to that time, few employees had direct interaction with computing devices.

Timesharing was possible in the 1960s, but on-line terminals were not widely installed in corporations, government agencies, or other organizations. Through the late 1970s, the low capacities of hard drives limited on-line access to small quantities of essential information. Data communication occurred at such low speeds that remote data entry, interactive information retrieval, file exchanges, and other communication-intensive operations took impracticably long amounts of time to complete. Desktop computers had not been developed. Electronic mail systems and local area networks were limited to experimental prototypes. Word processing relied on typewriter-like devices that were cumbersome and expensive. Document scanners, optical disk drives, and other components of desktop publishing and electronic document imaging systems did not exist. With the exception of voice dictation equipment, audio and video recording devices were largely relegated to professional applications in studio installations.

Problems of Electronic Records

- Inadequate controls over creation and maintenance
- Redundancy of information in electronic and nonelectronic formats
- Dependence on specific hardware and/or software for utility
- Transparent arrangement within given storage medium
- Remote access complicates security
- General records management concerns:
  - Storage space
  - Vulnerability to damage or loss
  - Organization for effective retrieval

Today, computers and other information processing machines are considered indispensable, productivity-enhancing tools to be made available to the broadest spectrum of the work force. Many employees have direct, hands-on involvement with information processing hardware and software, but few organizations have implemented formalized controls for the creation, storage, retention, and other management of electronic records associated with such devices. Desktop computers are commonplace, but detailed operational guidelines for creation, storage, retention, organization, and protection of electronic records are rare. Individual users typically determine the types of electronic recording media to be employed in specific situations, the names to be used for computer files, back-up procedures to be implemented for valuable information, criteria and methods for deleting obsolete records, and other routinely encountered aspects of creating and maintaining electronic records. In the absence of formalized procedures, end-user computing operations are often performed in a highly discretionary manner. Many computer users view the electronic records they create and maintain as "personal" files to be stored, discarded, or otherwise managed as they see fit, without regard to broader organizational needs or the relationship of electronic records to reports or other paper documents produced from them.

Information Redundancy

A comparison of the electronic and nonelectronic records maintained by a given organization typically reveals considerable redundancy of information in machine-readable and human-readable formats. Many paper documents are produced by word processing software, database management systems, and other computer programs. A substantial percentage of microforms likewise consist of computer-output microfilm (COM) or microfiche produced from machine-readable data sources. Such paper and microform records are created from computer-stored information, which they partially or fully replicate.

In a word processing installation, for example, a managerial or professional employee may use voice dictation equipment to create an audio recording of a document for subsequent transcription. An administrative employee, using a word processing program, creates a machine-readable version of the document, which is stored in a computer file on a hard drive or some other medium. A paper copy may then be printed for review and markup by the document's originator. If revisions are required, the word processing file is retrieved and edited. The new electronic version may replace the old one; alternatively, it may be stored as a separate computer file, thus permitting a return to the original version at a later time if required. In any case, the revised document will be printed for review and possible further changes. This cycle of revision, recording, and printing is repeated until a satisfactory final version is obtained, at which time the document will exist in multiple versions of varying content and completeness: an audio recording, one or more computer files, and one or more printed copies. As additional complications, back-up copies may also be produced of the various computer files, and one or more printed copies may subsequently be photocopied, microfilmed, or even scanned.

In some circumstances, such redundancy is both necessary and useful. Different versions of electronic documents and their paper counterparts may need to be retained until the final versions are prepared. The various versions reflect the developmental history of a document. Redundant recordkeeping poses both obvious and subtle problems for information management, however. The former include the increased space consumption—file cabinet and floor space for human-readable records and media space for electronic records—associated with duplicate information; the difficulty of controlling multiple human-readable and electronic versions of information and of identifying the version required for a given purpose; and the need to establish and coordinate retention periods for all versions. Other implications of records redundancy are easily overlooked but no less significant. In many countries, for example, electronic records—like their paper and microfilm counterparts—are routinely subject to discovery actions associated with court trials and other legal proceedings. Such discovery actions give the opposing party in a legal action the opportunity to inspect documents or other information pertinent to a given matter. If a business, government agency, or other organization possesses the information in question, it must disclose it. An organization may take great pains to discard specific paper and microfilm records in a timely manner to reduce its vulnerability to discovery actions, only to have the undiscarded electronic counterparts of those records—word processing versions of documents, for example—be subject to subpoena.

System Dependence

Electronic records contain machine-readable, digitally or analog-encoded information derived from electronic signals. As described in Chapter Two, such machine-readable information is represented by microscopic alterations in the physical or chemical characteristics of magnetic or optical storage media, which are the visible carriers of electronic records. The electronic records themselves are invisible. As a significant complication, electronic storage media and the information they contain are designed to be recorded and read by specific devices and software. Database records on magnetic tape, for example, must be processed by designated application programs that run under specific operating systems on compatible computers equipped with an appropriate magnetic tape drive. Video and audio recordings are similarly intended for playback by specific devices.

Given this dependent relationship, electronic records cannot be properly understood or evaluated without a thorough knowledge of their associated hardware/software environments. To manage electronic records effectively, records managers must understand the characteristics and capabilities of systems that create and store machine-readable information. Some records managers will consequently require additional training, particularly training in computer-based information processing, which may be obtained through formal courses of study or individual reading. As an additional, potentially significant complication, the future utility of electronic records is dependent on the continued availability of compatible hardware and software. The continued utility of electronic records is obviously imperiled by technological advances, which promote product obsolescence and discontinuations.

Media Stability

In many records management applications, the useful life of paper and photographic media equals or exceeds the retention periods for information that such media contain. When processed and stored in a manner specified in American National Standards, silver gelatin microfilm will retain its original information-bearing characteristics for centuries; diazo, vesicular, and thermally processed silver microfilms will remain stable for at least 100 years when stored in controlled environments. American National Standards similarly define the characteristics of permanent papers.

With exceptions noted in Chapter Five, the useful lives of magnetic and optical media that store electronic records are much shorter than those of paper and photographic films. In many cases, the stable life spans of electronic media are shorter than the retention periods for information recorded on such media. Electronic records must consequently be recopied, or migrated, onto new media at predetermined intervals to extend their lives for the designated term. This periodic recopying requirement, which has no counterpart in nonelectronic recordkeeping systems, complicates the management of electronic records and may prove impractical or impossible to implement in specific situations. Where electronic records must be retained for long periods of time, periodic recopying involves a future commitment of labor and economic resources of uncertain availability.

Transparent Arrangement

In paper filing systems, folders, documents, and other filing units are typically arranged in alphabetic, numeric, or other sequences that can be determined—though not necessarily understood fully—when the records are inventoried or otherwise inspected. Often, an examination of physical file arrangements provides information about the ways in which paper records are referenced or otherwise processed. By contrast, the physical arrangement of electronic records within a given magnetic or optical storage medium may be transparent to users. With magnetic and optical disks, for example, related information is not necessarily stored in contiguous sectors or tracks. Instead, the computer's operating system manages available storage resources, allocating space to specific information on an as-available basis. Unrelated records may consequently be intermixed within sectors of a magnetic or optical disk. Related information may be spread across several platters within a given hard drive, with access provided by directories that contain pointers to the physical locations of specific records. When inventorying electronic records, relating specific data files to their physical storage locations is consequently difficult or impossible. This intermixing of records can pose problems when defining retention periods, purging electronic records, or removing specific media for off-line storage.

Remote Access

To access paper or microfilm records, users typically go to the filing areas or other physical locations where the desired records are kept. Such records are customarily removed from their cabinets or other storage containers for reference; depending on application requirements, they may be taken to another work area for varying periods of time. In networked computer installations, by contrast, electronic records may be accessed from remote workstations and are never physically removed from their original repositories. Such records may be stored at considerable physical distances from prospective users, who never see the physical media on which electronic records are stored and may not be aware of the type of media employed. Although some computer storage media are removable from their drives and may be carried, shelved, mailed, or otherwise handled by users in the manner of paper files, others, such as hard drives, are not meant to be handled as physical objects. Remote access to computer-stored records is a significant functional advantage in many applications, but it also poses significant security problems, including the possibility of intrusion and contamination by computer viruses.

General Concerns

Certain widely recognized records management concerns are equally applicable to electronic and nonelectronic records. The proliferation of electronic records, for example, requires increasing quantities of storage equipment and media. Storage space, regardless of record type, is not an infinitely available resource. Unfortunately, some computer system managers and other information specialists trivialize this issue. They contend that storage requirements for voluminous electronic records can be easily satisfied by purchasing additional storage devices and media at ever-declining prices. That view reflects the primitive nature of much current thinking about managing electronic records. Half a century ago, professional records management abandoned the acquisition of additional space as an effective solution for the growing volume of paper records, yet it is often suggested as a viable approach to the problem of storing large quantities of electronic records. Although the costs of electronic storage devices and media are declining, they are not negligible, particularly when the total cost of ownership, including the labor for data backup, data migration, and other maintenance operations, is considered. In any case, the availability of inexpensive storage technology does not eliminate concerns about electronic records retention. Even if sufficient space were available to accommodate an organization's electronic records indefinitely, retaining all of them would not necessarily be advisable. Space conservation is only one of the motives for timely destruction of obsolete information.

Among other general concerns, vital electronic records, like their paper counterparts, are vulnerable to damage or other loss. Magnetic and optical media must be stored and handled in a manner that will safeguard the valuable information they contain. Further, the mere availability of records in electronic form is no guarantee that required information will be conveniently accessible when needed. Electronic records, like their paper counterparts, must be organized for effective retrieval.

PROGRAM COMPONENTS

Most records management concepts and program components were originally developed for paper documents; however, they are equally applicable to electronic records. Records management is concerned with the systematic control of recorded information. Records management programs should have broad authority over all records, regardless of format or media type. Electronic records are one of three major types of records maintained by corporations, government agencies, and other organizations; the other two types are human-readable paper documents and photographic records, including microforms. In U.S. government agencies, the definition of *records* presented in 44 U.S. Code 3301 specifically includes "machine-readable materials, or other documentary materials, regardless of physical form or characteristics." The National Archives of Canada defines records in a virtually identical manner. In the United Kingdom, the Public Records Act of 1958 applies to records that convey information by any means. In Australia, digital data is considered a Commonwealth record under the Archives Act of 1983. Comparable definitions and authority statements have been adopted by other countries, by state and local governments, and by many corporations and other organizations.

Records managers should examine the policy statements or other foundation documents that define the scope of their programs to determine their authority and responsibilities with respect to electronic records. If the foundation documents do not explicitly extend records management authority to electronic records, they should be modified to do so. Such amendments should define *electronic records* broadly to encompass any machine-readable media, including audio and video recordings as well as the more obvious computer-processible media. As with paper and photographic records, an enterprise-wide records management program must assert its authority over, and responsibility for, all electronic media, regardless of their location within the organization. Electronic records created by personal computers should be specifically included.

Elements of an Electronic Records Management Program

- Systematic inventory of electronic records
- Preparation and implementation of retention schedules
- Identification and protection of vital records
- Selection of appropriate electronic media
- Implementation of proper storage, care, and handling procedures for electronic media

Like its counterpart for human-readable records, a formally established program for the systematic management of electronic records must provide comprehensive coverage of the *information life cycle* from creation through utilization, destruction, or permanent preservation of such records. Addressing and elaborating on the issues and concerns raised in the preceding sections, subsequent chapters describe and discuss various facets of this information life cycle as they apply to electronic records. The systematic management of electronic records begins with records creation and the selection of appropriate records storage media for specific information processing applications. Records managers must develop and implement specifications for the types and characteristics of media to be purchased and utilized for particular electronic records. Those specifications must provide application-oriented guidance based on such factors as the volume of records to be stored, their retention periods, and the nature and frequency of anticipated reference activity.

To develop guidelines for electronic records, records managers must know and understand the technical and application characteristics of available electronic storage media and the types of information such media contain. Records managers must be familiar with the storage capacities, recording capabilities, stability, and other characteristics of available magnetic and optical media. They must also understand the types and characteristics of files that contain electronic records, as well as the methodologies and formats used to create such files. Further, records managers must be able to communicate their requirements and concerns to computer systems specialists, computer network managers, and other information professionals.

The preparation of retention schedules has been a critical component of professional practice since the inception of records management as a specialized information management discipline. Retention schedules establish the essential infrastructure on which many other records management activities are based. They provide an indispensable, formalized foundation for the systematic preservation or destruction of specific electronic records, as well as the conversion of records from one format to another. Records management programs typically devote considerable professional resources to schedule preparation, and many well-established programs have prepared retention schedules for the majority of nonelectronic records maintained by their organizations. To be truly complete, however, such schedules must encompass electronic records.

The identification and protection of vital records is likewise a long-standing records management responsibility. Briefly defined, **vital records** contain information essential to an organization's mission. Many electronic records support mission-critical applications, and such records are properly considered vital records. Chapter Six surveys the principal components of a vital electronic records program. These components include a systematic approach to the identification and enumeration of vital records, the analysis of risks to which vital records are exposed, and the development and implementation of appropriate protection methods. In data processing applications, vital records protection is often regarded as one facet of the broader issue of computer security.

Records managers are often asked to design filing systems and select equipment and supplies to facilitate the organization and retrieval of paper documents associated with specific applications. With computer-stored files, the arrangement of records is typically controlled by application programs with which the records are associated; but records managers must develop procedures for file naming, directory organization, and media labeling. Proper care and handling procedures must likewise be implemented for storage and working copies of such removable media as magnetic tapes, diskettes, and optical disk cartridges. These topics are examined in Chapter Seven.

SUMMARY

Electronic records contain machine-readable information generated by computer systems, special-purpose instrumentation, video recorders, audio recorders, and other devices. Such records are commonly stored on magnetic disks, magnetic tapes, and optical disks, although other media have been utilized in the past. Since the 1960s, electronic records created and maintained by corporations, government agencies, and other organizations have increased in both number and importance. The increased quantity of electronic records is attributable to the dramatic proliferation of hardware and software capable of generating such records; their importance is derived from their role in mission-critical applications. In most organizations, mission-critical applications receive the highest priority for automation. Electronic records associated with such applications are increasingly viewed as the most valuable and authoritative sources of information pertaining to particular operations or activities. In many cases, they contain information that is not included in paper documents.

Although their numbers and importance are increasing, certain characteristics of electronic records complicate their effective management. Few organizations, for example, have implemented formalized controls for creation, storage, and retention of electronic records. Personal computer users, in particular, may view the electronic records they create as "personal" files to be managed in a discretionary manner. Because they often contain information extracted from source documents and are themselves used to produce paper or microfilm printouts, electronic records may replicate information contained in other formats. In addition to wasting storage space, such redundant recordkeeping can make controlling and identifying the versions of information appropriate to specific operations difficult. Redundancy also necessitates the coordination of retention periods for electronic records and their nonelectronic counterparts.

As a significant complication, electronic records are entirely dependent on specific hardware devices and/or software configurations for their continued utility. Product obsolescence and discontinuations consequently imperil the future utility of electronic records. In addition, the continued retrievability of electronic records may be affected by the relatively limited stability of magnetic and optical media. In centralized computer installations, electronic records are accessed by remote workstations. Remote access is unquestionably convenient; however, it poses potential security problems. Finally, certain general records management concerns pertaining to storage space consumption, vital records protection, and proper media handling pertain equally to electronic and nonelectronic records.

A formally established program for the systematic management of electronic records must provide comprehensive coverage of the information life cycle from creation through utilization, destruction, or permanent preservation. Records managers must be familiar with the formats, storage capacities, recording capabilities, stability, and other characteristics of electronic media. They must also understand the types and characteristic of files that contain electronic records. The preparation of retention schedules is a critical component in any systematic program to manage electronic records, as is the identification and protection of vital electronic records. Retention recommendations and vital records protection plans must be based on information obtained through a comprehensive inventory of electronic records. Among their other responsibilities, records managers must develop and implement procedures for the care and handling of both storage and working copies of electronic media. Guidelines are likewise required for file naming, directory organization, and media labeling.

CHAPTER TWO

STORAGE MEDIA FOR ELECTRONIC RECORDKEEPING

As noted in Chapter One, electronic records may be stored on magnetic or optical media. Magnetic recording has dominated computer storage technology since the 1950s. It is also the most widely utilized technology for video and audio recording. Magnetism, one of the earliest known physical phenomena, has been the subject of scientific investigation and practical experimentation since the sixteenth century. Audio recorders, which utilized steel wires and bands as recording media, were invented in the late nineteenth century. Magnetic tape recorders, developed in the 1930s, were widely available by the 1950s. Prototype videotape recorders were demonstrated in the early 1950s, and operational equipment was in use by the end of that decade. Magnetic disks and tapes for computer applications likewise date from the 1950s.

Optical storage products use light generated by lasers, to record and/or retrieve **machine-readable information**. As their principal advantage for electronic recordkeeping, optical storage products offer high recording density and correspondingly high media capacity. This characteristic is particularly important for storage-intensive records management applications such as electronic document imaging. Optical storage media also have longer life spans than their magnetic counterparts, but the resulting advantages for records retention are diminished by hardware dependencies. The earliest optical disk systems, designed for video recording, date from the late 1970s. Optical disks for computer and audio applications were introduced several years later. Optical tapes and optical memory cards have also been developed, but they are used much less often than optical disks.

To knowledgeably evaluate and recommend electronic recordkeeping practices, records managers must be familiar with the physical and functional characteristics of magnetic and optical media that store computer, video, and audio information. When inventorying or otherwise examining electronic records, they must be able to recognize various types of storage media and make informed decisions about their suitability for information processing operations, records retention, vital records protection, or other purposes. The following sections survey the most important magnetic and optical devices and media employed by corporations, government agencies, and other organizations. The discussion emphasizes characteristics, such as media capacities, that are most significant for records management. Other characteristics, such as the access times and data transfer rates supported by devices that read and record specific media, are omitted or summarized very briefly; those characteristics are more important for computer system administrators than for records managers.

The media characteristics described in the following sections reflect the state of the art in electronic information storage at the time of this writing. Readers are cautioned that some characteristics are likely to change in the future—storage capacities, in particular, are subject to continuing improvements—and that new media formats with different attributes may be developed. Although the following discussion emphasizes the latest models of magnetic and optical storage devices and media, older configurations and obsolete products are also covered. Records managers cannot ignore electronic technologies of the past because discontinued media are often encountered during inventories of electronic records.

MAGNETIC MEDIA

Magnetic storage media suitable for computer, audio, or video records consist of three physical components:

1. A recording material capable of being magnetized when placed in a magnetic field and of retaining magnetization when the field is removed;
2. A **substrate** or base material, such as an aluminum platter or piece of polyester film, on which the recording material is coated; and
3. A binder, which functions as a carrier for the recording material and bonds it to the substrate.

Broadly defined, a *magnet* is a metal that generates a magnetic field capable of attracting or repelling other metals. The ability to be attracted to or repelled by magnets is a property of all matter, but the magnetic susceptibility of most substances is too weak to have practical significance. Most organic compounds and many metals have weak magnetic susceptibility. The magnetic recording materials used in computer applications are characterized by strong, easily detectable magnetization, even in the absence of an external magnetic field.

With iron crystals, for example, atoms are aligned in microscopic regions called *domains*. When iron crystals are in an unmagnetized state, their domains are randomly arranged. To record information, an external magnetic field of sufficient strength selectively orients the domains toward a magnet's north or south pole where the attractive forces are strongest. To represent the one bits in digitally coded data, domains may be aligned toward the magnet's north pole; the zero bits are represented by aligning domains toward the magnet's south pole. With computer storage devices, the external magnetic field is generated by an electromagnet called a *read/write head*. When the external field is removed, some magnetism, termed the **remanence**, remains in the recording material. Retrieval is based on detection of this residual magnetism.

Other examples of magnetic recording materials include the gamma form of ferric oxide, cobalt-modified iron oxide, **chromium dioxide**, pure iron particles, and barium ferrite. These recording materials may be coated on platter-shaped substrates (magnetic disks) or on thin ribbons of polyester (magnetic tapes). Magnetic disks are principally encountered in computer applications. Magnetic tapes are widely utilized for data storage, as well as for audio and video recording.

Hard Disks

A magnetic disk features a platter-shaped substrate coated with a magnetizable recording material. The disk's recording surface is divided into concentric rings or tracks. An electromagnetic read/write head is used for recording and playback. On instructions received from a host computer, a magnetic disk drive positions the read/write head above a designated track while the rotating platter brings the desired disk segment under the electromagnetic mechanism. The individual bits may represent character-coded text, quantitative values, document images, or other computer-processible information. They are usually recorded linearly— sometimes described as *longitudinally* or *horizontally*—within each track. Much less commonly, some magnetic disk drive manufacturers employ perpendicular or vertical recording to increase platter capacity.

Magnetic disk substrates may be rigid (**hard disks**) or flexible (**floppy disks**). With the most widely encountered type of hard disk system, one or more platters are built into the drive mechanism that records and reads information. Because the platters cannot be removed, the resulting computer storage device is properly characterized as a rigid **fixed magnetic disk drive**. It is popularly described as a *hard disk drive* or, simply, a **hard drive**; the storage device and the recording medium are considered an indivisible unit. In mainframe and larger minicomputer configurations, a hard drive is often described as a **direct-access storage device** or **DASD** (pronounced "dazdee"). Although hard drives for smaller computers similarly support direct access for recording and retrieval, the DASD designation is rarely applied to them. Removable hard disks and floppy disks combine the direct-access characteristics of platter-shaped media with off-line storage capabilities for **data archiving**, **back**up, data distribution, or other purposes. They are mainly encountered in small computer installations.

Since their introduction in the 1950s, hard disk drives have been the principal storage devices for digitally coded information and programs that need to be immediately and continuously available to computer users. They are intended for active records; hard drives provide convenient on-line access to electronic records that will be referenced frequently or unpredictably. The earliest hard drives had recording layers composed of iron oxide particles in an epoxy binder. Various other oxide compounds—including barium ferrite, metal particles, and cobalt-modified iron oxide— have also been used as hard disk coatings. Since the 1960s, steady reductions in the size and thickness of recording layers have been accompanied by significant improvements in the recording densities of hard disks. With particulate materials, however, reductions in coating thickness are accompanied by diminished magnetic field strength, as small particles become diluted in nonmagnetic binder materials. Manufacturers of newer high-performance magnetic disks consequently prefer thin metallic films to particulate materials. Composed of iron, nickel, cobalt, or other metals or alloys, such films are coated in a thin, undiluted layer on a hard disk platter. They are durable and offer excellent magnetizable properties.

The historical development and continuing evolution of hard disk storage can be summarized in four words: smaller, denser, faster, cheaper. Once considered a luxury to be carefully rationed among mission-critical applications, hard drives have become increasingly affordable necessities in virtually every computer configuration. Since the 1990s, storage capacities of hard drives have been measured in gigabytes. The principal determinants of hard disk capacity are the number of platters per drive, the platter size (diameter), and the areal density within each recording surface. Most hard disk drives contain multiple platters. Through the early 1990s, for example, full-height hard disk drives for microcomputers typically featured 10 platters, while half-height models incorporated a shorter stack of five platters. In the mid-1990s, several manufacturers introduced hard disk drives with just two or three platters. Their low heights permit compact equipment designs, an especially important consideration for notebook computers, personal digital assistants, and other mobile computing devices. The number of platters aside, the top and bottom surfaces of individual platters are used for data recording.

With their greater surface areas, large hard disk platters can store more information than smaller ones, assuming comparable areal recording densities. Since the 1950s, however, the sizes of hard disk platters have decreased steadily; technological innovations and improved product designs have dramatically enhanced recording densities and storage capacities per platter. The earliest hard disk drives, introduced by IBM in the mid-1950s, utilized 24-inch platters. In the decades that followed, they were replaced by mainframe and minicomputer disk drives with 14-inch, 12-inch, and 8-inch platters. Today, high-capacity direct-access storage devices for mainframe and minicomputer installations employ multidrive disk arrays with 3.5-inch platters. Introduced in the 1980s for small computer installations with limited storage requirements, the areal recording densities and storage capacities of small hard disk platters have improved dramatically in recent years. Multigigabyte models have been commonplace since the mid-1990s, and capacities are doubling at 12- to 18-month intervals.

In array configurations, small hard drives can satisfy mainframe-class storage requirements previously served by large-platter devices. A computer's operating system treats the multiple physical drives in a **hard disk array** as a single logical drive for recording and retrieval purposes. Compared with devices with larger platters, 3.5-inch hard drives are more widely available, require less floor space, consume less power, and are much less expensive to purchase, install, operate, repair, and replace. They are more reliable, can be scaled to address varied storage requirements, and support faster access times for reading and recording. Arrays of multiple 3.5-inch hard drives are often supplied in RAID configurations, which incorporate redundant recording and storage procedures for fault-tolerant operation and data protection. The **RAID** acronym originally stood for **redundant array of inexpensive disks**; more recently, vendors have substituted **redundant array of independent disks**. RAID technology is not limited to mainframe and minicomputer installations. RAID configurations are also available for network servers and, less commonly, desktop computers.

Personal computers have relied on hard drives for on-line storage of information and programs since the early 1980s. The much-publicized complexity of newer operating systems and application software, combined with the growing volume and variety of electronic records generated by such programs, have led to dramatically increased hard disk requirements in small computer installations. Desktop computers now provide storage capacities that would have been unusually high in minicomputer configurations a decade ago. When equipped with hard disk arrays, desktop computers and personal computer-based network servers can accommodate voluminous collections of electronic records. Although most hard drives for desktop computers and network servers employ 3.5-inch platters, drives with 2.5-inch, 1.8-inch, or smaller platters are also available. They are principally utilized in notebook computers, personal digital assistants, and other mobile information processing devices where compact drive dimensions and light weight are important concerns.

Removable Hard Disks

As a potentially significant limitation, fixed magnetic disks can become full, necessitating their replacement with higher-capacity models or the purchase of additional hard drives. Alternatively, some electronic records must be deleted or transferred to magnetic tapes or other media for off-line storage, thereby freeing space for new information. Hard drives with removable recording media address this problem. With such devices, a single drive can support an infinite number of disks, any of which can be inserted into the drive as required for recording or retrieval. Hard drives with removable media consequently provide unlimited capacity— provided, of course, that off-line storage is acceptable for some electronic records. When greater hard disk capacity is required, a customer merely purchases additional recording media rather than upgrading or replacing an entire drive.

Among their other advantages for electronic recordkeeping, removable hard disks may be stored in locked cabinets, vaults, or other secure locations to protect sensitive or valuable electronic records against unauthorized access when not in use. Removable hard disks provide a convenient method of transferring electronic records from one computer system to another equipped with compatible drives. They can be used for physical exchange of information and to back up the contents of conventional hard drives. Compared with magnetic tapes, removable hard disks permit faster restoration of electronic records in the event of hard drive failure. Removable hard disks also offer a measure of fault tolerance; if a removable hard disk drive fails, its recording media can be mounted onto an identical device.

In most computer installations, removable hard disk drives serve as supplements or complements, rather than replacements, for conventional hard drives.

Because removable hard disks must be retrieved from their storage locations and mounted into a drive when required, they are not suitable for electronic records that must be immediately and continuously accessible on-line. Unlike optical disks and certain magnetic tapes, **jukebox**-type **autochangers** that provide unattended access to individual media are not available for removable hard disks.

Removable hard disk systems have a long history. IBM introduced the first magnetic disk drive with removable recording media in 1962. Intended for small mainframe installations that could not afford enough fixed disk capacity to meet their information storage requirements, it featured removable 14-inch disk packs with multiple platters mounted onto a spindle. Similar products were widely encountered in mainframe and minicomputer installations through the early 1980s. When not mounted into their drives, the individual disk packs were stored on shelves under a protective, translucent plastic cover that resembled a hatbox. A variant form of removable hard disk drive, more common in minicomputer installations than mainframe sites, employed 14-inch platters encapsulated in opaque plastic cartridges.

As computer storage media, hard disk packs and 14-inch **hard disk cartridges** are defunct products. Although drives that accepted hard disk packs and 14-inch cartridges remained available for sale through the late 1980s, new models are not being manufactured. Records managers may occasionally encounter hard disk packs and 14-inch cartridges when inventorying media stored off-line by data processing centers. Such media may also be packed in containers transferred to records centers or other off-site storage facilities. In most cases, their contents are not retrievable, because compatible drives are not available.

Removable hard disk technology is a viable contemporary storage option for small computer configurations, however. Available products separate a drive's read/write head assembly from its platter-shaped recording medium, which is encapsulated in a removable plastic cartridge. Principally intended for desktop computer installations, these hard disk cartridges can store electronic records such as computer-aided design (CAD) or desktop publishing files that do not need to be immediately and continuously available on-line. They can also be used to transport information, such as databases or typesetter files, between compatible computer systems or between an in-house computer system and a service bureau. Hard disk cartridges permit grouping of information by type or activity on individual cartridges. Other applications include hard disk backup; digital photography; and recording of music, compressed video, or multimedia programs. The newest products offer gigabyte-level storage capacities.

As removable media, hard disk cartridges permit off-line retention of electronic records, but their suitability for such data archiving depends on the continued availability of compatible equipment to read the archived information. Hard disk cartridge drives and media are proprietary products. Cartridges and drives of different manufacturers are incompatible with one another. Some products that were widely utilized in the 1980s and 1990s have been discontinued. The suitability of hard disk cartridges for data archiving is further undermined by technological improvements that enhance their functionality for other purposes. As with conventional hard drives, platter sizes have decreased and media capacities have increased since the first models were introduced in the 1980s. Within a given manufacturers' product line, some larger- and lower-capacity hard disk cartridges recorded by prior generations of equipment cannot be read by newly developed drives. These cartridges have no guarantee of backward-compatibility and no safeguards against future discontinuation of specific products. *Backward-compatibility* is the ability of future computer, audio, and video products to read information recorded in particular formats. These issues are significant concerns for long-term retention of electronic records.

Floppy Disks

Floppy disks, also known as **diskettes**, are circular pieces of polyester coated with a magnetizable material. Diskette manufacturers have utilized **gamma ferric oxide**, cobalt-modified iron oxides, and barium ferrite, among other recording compounds. Introduced in the early 1970s, floppy disks were initially intended as lower-cost alternatives to hard drives in minicomputer installations. They were subsequently adopted as the principal direct-access storage devices by dedicated word processors and first-generation microcomputers. Diskettes remain the most widely encountered examples of removable magnetic disks in personal computer installations. Some Unix-based network servers are equipped with floppy disk drives, but they are rarely encountered in minicomputer configurations.

Like their rigid counterparts, floppy disks have decreased in size since the 1970s, while their recording densities and storage capacities have risen steadily and significantly. The earliest diskettes measured eight inches in diameter and stored approximately 80 kilobytes of computer-processible data. Within several years, however, improved head designs and thinner magnetic coatings had raised their capacities to megabyte levels, although some products stored considerably less than a megabyte. Eight-inch diskettes were utilized in minicomputer, microcomputer, and word processing installations through the early 1980s. They were sometimes described as the *standard* size to distinguish them from 5.25-inch and 3.5-inch diskettes, which came after them. Apart from their external dimensions, however, nothing was standard about 8-inch diskettes. Individual computer systems formatted them for their own purposes, and certain word processors and small business computers required proprietary, preformatted 8-inch diskettes that could be purchased only from designated suppliers.

Eight-inch diskettes are obsolete media. They were ultimately supplanted by 5.25-inch floppy disks, the so-called **minifloppy disk** variety. Introduced in the mid-to-late 1970s, 5.25-inch floppy disk drives were initially utilized in low-performance personal computer systems intended for educational or consumer markets rather than business applications. The earliest models employed single-sided 5.25-inch diskettes with 70 to 120 kilobytes of storage capacity. Manufacturers of business-oriented computers and word processors continued to favor the 8-inch format until the early 1980s, when IBM selected 5.25-inch floppy disk drives for its Personal Computer (PC). Business acceptance followed quickly, as 5.25-inch floppy disk drives became standard equipment on IBM-compatible microcomputers.

At first, 5.25-inch diskettes were limited to single-sided recording, but a double-sided, double-density (DS/DD) format with 360 kilobytes of storage capacity was soon developed. A double-sided, high-density (DS/HD) 5.25-inch diskette with 1.2 megabytes of recording capacity was introduced in the mid-1980s.

Although they were occasionally encountered through the 1990s, 5.25-inch diskettes have joined their 8-inch counterparts on the list of defunct computer storage media. In personal computer configurations, they have been replaced by 3.5-inch **microfloppy disks**. In their original double-sided, double-density configuration, introduced in the early 1980s, 3.5-inch diskettes could store 720 kilobytes when formatted by the MS-DOS operating system or 800 kilobytes in Macintosh installations, although double-density Macintosh diskettes were also available in a single-sided, 400-megabyte version. Double-sided, high-density 3.5-inch diskettes, the dominant floppy disk format since the early 1990s, store 1.44 megabytes. A double-sided, quad-density (DS/QD) 3.5-inch format, introduced in the late 1980s, stores 2.88 megabytes, but it is rarely encountered in personal computer installations.

Smaller diskette formats have not been commercially successful. Early digital cameras used 3-inch floppy disks, but they were ultimately replaced by semiconductor memory cards. Two-inch floppy disk drives and media, in capacities up to one megabyte, were introduced in the late 1980s and early 1990s by several companies. Principally intended for mobile computing devices and digital photography, 2-inch products were not widely adopted.

Although the megabyte-level storage capacities of high-density and quad-density diskettes were viewed as impressive technical developments in the 1980s, they now limit the usefulness of floppy disk technology for file backup, data archiving, and software distribution. Multimegabyte databases, complex desktop publishing documents, document image collections, multimedia presentations, and other large files will not fit onto a single floppy disk. Personal computer software packages, formerly distributed on one or two diskettes, now require a dozen or more. To address this problem, several manufacturers of computer storage peripherals and media have developed higher-capacity 3.5-inch floppy disk drives that employ innovative recording technologies.

During the late 1980s and early 1990s, several computer storage vendors introduced floppy disk drives and media with 10 to 20 megabytes of recording capacity. These higher-capacity diskette formats attracted intermittent attention but comparatively few customers. Their records management significance is consequently limited; they had so few installations that they are unlikely to turn up in inventories of electronic records. So-called floptical disk drives, developed in the late 1980s, use optically encoded control information to greatly increase track density when compared to conventional diskettes. Despite their name, floptical media feature a magnetic rather than an optical recording layer. The earliest models offered 21 megabytes of storage capacity per 3.5-inch diskette, but they were not widely adopted. A second-generation floptical disk with 120 megabytes of storage capacity was introduced in 1996. Known as the *LS-120 laser servo diskette* or, more commonly, the **SuperDisk**, it is intended for personal computer configurations. A third-generation model doubles the recording capacity to 240 megabytes per diskette. Higher-capacity SuperDisk drives can read 120-megabyte media.

The Bernoulli product line, one of the most successful high-capacity diskette technologies, was introduced by Iomega Corporation in 1981. It took its name from a nineteenth century Swiss physicist who formulated a famous fluid-dynamics theorem; within a Bernoulli drive, spinning motion creates air pressure that lifts a flexible magnetic storage medium toward read/write heads. Because Bernoulli disks are encapsulated in protective plastic cartridges, they are often mistaken for removable hard disks, but they are flexible media. The original Bernoulli drive, called the *Bernoulli Box*, used 8-inch cartridges with 10 or 20 megabytes of storage capacity. Although they remained available through the late 1980s, 8-inch Bernoulli drives were eventually supplanted by more compact models that initially provided five megabytes of storage per 5.25-inch cartridge. Successively improved versions increased the capacities of Bernoulli cartridges to 230 megabytes by the mid-1990s, when the last drive in the Bernoulli series was introduced.

In late 1994, Iomega announced its Zip® drive, the most successful high-capacity floppy disk product. Like the Bernoulli Box, which it ultimately supplanted, the Zip drive employs flexible media encapsulated in protective plastic cartridges. Zip cartridges measure 3.5 inches per side but are thicker than conventional floppy disks. First-generation products, which remained available at the time of this writing, stored 100 megabytes per cartridge. A second-generation 250-megabyte version can read 100-megabyte media. The recently released 750-megabyte Zip drive can read the 100- and 250-megabyte Zip disks.

For those formats that conform to published national and international standards for particular sizes and recording densities, floppy disk technology provides excellent compatibility between the unrecorded diskettes of one manufacturer and the drives of other manufacturers. Once floppy disks are formatted for recording by a particular computer operating system, however, media interchangeability is limited to compatible computer configurations. Addressing this limitation, popular utility programs permit the interchange of 3.5-inch double-density and high-density diskettes formatted for different operating systems. Such programs allow Macintosh computers to load DOS-formatted diskettes, for example. Certain higher-capacity floppy disk products, such as quad-density 3.5-inch drives and SuperDisk drives, are compatible with double-sided, double-density diskettes for reading and/or recording. Other higher-capacity floppy disk drives, such as Iomega's Bernoulli and Zip products, are based on proprietary technology. They do not accommodate diskettes in other formats.

Subject to capacity limitations, floppy disks can be used for off-line electronic records retention. For 3.5-inch double-sided, high-density diskettes, continued availability of compatible hardware to read previously recorded information is of little concern. Given their widespread implementation in personal computer configurations, 3.5-inch double-sided, high-density floppy disk drives likely will be widely available for the foreseeable future. As proprietary products, the higher-capacity diskettes are poorly suited to long-term electronic records retention. Future products may not provide backward-compatibility with existing media. Further, product discontinuation is a risk with any proprietary technology. Eight-inch diskettes, 5.25-inch diskettes, and Bernoulli cartridges are obsolete media. They are unsuitable for electronic records retention.

Nine-Track Computer Tapes

Broadly defined, a **magnetic tape** is a long strip of polyester film coated with a magnetizable recording material. Magnetizable layers composed of particulate materials, such as gamma ferric oxide, have been utilized since the technology's inception. Newer magnetic tape products utilize chromium dioxide, metal particles, or other media formulations.

Magnetic tape devices and media have a long history in information storage. Audio recording equipment dates from the 1920s. Video recording applications followed in the 1950s. Magnetic tape drives were the principal auxiliary storage devices in early computer installations, but their serial access characteristics rendered them unsuitable for on-line applications requiring rapid retrieval of information in unpredictable sequences. To access information recorded on a given portion of a magnetic tape, the tape drive must pass through all preceding information. As higher performance magnetic disk technology became more widely available and affordable, magnetic tapes were relegated to batch processing applications, which have been steadily replaced by on-line systems. Today, computer tapes enjoy a well-established position in electronic recordkeeping; they are the most widely utilized media for back-up protection and off-line storage of machine-readable data. As such, they complement rather than compete with magnetic disk technologies. Magnetic tapes are also used for distribution of information and software, particularly in mainframe and minicomputer configurations.

These information management applications are supported by a diverse group of magnetic tape formats, some of which have multiple varieties. Half-inch magnetic tapes wound onto plastic reels have been used for computer storage since the 1950s. The most widely utilized reels measure 10.5 inches in diameter and contain 2,400 feet of tape. Smaller reels (7 inches and 8.5 inches) and different tape lengths (600, 1,200, and 3,600 feet) are available, but they are less commonly encountered. These variations aside, information is recorded and read by a computer peripheral device that is variously termed a *reel-to-reel tape drive*, a *half-inch reel tape drive*, or a **nine-track tape drive**. The tapes themselves are described as **nine-track tapes** or *nine-track reels* to differentiate them from other half-inch magnetic tapes, which are packaged in cartridges. Across the tape width, the bits that encode individual characters are recorded in nine parallel tracks. Eight of the tracks store data bits that encode characters. The ninth track is reserved for a parity bit that facilitates detection of recording and playback errors.

Individual characters follow one another down the length of nine-track tape. The linear recording density is measured in **bits per inch (bpi)** along the tape's length. Depending on the model, available nine-track magnetic tape drives support linear recording densities of 800, 1,600, or 6,250 bpi. For a 2,400-foot reel of nine-track tape, approximate storage capacities are 20 megabytes at 800 bpi, 40 megabytes at 1,600 bpi, and 160 megabytes at 6,250 bpi. Higher recording densities and storage capacities are technically possible; however, their introduction is unlikely. Since the 1970s, manufacturers of magnetic tape products have shifted their research and marketing efforts from half-inch reels to more compact cartridge formats. Discontinued formats for half-inch magnetic tapes were based on recording densities of 100, 200, or 556 bpi. The earliest computer tape drives employed a seven-track recording format. Although such devices have not been manufactured for several decades, magnetic tapes created by them may be encountered when inventorying electronic records in computer centers or off-site storage repositories. In most cases, magnetic tapes recorded at any density below 800 bpi should be considered obsolete media that are unreadable by available equipment.

Characteristics of unrecorded nine-track magnetic tapes are specified in national and international standards. Because nine-track magnetic tape technology offers excellent compatibility of recording equipment and media, it is a popular choice for data and software distribution, as well as for data archiving and off-line electronic records retention. The nine-track tape's position as a mature product limits its storage capacity, but it avoids future problems of backward-compatibility associated with computer storage technologies that are subject to continuing development. Further, nine-track tapes have little risk of product discontinuation. Alternative media have virtually supplanted nine-track tapes for new computer applications; however, hundreds of millions of previously recorded tapes currently residing in storage areas will remain subject to occasional reference, if only to convert their contents to other media. In particular, legacy data recorded on nine-track tapes must be transferred to other media when mainframe and minicomputer applications are converted to client/server implementations.

Half-Inch Data Cartridges

Half-inch data cartridges are based on magnetic tape formats developed by IBM and subsequently adopted by other computer equipment and media manufacturers. Half-inch data cartridges are principally encountered in mainframe and minicomputer installations where they offer compact, convenient, higher-capacity alternatives to nine-track magnetic tape drives and media. The first half-inch data cartridge drive, the IBM 3480 Magnetic Tape Cartridge Subsystem, was introduced in 1984. Its chromium-dioxide recording medium is packaged in a plastic cartridge that measures 4 inches by 5 inches by 1 inch. The tape's half-inch width is divided into two parallel sets of nine tracks each. One set of tracks is recorded from the beginning to the end of the cartridge, using one-quarter inch of tape width. The tape is then rewound, and the other set of tracks is recorded from beginning to end. This recording format is called **serpentine recording**. A nine-track tape and a half-inch data cartridge are shown in Figure 2-1.

Most 3480-type data cartridges contain 550 feet of magnetic tape. The nominal cartridge capacity is 200 megabytes, which is equivalent to five reels of nine-track magnetic tape recorded at 1,600 bpi or 1.25 reels recorded at 6,250 bpi. Longer tapes with storage capacities up to 300 megabytes are available. Two related data cartridge formats, the 3490 and 3490E, were introduced in 1989 and 1991, respectively. The 3490 format is a version of the 3480 format with **data compression** capabilities, which can triple cartridge capacity. The 3490E format employs 36-track bidirectional recording and a longer tape than its 3480 and 3490 counterparts. A 3490E data cartridge can store 800 megabytes in the uncompressed recording mode or up to 2.4 gigabytes when compression is employed.

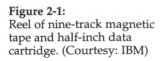

Figure 2-1:
Reel of nine-track magnetic
tape and half-inch data
cartridge. (Courtesy: IBM)

The 3480, 3490, and 3490E data cartridge formats are collectively categorized as *34XX formats.* Since the 1980s, they have steadily supplanted nine-track
reels as the magnetic tape formats of choice for data archiving and back-up operations in mainframe and minicomputer installations. Compared with nine-track
reels of magnetic tape, half-inch data cartridges require less shelf space for a given
quantity of computer-processable information. Their space-saving advantages are
particularly significant where large numbers of magnetic tapes must be stored in
environmentally controlled vaults, computer rooms, or other expensive facilities.
Replacing nine-track reels with half-inch data cartridges can expand a vault's
capacity, thus avoiding or minimizing costly construction or procurement of additional storage facilities.

Half-inch data cartridges have excellent compatibility with unrecorded media
and 34XX cartridge drives of different manufacturers. The 34XX formats are well
suited to distribution or exchange of recorded information among different computer systems, and they are good choices for long-term electronic records retention. The
U.S. National Archives, which formerly accessioned electronic records only on nine-
track reels, now accepts 3480-type data cartridges as well. For continued utility of
information recorded on half-inch data cartridges, drive manufacturers routinely
provide backward-compatibility with predecessor formats for reading and/or
recording. Thus, 3490-type drives can read cartridges recorded in the 3480 format;
3490E-type drives can read cartridges recorded in the 3480 and 3490 formats.

The 3590 data cartridge format was introduced in 1995. Developed jointly by
IBM and the 3M Company, the 3590 data cartridge is identical to its 34XX counterparts in size, but it contains a metal particle tape designed specifically for high-
density recording. A 3590 data cartridge employs a 128-track recording format to
store 10 or 20 gigabytes of computer-processable information, depending on the
tape length. When data compression is applied, the cartridge's capacity is tripled.
The 3590E data cartridge format, an enhanced version introduced in 1999, employs
a 256-track recording format, which yields a storage capacity of 40 or 60 gigabytes,
depending on tape length, without data compression or up to 180 gigabytes with

compression. For backward-compatibility with the many millions of half-inch data cartridges currently in storage, 3590 and 3590E tape drives can read media record-ed in the 36-track 3490E format and the 18-track 3480 and 3490 formats.

Digital Linear Tape

Digital linear tape (DLT) was introduced in the early 1990s by Digital Equipment Corporation as a higher-capacity alternative to the 34XX formats. In 1994, Digital Equipment sold digital linear tape technology to Quantum Corporation. Since that time, DLT has become the dominant data back-up format in midrange com-puter and network server installations. DLT products are available from many storage peripheral vendors. Like their 34XX and 3590 counterparts, DLT car-tridges measure 4 inches by 4 inches by 1 inch and contain half-inch tape. The tape's recording layer features a high-density metal particle material.

DLT capacities, which depend on specific equipment and media configura-tions, have increased since the technology was introduced. At the time of this writ-ing, the highest capacity DLT cartridges—sometimes characterized as *super digital linear tape (SDLT)*—could store 110 gigabytes in an uncompressed format. Cartridge capacity doubles with data compression. Older DLT cartridge formats provided 10 to 40 gigabytes of uncompressed storage capacity. Characteristics of unrecorded digital linear tape cartridges are specified in several international standards. At the time of this writing, higher-capacity DLT drives provided back-ward-compatibility with selected lower-capacity DLT formats for both reading and recording. Digital linear tape is shown in Figure 2-2.

Linear Tape–Open Technology

Linear tape–open (LTO) technology is a joint development of IBM, Hewlett-Packard, and Seagate Technology. Introduced in the late 1990s, it provides high capacity for voluminous data back-up requirements in large computer and network

Figure 2-2:
Digital linear tape (DLT).
(Courtesy: Imation)

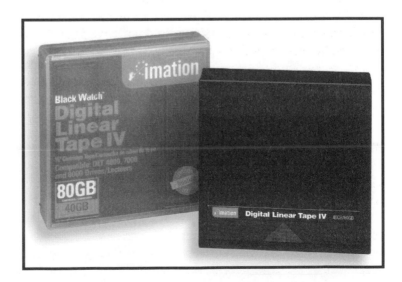

server installations. LTO specifications have been developed for two different magnetic tape cartridge formats: Ultrium and Accelis. An LTO Ultrium cartridge is shown in Figure 2-3.

The LTO Ultrium format features half-inch tape and a single-reel design. First-generation Ultrium cartridges can store up to 100 gigabytes of uncompressed data or twice that amount when compressed. According to the migration path of this technology, Ultrium cartridges will eventually store up to 800 gigabytes of uncompressed data or 1.6 terabytes compressed.

Although the Ultrium format emphasizes high storage capacity, the LTO Accelis format is designed for tape automation installations requiring fast access to recorded information. The Accelis cartridge features eight-millimeter tape and a double-reel design. First-generation Accelis media can store up to 25 gigabytes of uncompressed data. The planned migration path calls for 200 megabytes of cartridge capacity in future products.

Quarter-Inch Cartridges

Quarter-inch magnetic tape cartridges, the most diverse group of magnetic tape products, were introduced in the early 1970s as a lower-cost alternative to nine-track magnetic tape reels in minicomputer installations. Today, they are used for hard disk backup, data archiving, and other information storage activities in small-to-midrange computer configurations, including desktop computers and network servers. Although the earliest quarter-inch cartridge drives and media employed proprietary recording formats, newer products are standardized. Quarter-Inch Cartridge Drive Standards Incorporated promotes the technology and develops specifications for quarter-inch cartridge formats. Those specifications are known as *QIC development standards* or **QIC formats**; compliant quarter-inch cartridge drives and media are described as *QIC products*. Since the 1990s, QIC products have replaced older quarter-inch cartridge drives based on proprietary recording formats. Records managers may encounter proprietary quarter-

Figure 2-3:
LTO Ultrium cartridge.
(Courtesy: Imation)

inch cartridges, however, when inventorying older electronic records in magnetic tape storage vaults, computer rooms, or other media repositories. Quarter-inch cartridge tape is shown in Figure 2-4.

With notable exceptions, quarter-inch cartridges contain magnetic tape that measures one-quarter inch wide. Though described as cartridges, quarter-inch media are actually cassettes that incorporate both a tape supply spool and a take-up spool in a single plastic shell. True cartridges, by contrast, contain only the supply spool; the magnetic tape passes out of the cartridge during use and must be rewound prior to removing the cartridge from its drive. Imprecise descriptive terminology aside, quarter-inch magnetic tape cartridges are available in two configurations:

1. Quarter-inch data cartridges that measure 4 inches by 6 inches by 0.625 inch. They are intended for magnetic tape drives in the 5.25-inch form factor.
2. Quarter-inch minicartridges that measure 2 inches by 3 inches by 0.5 inch. They are intended for magnetic tape drives in the 3.5-inch form factor.

QIC recording formats for data cartridges are identified by the suffix *DC*, while the suffix *MC* identifies recording formats for QIC minicartridges.

Since their inception, QIC products have been designed to back up hard disk drives in one operation with a single recording medium. The media capacities of newly developed QIC formats consequently approximate prevalent hard drive capacities. Through the mid-1980s, when hard drives stored much less information than at the time of this writing, QIC formats for 5.25-inch data cartridges provided less than 200 megabytes of recording capacity, while minicartridge capacities were even lower. As hard drive capacities increased, however, denser QIC formats were developed. Gigabyte-level QIC media have been available since the early 1990s. Although lower-capacity QIC formats employ gamma ferric oxide tapes, high-capacity QIC media employ cobalt-modified iron oxide or metal particle recording materials. Specifications for certain QIC formats permit data compression, which approximately doubles cartridge capacity.

As a group, data cartridge capacities exceed their minicartridge counterparts, although the latter, which require smaller drives, are typically preferred by desktop

Figure 2-4:
Quarter-inch cartridge tape.
(Courtesy: Imation)

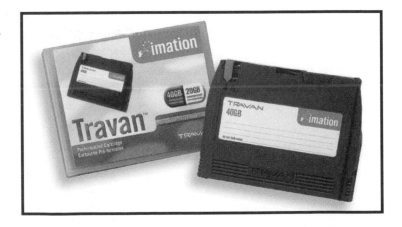

computer users. To achieve higher media capacities, several manufacturers have introduced variant QIC technologies that package a wider and/or longer magnetic tape in a minicartridge shell. Although the resulting cartridges may not contain quarter-inch tape, they are typically categorized as QIC products and are covered by QIC standards. The wider tape measures eight millimeters (0.315 inch) across. It increases minicartridge capacity by accommodating more parallel recording tracks than quarter-inch tape.

Travan technology, the best known QIC variant, was introduced in 1994. It was quickly adopted by manufacturers of QIC drives and media. At the time of this writing, uncompressed storage capacities ranged from 400 megabytes per minicartridge for the Travan TR-1 format to 10 gigabytes per minicartridge for the Travan TR-5 format. These amounts double when data compression is applied; thus, media manufacturers typically cite 20 gigabytes as the storage capacity of Travan TR-5 tapes. The migration path for Travan technology projects future storage capacities up to 30 gigabytes per minicartridge.

Among other QIC variants, the QIC-Wide format was introduced by Sony in 1993. It modifies the physical characteristics of a conventional QIC minicartridge, increasing the tape width to 0.315 inch and increasing the tape length by 33 percent, from 300 to 400 feet. The resulting storage capacity increases by as much as 75 percent, depending on the QIC minicartridge format with which it is compared. QIC-Wide drives incorporate redesigned guides and rollers to accommodate the wider tape. The QIC-EXtra format, also known as the *QIC-EC* or *EC1000 format*, was developed by Gigatek Memory Systems and Verbatim. It packages 1,000 feet of magnetic tape in a modified quarter-inch minicartridge. The QIC-EXtra cartridge is longer than conventional minicartridges, but it fits into existing QIC drives. The QIC-EXtra format can increase minicartridge capacity by more than 200 percent when compared with conventional QIC minicartridge formats.

With an installed base of 15 million units, QIC drives outnumber all other magnetic tape devices combined. Hundreds of millions of QIC cartridges store electronic records. Records managers are cautioned, however, that QIC product designations encompass a variety of formats that were developed at various points in time. Some older formats are now considered obsolete. QIC drives and media continue to evolve to satisfy emerging capacity requirements. Quarter-Inch Cartridge Drive Standards Incorporated has defined migration paths for QIC products with progressively greater recording densities and media capacities. To permit continued access to previously recorded information, new QIC standards specify read-compatibility with certain earlier QIC formats. As a complicating factor for long-term electronic records retention, however, new standards do not specify compatibility with all earlier QIC formats, and a given QIC-compliant drive may not implement fully backward-compatibility specified by a particular QIC standard.

Eight-Millimeter Data Cartridges

Several computer storage products are based on helical scan technologies adapted from video and audio recording formats. The quarter-inch and half-inch magnetic tape drives discussed previously employ **longitudinal recording** methods. Their stationary magnetic heads record data in parallel tracks that run the entire length of a tape. **Helical scan recording** technologies, by contrast, record computer-processible information in narrow tracks positioned at an acute angle with respect to the edges of a tape. As their principal advantage for electronic recordkeeping, helical scan technologies offer higher densities than are possible with longitudinal tape recording.

The most widely encountered helical scan formats for computer storage applications are eight-millimeter data cartridges and digital audio tape (DAT). Eight-millimeter data cartridges are based on eight-millimeter video cassette technology, but they contain a metal particle or evaporated metal tape specifically designed for high-density data recording. The cartridges, which are actually cassettes, measure 3.7 inches by 2.5 inches by 0.6 inch. Eight-millimeter data cartridge drives are widely used for back-up operations and data archiving in midrange computer and network server installations. As such, they compete with digital linear tape, the higher-capacity QIC data cartridge formats, and the DAT products. Incompatible eight-millimeter data cartridge drives are manufactured by Exabyte and Sony. The Exabyte product line, introduced in 1987, is more widely implemented. Sony's **advanced intelligent tape (AIT)** system was introduced in 1996. An eight-millimeter tape drive and a cartridge are shown in Figure 2-5.

Exabyte's first-generation eight-millimeter product could store 300 megabytes to 2.5 gigabytes per data cartridge, depending on tape length. Second-generation models offered improved recording techniques and data compression capabilities, which significantly increased media capacity. By the early 1990s, Exabyte's eight-millimeter data cartridges could store 5 gigabytes in the uncompressed recording mode and 10 gigabytes with compression. A longer tape, introduced in the mid-1990s, increased the maximum cartridge capacity to 7 gigabytes uncompressed and 14 gigabytes compressed. In 1996, Exabyte introduced its Mammoth line of eight-millimeter data storage products with 20 gigabytes of

Figure 2-5:
Eight-millimeter tape drive and cartridge.
(Courtesy: Exabyte)

uncompressed cartridge capacity. Exabyte's second-generation Mammoth-2 (M2) format has an uncompressed cartridge capacity of 60 gigabytes.

Sony's first-generation AIT system, introduced in 1996, can store 25 gigabytes per eight-millimeter cartridge. The second-generation AIT-2 product can store up to 50 megabytes per data cartridge. Third-generation AIT-3 technology capable of storing 100 gigabytes per data cartridge was in development at the time of this writing. Future AIT products, to be introduced over the next five years, are expected to store up to 800 gigabytes per data cartridge. Like Exabyte's Mammoth product line, AIT technology employs evaporated metal recording media.

As with other computer storage products, new eight-millimeter drives eventually render their predecessors obsolete. As an advantage for long-term electronic records retention, however, Exabyte's new drives offer backward-compatibility with selected eight-millimeter data cartridges recorded by earlier models. Sony's newest AIT drives can likewise read older AIT media, but media recorded by AIT and Exabyte drives are not interchangeable.

Digital Audio Tape

As their name implies, **digital audio tape (DAT)** products for computer storage are based on technology originally developed for audio recording. The first DAT systems for computer applications were introduced in 1988. Competing industry groups initially proposed different and incompatible data recording methods, but the digital data storage (DDS) format, which was co-developed by Sony and Hewlett-Packard, became the basis for subsequent product development.

Digital audio tape is four millimeters wide and features a high-coercivity, metal particle recording material. **Coercivity** is the amount of force, usually measured in **oersteds**, that is required to orient magnetic particles. Tape lengths range from 60 to 120 meters. DAT cartridges, which are actually cassettes, measure 3 inches by 2 inches by 0.4 inch. Specifications for DAT recording formats and media capacities are defined by the **Digital Data Storage (DDS) Manufacturers Group**, which is comprised of DAT drive and media manufacturers. The original DAT recording format, now known as DDS-1, provided 1.3 gigabytes of storage capacity per 60-meter tape. With 90-meter tape, the cartridge capacity is increased to two gigabytes. A DDS-DC format, introduced in 1992, uses data compression that approximately doubles cartridge capacity. The DDS-2 format was introduced in 1993 as an extension of the DDS-DC format with a higher track density and a longer tape. The DDS-2 storage capacity is four gigabytes per cartridge in the uncompressed mode, or approximately eight gigabytes with data compression.

The DDS-3 format, introduced in 1994, provided an uncompressed storage capacity of 12 gigabytes per DAT cartridge. With data compression, the cartridge capacity is 24 gigabytes. The DDS-4 format, introduced in 1997, offers 24 gigabytes of uncompressed cartridge capacity, with data compression raising that amount to 48 gigabytes. At the time of this writing, newer DAT drives provided backward-compatibility with earlier DDS formats. Thus, a DDS-4 drive can read DAT cartridges recorded in the lower-capacity DDS-1, DDS-2, and DDS-3 formats. Digital audio tape cartridges are shown in Figure 2-6.

Figure 2-6:
Digital audio tape cartridges.
(Courtesy: Maxell)

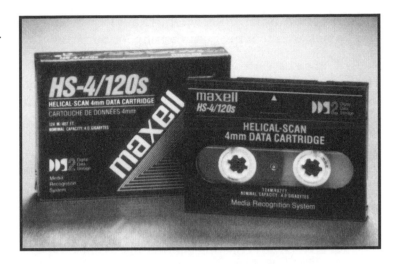

Other Computer Tape Formats

Although they are not as widely encountered as eight-millimeter or DAT products, other helical scan technologies are based on equipment and media originally developed for video recording. Several vendors, for example, offer high-capacity data storage products based on digital video recording media, including D-2 and D-3 tape cartridges. These products are intended principally for remote sensing, medical imagery, technical data retrieval, film animation, and other mass storage applications where huge quantities of computer-processable information are generated by scientific or medical instrumentation. Data storage products based on half-inch video cassette technology were introduced in the mid-1980s, but they have since been supplanted by the formats described previously. The earliest products could store 2.5 gigabytes on a VHS-format cassette. With later models, the cassette capacity exceeded 20 gigabytes.

Other half-inch data cartridge formats have been discontinued, although they may be encountered when inventorying electronic records generated by older minicomputer systems. The TK50 magnetic tape drive, introduced by Digital Equipment Corporation in 1985 for its widely installed VAX computer systems, stored 95 megabytes on 600-foot cartridges. An improved version, the TK70, provided 300 megabytes of storage capacity per cartridge. Half-inch streaming tape systems were manufactured by several companies through the early 1990s. Their cartridge capacities ranged from less than 100 megabytes to more than 500 megabytes.

Audio Tapes

For many organizations, voice dictation tapes are the oldest category of electronic records. In some corporations and government agencies, voice dictation equipment preceded computer installations by several decades. They were among the first applications of magnetic recording technology. During the 1960s and 1970s, several companies marketed voice dictation systems that utilized magnetic-coated belts, small magnetic disks, and continuous loops of magnetic tape. Such media may be encountered in off-site storage locations and archival repositories, but they are no longer manufactured or sold. Today, voice dictation systems, telephone answering machines, and other office-oriented audio recording products employ magnetic tape cassettes in C-type, microcassette, or minicassette configurations.

C-type cassettes are also described as standard size or **Philips-type cassettes**. They measure 3.9 inches by 2.5 inches by 0.5 inch and contain magnetic tape that measures four millimeters wide. Although manufacturers' product designations vary, C-type audio cassettes are typically identified by a code that indicates their recording time in minutes. C-90 cassettes, for example, provide 90 minutes of double-sided recording time (45 minutes per side). C-30 and C-60 are also popular sizes for voice dictation. Other cassette designations range from C-05 to C-120; the longer the recording time, of course, the longer the tape the cassette contains.

During the 1970s and early 1980s, C-type cassettes were used for data recording by early personal computers and word processing systems, automatic send-receive (ASR) computer terminals, point-of-sale terminals, key-to-tape data entry devices, desktop calculators, and some scientific instruments. Cassettes intended for data recording were typically described as digital or data-grade cassettes to distinguish them from their audio counterparts, which are designed to record analog signals. For the most part, data-oriented cassette recorders were hampered by low media capacities and marginal performance. Other storage devices discussed in this chapter have replaced them in computer installations. Digital cassettes may be encountered when inventorying older electronic records, however. Such media must be viewed as obsolete. Compatible devices are unlikely to be available to read their contents.

As their names suggest, microcassettes and minicassettes are smaller than their C-type counterparts. Audio **microcassettes** measure 2 inches by 1.25 inches by 0.25 inch. They were originally developed for portable dictation equipment, although they are also used by desktop audio recording devices and transcribers. Audio **minicassettes** measure approximately 3 inches by 2 inches by 3/8 inch. Depending on tape length, they can record 30 or 60 minutes of voice dictation.

Microcassettes and minicassettes are designed to record speech rather than music. C-type audio cassettes may be used for music recording as well as voice dictation. Standards developed by the **International Electrotechnical Commission (IEC)** specify the magnetic recording media contained in such cassettes. IEC **Type I magnetic tape cassettes**, widely described as *normal bias cassettes*, contain tape coated with gamma ferric oxide, the same recording material used by nine-track computer tape and some floppy disks. The least expensive Type I cassettes are suitable for voice dictation systems and telephone answering machines where recordable frequencies are limited to a narrow range and high fidelity is rarely required. For music recording, which involves a broader range of audio frequencies, most media manufacturers offer Type I cassettes with improved gamma ferric oxide formulations. IEC **Type II** and **Type IV magnetic tape cassettes** are intended exclusively for music recording in applications where high audio quality is an important consideration. Type II cassettes, sometimes described as *high bias cassettes*, contain chromium dioxide tapes. Type IV cassettes contain metal particle tapes. Type II and Type IV cassettes require tape recording equipment compatible with their particular magnetic materials. IEC Type III audio cassettes have been discontinued.

Where superior audio performance is desired, DAT systems utilize digital rather than analog recording techniques to create magnetic tapes with sonic properties similar to those of compact discs. Digital audio tapes are packaged in cassettes, and, like IEC Type IV cassettes, they contain metal particle tape. Audio recording times vary with the tape length. Professional music studios have utilized DAT systems since the late 1980s.

Open-reel magnetic tapes for audio recording are likewise used principally by music studios, although inventories of electronic records may reveal older audio tape reels that contain dictation, interviews, depositions, or other voice recordings. Some government agencies, for example, have produced audio tape recordings of meetings, hearings, and other proceedings for decades. Widths of open-reel tape range from one-quarter inch to two inches. Lengths vary with reel sizes, which may exceed 10 inches in diameter. In most cases, open-reel audio tapes are coated with gamma ferric oxide.

Video Tapes

Magnetic tapes for video recording are usually coated with cobalt-modified iron oxide or metal particles, although gamma ferric oxide materials are also encountered. Like their audio counterparts, studio-oriented video tape recorders utilize open-reel media. As previously noted, video recording equipment dates from the 1950s. Early four-head video recorders, typically described as **quadraplex recorders**, employed 2-inch tape supplied in 2,400-foot lengths. Since the 1970s, they have been supplanted by helical-scan devices known as *C-format recorders*. They record video signals on a magnetic tape that measures one-inch wide. Individual reels may contain up to three hours of video recording.

U-Matic systems, introduced by Sony Corporation in 1971, were the first video recording devices to utilize magnetic tape cassettes. U-Matic tape is three-quarters of an inch wide. Recording times range from a few minutes to over one hour per cassette, depending on tape length. U-Matic is an obsolete format; however, some corporations, government agencies, and other organizations have large collections of previously recorded U-Matic cassettes. For continued utility, such video recordings can be converted to C-format tapes or to one of the cassette formats described next. Video service bureaus offer appropriate conversion capabilities.

Sony introduced the first commercially successful half-inch video cassette recorder, the Betamax, in 1975. Two years later, the Victor Company of Japan (JVC) introduced the **VHS** video cassette format, which ultimately supplanted its **Beta format** counterpart in business and consumer applications. VHS cassettes measure 7.4 inches by 4 inches by 1 inch. As with audio cassettes, tape lengths are typically identified by a code that indicates the recording time in minutes when the VHS recorder is operated at the standard play (SP) speed. The most popular length, designated T-120, provides two hours of recording time per cassette at the SP speed, three times that amount at the extended play (EP) speed. Other VHS cassette designations range from T-15 through T-180.

Two versions of the VHS format, **Super-VHS (S-VHS)** and **VHS-Compact (VHS-C)**, have been developed for special situations. The Super-VHS format is intended for applications where image quality is a paramount consideration. S-VHS cassettes are identical to their conventional VHS counterparts in size and appearance, but they contain higher-grade recording materials. A special S-VHS cassette recorder or **camcorder** is required. VHS-C is an implementation of the VHS format designed specifically for use in camcorders. VHS-C cassettes measure approximately 4 inches by 2.5 inches by 0.5 inch. Tape lengths are identified by a code that indicates the recording time in minutes at the standard play (SP) speed. TC-20 cassettes, for example, provide 20 minutes of recording time. A VHS-C cassette is inserted into an adapter for playback on a conventional VHS-type video cassette recorder. S-VHS-C, a related format, is a compact implementation of Super-VHS cassette technology. S-VHS-C cassettes are the same size as their VHS-C counterparts.

The Beta format continues to be used by professional video studios and in occasional business applications. Beta-format video cassettes measure 6.1 inches by 3.8 inches by 1-inch deep. As with VHS cassettes, recording capacities vary with tape length and recording speed. Beta video cassettes are identified by a code that indicates the tape length in feet. At the Beta II speed, the recording mode utilized by many prerecorded Beta-format tapes, an L-750 cassette provides three hours of recording time. Other Beta cassette designations range from L-250 to L-830.

The Betacam format, which was introduced by Sony in 1982, and BetacamSP format, which was introduced in 1986, use a larger cassette that measures 5.5 inches by 10 inches by 1-inch deep. The Betacam and BetacamSP formats are principally encountered in professional broadcast recording rather than business applications. The MII video format, which was introduced by Matsushita in 1986, is also used primarily for professional broadcast recording. M-II cassettes measure 4 inches by 8 inches by 1 inch.

Like the VHS-C format, eight-millimeter video cassettes are primarily intended for camcorder applications. The cassettes are identical to their data recording counterparts. Their small size permits the design of very compact, lightweight camcorders. **Eight-millimeter tape** lengths are identified by a code that indicates the recording time in minutes; the possibilities range from about 15 minutes to 2 hours per cassette. Eight-millimeter video cassettes employ metal particle recording media. The Hi-8 format is an implementation of eight-millimeter video cassette technology designed specifically for applications where high image quality is required. It is, in effect, the eight-millimeter counterpart of the S-VHS format. Hi-8 cassettes are identical to their conventional eight-millimeter counterparts in size and appearance, but they contain metal-evaporated tape rather than metal particle tape.

The video recording formats and media described previously employ analog coding, the historically dominant encoding method in video applications. Digital video tape technologies date from the mid-1980s. Early examples, such as the D1, D2, and D3 formats, were intended for professional broadcast videotaping. Some digital video tape formats have been adapted for high-capacity data recording. **Digital video (DV) cassette** formats for business and consumer applications date from 1996. Conventional DV cassettes measure 3 inches by 5 inches by 0.6 inch deep. **Mini-DV cassettes**, intended for use in digital camcorders, measure 2 inches by 2.2 inches by 0.5 inch deep. DV tape is one-quarter inch wide.

Several other digital video tape formats were commercially available or emerging at the time this chapter was written. Digital 8 camcorders, for example, utilize the eight-millimeter video cassettes described previously. D-VHS and Digital S media are based on VHS and Super-VHS cassettes. Betacam SX is the digital counterpart of the Betacam format.

Common types of magnetic media used for computer recordkeeping are listed in Table 2-1. Recording material, storage capacity, and information management applications are listed for each media type.

Table 2-1:
Magnetic Media for Computer Recordkeeping

Media Type	Recording Material	Storage Capacity	Information Management Applications
Fixed hard disk	gamma ferric oxide, metallic thin film	multigigabytes	On-line access to frequently referenced information
Hard disk cartridges	gamma ferric oxide, metallic thin film	1 GB+	On-line access to frequently referenced information; data archiving and backup
Floppy disks	gamma ferric oxide, cobalt-modified iron oxide, barium ferrite	1.44 to 250 MB+	Data and software distribution; data archiving and backup
9-track magnetic tape	gamma ferric oxide	40 to 180 MB	Data archiving and backup; data and software distribution
34XX data cartridges	chromium dioxide	200 MB to 2.4 GB	Data archiving, backup, and distribution
3590 and 3590E data cartridges	metal particle	10 to 50 GB+	Data archiving, backup, and distribution
Digital linear tape (DLT)	metal particle	10 to 110 GB+	Data archiving, backup, and distribution
Quarter-inch cartridges (QIC)	gamma ferric oxide, cobalt-modified iron oxide	40 MB to multi-gigabytes	Data archiving, backup, and distribution
Linear tape–open (LTO)	metal particle	25 to 100 GB+	Data archiving, backup, and distribution
8mm data cartridges	metal particle, evaporated metal	up to 1 hour of video; 20 GB+ of data	Video recording, data backup, and archiving
Digital audio tape (DAT)	metal particle	12 GB+ of data; up to 2 hours of audio	Data backup and archiving; audio recording

Obsolete Magnetic Media

Various magnetic media were utilized by older office machines, video recorders, and other information processing devices that are no longer manufactured or marketed. In the absence of a formal retention program for electronic records, some corporations, government agencies, and other organizations continue to maintain files of such obsolete media, even though the equipment required to record and read them is unavailable. Often, such media were shipped to off-site storage locations or otherwise packed away when the devices that used them were replaced by new technologies. Examples of obsolete magnetic media that may be encountered during inventories of electronic records are described next. A complete listing is beyond the scope of this book; for every obsolete medium mentioned, several dozen additional examples could have been cited. When making retention decisions about obsolete media, records managers should be guided by common sense. If information recorded on a given medium has not been retrieved for years or decades, its continuing reference value must be suspect. If the device required for reading the medium no longer exists, the electronic records it contains cannot be retrieved. No business purpose is served by retaining such records. In any case, some obsolete magnetic media have been in storage for many years. Physical or chemical damage probably renders them unusable.

The magnetic tape/selectric typewriter (MT/ST), a word processing system introduced by IBM in the 1960s, stored character-coded text in specially designed magnetic tape cartridges. During the 1970s, the MT/ST was replaced by word processing systems that utilized **magnetic cards** that were magnetic-coated tabulating-size cards, popularly described as *mag cards*. As originally developed for the IBM magnetic card/selectric typewriter (MC/ST), each card could store 5,000 characters, the approximate equivalent of two double-spaced typewritten pages. Magnetic cards utilized by other word processing systems offered higher storage capacities. Through the mid-1970s, magnetic cards competed with magnetic tape cassettes as the dominant media in early word processing installations, but both were eventually supplanted by floppy disks. During the 1960s and early 1970s, some electronic accounting machines utilized paper cards coated with magnetic strips for data recording; such pre-computer devices and media are no longer manufactured. Small magnetic-coated cards were likewise used by some calculators during the 1970s. Today, credit cards contain a strip of magnetic recording materials, but such media have little records management significance.

Small, removable **magnetic disks** were employed in the System 6:5, a voice dictation product marketed by IBM during the 1970s. Each disk offered six minutes of audio recording capacity, which is about the time required to dictate a typical business letter. For transcription, individual disks were stacked in cartridges, which had a total playback capacity of five hours. Other dictation equipment utilized magnetic-coated belts or loops of tape in varying lengths. A typical magnetic belt measured three inches wide and provided up to 20 minutes of audio recording time. Dictation systems that utilized such magnetic belts were discontinued in the mid-1970s.

During the late 1960s and early 1970s, various video recording products were briefly and unsuccessfully marketed under such trade names as Instavision,

Cartravision, Betacord, and V-Cord. Remembered only by a small number of embittered customers, they had no impact on records management operations. A quarter-inch video tape format, called the *compact video cassette* (CVC), was developed by Funai in the early 1980s. Marketed in the United States by Technicolor Audio-Visual, it was not a commercial success. The European V-2000 format, which was utilized in video cassette recorders manufactured by Grundig, was never available in the United States. The eight-track audio cartridge, perhaps the best-known example of a defunct magnetic recording medium, played no role in records management applications.

OPTICAL DISKS

Optical storage technology uses lasers to record information by selectively altering the light reflectance characteristics of a platter-shaped storage medium. Within an optical storage device, the recorded information is read by a laser and pick-up mechanism that detects variations in reflected light, much as read/write heads sense variations in the alignment of metallic particles within magnetic disks and tapes. To prevent destruction of information, the playback laser operates at lower power or a different wavelength than the laser used for recording.

As their most important characteristic, optical media feature high areal recording densities—that is, individual bits that encode machine-readable information are very closely spaced, allowing many bits to be recorded within a given area. The result is high media capacity. When the first optical media were introduced in the early 1980s, they provided gigabyte-level storage at a time when most hard drives and magnetic tapes stored less than 200 megabytes. In recent years, magnetic recording technologies have caught up, but optical media still offer impressive storage capacities.

Optical disks in various formats are the most important optical storage media. In records management work, optical disks are most closely associated with storage-intensive applications, such as electronic document imaging, but they are suitable for other purposes as well. Any computer, audio, or video information that can be recorded onto magnetic tapes or magnetic disks can be stored on optical media, and vice versa. In corporations, government agencies, and other organizations, optical media can store huge quantities of character-coded text, computer databases, graphic images, and audio signals.

All optical disks are removable media. With the exception of compact disks and certain DVD formats, optical disks are encapsulated in protective plastic cartridges that facilitate handling. Consequently, the terms *optical disk, optical disk cartridge*, or simply *optical cartridge* may be used interchangeably. Like magnetic tapes, optical disks are stored off-line when not in use and must be inserted into a compatible drive for reading and recording. Jukebox units, also known as optical disk libraries or autochangers, automate this process.

Optical disks are a diverse product group that encompasses several formats with different attributes. At the time of this writing, the most important categories of optical disks were **magneto-optical (MO) disks**, compact disks, and DVDs. All magnetic media support direct recording, but optical disks are available in read-only and recordable varieties. **Read-only optical disks**, as their name implies, have no record-able properties. They are limited to playback of prerecorded information generated by a mastering and replication process. *Recordable optical disks*, by contrast, permit direct recording of machine-readable information. In this respect, they resemble their magnetic counterparts. Recordable optical disks may be write-once or rewritable media. **Write-once optical disks** are sometimes described as *WORM media*; the acronym variously stands for write once–read many or write once–read mostly. Such disks are not erasable. Once information is recorded in a given area of a write-once optical disk, that area cannot be reused. **Rewritable optical disks**, by contrast, are erasable and reusable. The contents of previously recorded media segments may be deleted or overwritten with new information.

The following sections describe the most important optical disk formats for electronic recordkeeping. Some obsolete formats are also covered. The chapter con-cludes with a brief discussion of other optical storage products, including optical memory cards and optical tapes.

Magneto-Optical Disks

Magneto-optical (MO) recording, also known as *thermo-magneto-optical (TMO)* recording, is a hybrid technology. Within a platter-shaped medium, information is stored magnetically but recorded and read by a laser. **Magneto-optical disks** are actually multilayered magnetic disks. Their glass or plastic substrates are coated with an active recording layer that combines iron with selected other metals. The magneto-optical recording layer is surrounded by additional layers that protect against contaminants and facilitate playback of recorded information. On an unrecorded magneto-optical disk, all particles have the same magnetic orienta-tion. To record information, a highly focused laser beam heats a spot on the disk, causing a loss of the initial magnetic direction. An electromagnet then generates a magnetic field to orient the particles into the desired direction. When read by a laser and pick-up mechanism, recorded areas of a magneto-optical disk rotate reflected light in a clockwise or counterclockwise direction to play back the one and zero bits in digitally coded data.

Magneto-optical disks are encapsulated in plastic cartridges to protect their recording surfaces during media loading, removal, filing, and other handling. Of the several available sizes, 5.25-inch (130-millimeter) magneto-optical disks are the most widely utilized in electronic document imaging implementations. Two smaller magneto-optical formats, 3.5 inches (90 millimeters) and 2.5 inches (64 millimeters) are also available.

The storage capacities of 5.25-inch magneto-optical disks have increased steadily and significantly from 650 megabytes for first-generation products intro-duced in the late 1980s to 5.2 gigabytes for fourth-generation media 10 years later. Fifth-generation products, capable of storing 9.1 gigabytes, were introduced in 2001. The industry's migration plans forecast eventual increases to 40 gigabytes or more over the next five years. International standards for 5.25-inch magneto-optical disks were first published in the early 1990s, and compliant drives are available from multi-ple manufacturers. Although newer models quickly supplanted their predecessors, successive generations of magneto-optical drives have maintained backward-compatibility with older formats for reading previously recorded information. Although 5.25-inch magneto-optical disks are double-sided media, all drives are single-headed devices. On-line availability is one-half the disk's storage capacity. Thus, a 5.2-gigabyte magneto-optical disk provides 2.6 gigabytes on-line. A given magneto-optical cartridge must be ejected, turned over, and reinserted to read from or record onto its opposite side.

Magneto-optical cartridges in 5.25-inch size are available in write-once and rewritable varieties. Magneto-optical drives can distinguish between write-once and rewritable cartridges and will automatically activate the appropriate recording mode. Smaller magneto-optical disks are available as rewritable media only. The storage capacities of 3.5-inch magneto-optical disks have increased from 128 megabytes for first-generation media introduced in 1990 to 1.28 gigabytes for fourth-generation products introduced 10 years later. The 2.5-inch MiniDisc was introduced by Sony in 1992 as the first optical disk designed specifically for audio recording. The MD Data format, a version for computer-processable information, was introduced in 1993, but it is rarely encountered in records management applications. A 5.25-inch magneto-optical disk drive and cartridge are shown in Figure 2-7.

Compact Disks

Compact disk (CD) is the collective designation for a group of interrelated optical storage formats and products based on technology developed during the 1970s and 1980s by Sony and Philips. The most widely encountered type of compact disk is a rigid plastic platter that measures 4.75 inches (120 millimeters) in diameter. The various compact disk formats are distinguished by the type of information they

Figure 2-7:
5.25 magneto-optical
disk drive and
cartridge. (Courtesy:
Pinnacle Micro)

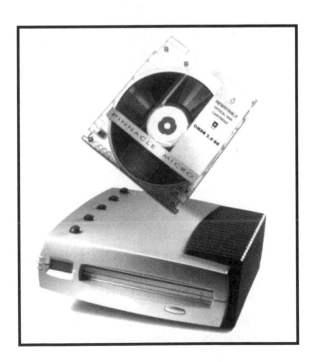

contain. Compact disk–digital audio (CD-DA), the first and best known type of optical disk, is a sonically superior alternative to long-playing phonograph records and audio tape cassettes. Principally a consumer product, it has no records management significance. **Compact disk–read-only memory (CD-ROM)**, **compact disk–recordable (CD-R)**, and **compact disk–rewritable (CD-RW)** are the compact disk formats for computer-processible information.

Of these, CD-ROM is the most widely encountered. Since the mid-1990s, CD-ROM drives have been standard storage peripherals in personal computer configurations. As a read-only technology, CD-ROM is essentially a publishing and distribution medium for software, databases, or other computer-processible information. Read-only optical disks contain prerecorded information. They are produced by a mastering and replication process. Computer-generated information, video images, or audio signals to be recorded on a given CD-ROM are organized, edited, and otherwise prepared for submission to a production facility, which produces a master disk from which individual copies are generated by injection molding or some other process. The copies have no recordable properties. They are read by playback devices (CD-ROM drives) that have no recording mechanisms. A 4.75-inch CD-ROM, the most common size, can store about 540 megabytes of computer-processible information. Some product specification sheets cite capacities up to 650 megabytes, but that amount is formatted capacity. A 3.5-inch (90-millimeter) CD-ROM, which can store about 190 megabytes, is rarely encountered in records management applications.

Compact disk–recordable (CD-R) and compact disk–rewritable (CD-RW) are recordable optical media. CD-R products are write-once optical disks that employ **dye-based recording** technology or *dye polymer recording* technology. They feature a transparent polymer that contains an infrared-absorbing dye. Information is recorded by a laser that operates at the dye's absorption wavelength. The laser's energy is converted to heat, which creates pits or bumps in the polymer layer. The pits or bumps typically represent the one bits in digitally coded data; zero bits are represented by spaces. CD-RW media, which are erasable, employ **phase-change recording** technology. With unrecorded media, phase-change compounds exist in either a crystalline or an amorphous state. A laser records information by heating selected areas of the recording layer, inducing a crystalline-to-amorphous or amorphous-to-crystalline transition. Crystalline and amorphous areas have different reflectivity characteristics, which represent the one and zero bits in digitally coded information.

Competitively priced and available from many suppliers, CD-R and CD-RW drives and media are widely encountered in desktop computer installations where they may be used for data backup, data archiving, or other purposes. Their formatted storage capacities range from 540 megabytes to 660 megabytes, depending on the type of medium selected. When used for digitized audio information, CD-R and CD-RW media provide up to 74 minutes of recording time. Unlike magneto-optical disks, CD-R and CD-RW media are not encapsulated in protective cartridges.

DVD Media

DVD—which originally stood for *digital video disk* and then *digital versatile disk*— is the replacement technology for compact disks, which they physically resemble.

DVD specifications were developed in the mid-1990s by a group of cooperating companies. At the time of this writing, the technology was still evolving, and new formats and products can be expected. DVD media, which measure 4.75 inches in diameter, can store video, audio, or computer-processible information. DVD-Video and DVD-Audio are consumer formats that have no records management significance. Among the computer formats, DVD-ROM is the higher-capacity successor to CD-ROM. Intended for publication and distribution of large databases, clip art libraries, document image collections, multimedia presentations, or other voluminous information, a single-sided DVD-ROM can store up to 4.7 gigabytes. A double-sided DVD-ROM format with 9.4 gigabytes of storage capacity has been proposed, but such media were not available at the time of this writing. Like its CD-ROM counterpart, DVD-ROM is a read-only format. DVD-ROM drives, which will ultimately replace CD-ROM drives in desktop computer installations, have no recording capabilities.

The recordable DVD formats are DVD-R, DVD-RAM, DVD-RW, and DVD+RW. They are the counterparts of CD-R and CD-RW, which they may eventually supplant. DVD-R, like CD-R, is a write-once medium that employs dye polymer recording technology. Single-sided storage capacities have increased from 3.95 gigabytes for first-generation DVD-R products introduced in 1997 to 4.7 gigabytes for second-generation media introduced in 1999. Double-sided DVD-R media can store up to 9.4 gigabytes. A DVD-RAM disk is shown in Figure 2-8.

As erasable optical disk formats, DVD-RAM, DVD-RW, and DVD+RW are the counterparts of CD-RW. They use phase-change recording technology but differ in capacity and are otherwise incompatible. DVD-RAM media are available in single- and double-sided versions, which can store 2.6 and 5.2 gigabytes, respectively. DVD-RW and DVD+RW media can store 4.7 gigabytes on single-sided disks or 9.4 gigabytes on double-sided disks. Like magneto-optical disks, double-sided DVD-RAM media are encapsulated in a protective cartridge. Other DVDs, like their compact disk predecessors, are not encapsulated in cartridges.

DVD drives offer selective compatibility with compact disk formats. DVD-ROM drives, for example, can read CD-ROM and CD-RW media, but they may have

Figure 2-8:
DVD-RAM disk.
(Courtesy
Maxell)

problems reading certain CD-R disks. Due to variations in dye polymer recording technologies, DVD-R drives may be incompatible with information recorded on certain CD-R media. Erasable DVD drives can read CD-RW and CD-ROM media. Several vendors offer optical disk jukeboxes that co-mingle DVDs and compact disks in various formats.

Types of optical media used for computer recordkeeping are listed in Table 2-2. Media sizes, storage capacities, and whether each media is recordable and/or erasable are also included.

Obsolete Optical Disk Formats

Other optical disk formats, introduced during the 1980s, have been discontinued or remain in very limited use. Optical disks in the 14-inch and 12-inch sizes were principally encountered in mainframe and minicomputer installations with voluminous storage requirements, where they competed with or supplemented hard drives. They were also used in some electronic document imaging installations. Their storage capacities ranged from 2 gigabytes to 25 gigabytes per optical disk cartridge. Fourteen-inch optical disks were write-once media only. Twelve-inch optical disks were available in write-once and rewritable versions, although the latter were seldom encountered. Eight-inch optical disks were discontinued shortly after their introduction in the 1980s.

Table 2-2:
Optical Disks for Computer Recordkeeping

Media Type	Media Size	Storage Capacity	Recordable?	Erasable?
Magneto-optical disks	5.25 inches	up to 9.1 GB	yes	yes
Magneto-optical disks	3.5 inches	up to 1.28 GB	yes	yes
CD-ROM	4.75 inches	540 MB+	no	no
CD-ROM	3.5 inches	190 MB	no	no
CD-R	4.75 inches	540 MB+	yes	no
CD-RW	4.75 inches	540 MB+	yes	yes
DVD-ROM	4.75 inches	4.7 GB	no	no
DVD-R	4.75 inches	4.7 or 9.4 GB	yes	no
DVD-RW	4.75 inches	4.7 or 9.4 GB	yes	yes
DVD+RW	4.75 inches	4.7 or 9.4 GB	yes	yes
DVD-RAM	4.75 inches	2.6 or 5.2 GB	yes	yes

A number of vendors introduced proprietary 5.25-inch write-once and rewritable optical disks during the mid-1980s and early 1990s, but most of those products were discontinued when magneto-optical technology was introduced in the late 1980s. Their storage capacities ranged from 200 megabytes to 650 megabytes. Given their relatively short life cycles—less than five years from introduction to discontinuation in most cases—obsolete optical disk products illustrate the perils of selecting storage media for electronic records.

Introduced in 1978, read-only analog **video disks** were the first optical storage products to be successfully commercialized. Originally intended as consumer products, analog video disks were produced by corporations, government agencies, and other organizations for training and other purposes. In their 12-inch versions, analog video disks could store 54,000 still-video images or 60 minutes of full-motion television with stereo audio on each of two sides. Eight-inch media could store 24,000 still-video images or 13.5 minutes of full-motion television and stereo audio per side. Although analog video disk technology remains in use, discontinuation is likely as applications move to DVD-Video, which with digital coding and video compression, can store 130 minutes of full-motion television on smaller media. During the 1980s, several companies developed special production techniques that could store digitally coded, computer-processable information, including databases and document images, on read-only video disks, but that technology was not commercially successful.

Optical Cards and Tape

Optical disks in the various formats are the most important optical storage products for electronic records. Two other optical storage media, **optical cards** and **optical tape**, play little or no role in records management applications. Optical cards, also known as *optical memory cards* and *optical digital data cards*, were introduced in the early 1980s as compact, portable storage media for desktop computers. Optical cards are the size and thickness of a credit card (approximately 2.1 inches by 3.4 inches by 0.03 inch). They are coated on one side with a reflective strip of optical recording material. The leading manufacturer is LaserCard Systems, a subsidiary of Drexler Technology, the developer of the LaserCard brand of optical memory cards and the Drexon optical recording material employed by such cards.

Optical memory cards are available in read-only and read/write versions. The latter are more common; like certain optical disks, they are write-once media. First-generation optical memory cards provided 2.86 megabytes of formatted capacity. A 4.1-megabyte version was introduced in 1993. Although their manufacturers emphasize the advantages of portability and reliability, widespread adoption of optical memory cards was initially impeded by the limited availability of reader/writer equipment for personal computer installations. Until the mid-1990s, such equipment could be purchased only in limited quantities. To date, the principal applications for optical memory cards have involved medical information. They have also been used for equipment maintenance records, cashless funds transfers, transaction processing, shipping manifest records, and as personal identification media in computer-controlled security and access systems.

An optical tape is a ribbon of film coated with an optical recording material. Optical tape's potential for electronic recordkeeping, particularly its high storage capacity, has been discussed for years, but, at the time of this writing, no optical tape products were commercially available. Only one optical tape system, developed by CREO in the late 1980s and discontinued in the mid-1990s, was ever available for sale. It could store one terabyte of computer-processible information on a 12-inch reel of optical tape that measured 35 millimeters wide by 880 meters (approximately 2,400 feet) long. The CREO optical tape system was principally intended for mass storage installations in aerospace, avionics, and other applications where huge quantities of information are generated by scientific instrumentation. Its high capacity permitted the consolidation of large magnetic tape libraries, with a resulting reduction in vault space requirements. A single reel of optical tape could store the equivalent of about 5,500 reels of nine-track tape recorded at 6,250 bits per inch. Other optical tape products have been demonstrated in prototype versions, but their market potential has been undermined by continuing improvements in magnetic tape capacities.

PAPER-BASED ELECTRONIC MEDIA

Electronic records are now stored on magnetic disks, magnetic tapes, or optical disks; however, various pre-computer and early computer systems relied on paper media. From the 1950s through the 1970s, for example, mainframe and minicomputer installations employed **punched card** technology for converting data and programs to machine-readable form. Data was recorded on such cards by keypunch machines that converted typed characters to predetermined patterns of holes in successive, numbered columns. Typically, the cards are both punched and interpreted; that is, human-readable representations of individual characters are printed at the tops of the columns in which punches are recorded. Punched cards are processed by a card reader, an on-line peripheral device that detects the pattern of holes punched in successive columns and converts their character content to computer-processible form. Punched cards have also been employed by tabulating machines, sorters, electromechanical accounting machines, programmable calculators, and other pre-computer devices.

Although punched cards are obsolete media, they are of more than historical interest. Hidden away in basements, closets, records centers, or other locations, punched cards are routinely discovered during inventories of electronic records. The most widely encountered examples are tabulating size (3.25 inches by 7.375 inches). They contain 80 columns punched with square holes. Sometimes called an IBM card, it was initially utilized in equipment manufactured by the Tabulating Machine Company, which later became International Business Machines. Versions with as few as 30 columns were employed by the U.S. Census Bureau in the late nineteenth century. Cards of different sizes and capacities have been utilized by specific computer systems. Remington Rand, for example, introduced a tabulating-size card with 90 columns for use with early UNIVAC computers and certain electromechanical accounting machines. Such cards are easily identified by their round holes. In the late 1960s, IBM introduced a 96-column punched card for use with its System/3 minicomputers. Measuring 3.25 inches by 2.75 inches, it featured three rows of punches representing 32 characters per row.

Punched **paper tape** is a ribbon of paper that uses predetermined patterns of holes and spaces to represent digitally coded data. The holes are generated by a paper tape punch and decoded by a paper tape reader. Five to eight holes, aligned across the width of the tape, are used to represent individual characters. Punched paper tape is one of the oldest electronic recordkeeping media. Its use in telegraphy dates from the nineteenth century. During the 1960s and early 1970s, punched paper tape was employed by computer terminals, TWX machines, and telex machines for off-line preparation of messages or other information to be transmitted to a computer system or through a telecommunications network. Punched paper tape and punched paper belts were also employed as text storage media by some early word processing systems, but they were quickly supplanted by magnetic media. Like punched cards, punched paper tapes that have not been processed for decades may be stored by corporations, government agencies, or other organizations. Originally supplied in 1,000-foot lengths, punched paper tapes in storage typically consist of relatively short strips or rolls.

SUMMARY

Magnetic storage media have dominated electronic recordkeeping for decades and are likely to continue to do so. Magnetic disk drives are the storage devices of choice in high-performance computer applications that require rapid, on-line access to active electronic records. Magnetic disks are platter-shaped media that may be fixed in or removable from the drives on which information is recorded and retrieved. Fixed magnetic disk drives, or hard drives, are equipped with one or more rigid platters. Their storage capacities have improved steadily and significantly since the 1950s. At the same time, platter sizes have decreased. Mainframes, minicomputers, and network servers increasingly employ high-capacity, multidrive arrays with small platters. Desktop and portable computers are routinely configured with hard drives in capacities formerly associated with large computer installations.

Removable magnetic disk systems provide infinite storage capacity within a given hardware configuration, although some information will necessarily be stored off-line at a given moment. Examples of removable magnetic disks include hard disk cartridges and floppy disks. Some removable magnetic disk products have been discontinued over the years. Media produced by such products can no longer be read.

Successfully employed for information storage since the 1920s, magnetic tape is a ribbon or strip of plastic film coated with a magnetic recording material. Utilized for computer, video, and audio recording, magnetic tapes may be packaged on open reels, in cartridges, or in cassettes. In computer applications, magnetic tapes are widely utilized for back-up copies, data archiving, and software or data distribution. Reels of nine-track magnetic tape have been employed in mainframe and minicomputer installations since the 1950s. Half-inch data cartridges, including 34XX and 3590 formats, offer greater storage capacity and more compact dimensions than their nine-track counterparts. Digital linear tape (DLT), which also uses half-inch tape, has been widely adopted in network server installations. It offers very high storage capacity. Quarter-inch data cartridges and minicartridges are the dominant magnetic tape formats for desktop computers. In their higher-capacity versions, quarter-inch tape drives and media are also suitable for network server installations, where they compete with eight-millimeter data cartridges, digital audio tape (DAT), and LTO technology. Very high-capacity computer tape formats have been developed for special situations.

C-type, or Philips-type, magnetic tape cassettes are the dominant magnetic media for audio recording, including voice and music. Microcassettes and minicassettes are used exclusively in voice dictation systems and answering machines. Open-reel audio tape and digital audio tape are principally utilized by professional music studios. The most widely encountered video tape formats feature half-inch magnetic tape packaged in VHS-compatible cassettes, although other cassette formats and open reels of video tape remain in use. Eight-millimeter video tape cassettes have facilitated the development of compact, lightweight camcorders. Newer video storage media employ digital coding rather than the analog coding that has historically dominated video recording.

As an alternative or supplement to magnetic disks and tapes, optical storage systems use lasers to record information by selectively altering the light reflectance properties of specially designed media. As their most significant characteristics for electronic recordkeeping, optical storage media offer high capacity. Optical disks—particularly, magneto-optical disks, compact disks, and DVDs—are the most important category of optical storage media. Optical memory cards and optical tapes are less commonly encountered. Optical disks are available in recordable and read-only varieties. The former permit both recording and playback of machine-readable information, while the latter are limited to playback of prerecorded information. Recordable optical disks are available in write-once and rewritable varieties. Write-once optical disks, or WORM media, are not erasable; rewritable optical disks, like magnetic media, permit deletion and/or overwriting of previously recorded information.

Obsolete machine-readable media may be encountered when inventorying electronic records. Examples include magnetic cards, MT/ST tape cartridges, magnetic tape belts, video cassettes in defunct formats, punched cards, and punched paper tape.

CHAPTER THREE

FILE FORMATS FOR ELECTRONIC RECORDS

Electronic records generated by computer, video, and audio systems are stored in a manner appropriate to and determined by the hardware and/or software that creates, retrieves, edits, or otherwise processes the recorded information. Following traditional records management practice, a collection of electronic records is called a **file**. The term may be preceded by an adjective that denotes the physical storage medium on which the information is recorded; hence, the use of such designations as *disk file* and *tape file*. Alternatively, and more meaningfully, a file descriptor may indicate the type of information the file contains and the type of applications it serves. Examples of such designations include a computer file, video file, or audio file. Additional adjectives, such as master, update, temporary, or backup, indicate a file's relationship to other files. Computer files may be further categorized by the type of information they contain. Widely encountered examples include text files, spreadsheet files, data files, and image files.

Within each file type, computer-processable information may be recorded in proprietary or nonproprietary formats. As their default operating mode, most computer programs record files in a proprietary format whenever a save command is initiated. When a word processing document created with Microsoft® Word is saved, for example, the file format for that version of Word is automatically applied, unless the computer operator selects a different format. Proprietary file formats are sometimes called *native formats*. They are associated with specific software developers and computer programs.

Nonproprietary file formats, by contrast, are supported by multiple software developers and computer programs. Nonproprietary formats are sometimes characterized as *neutral formats* or *transfer formats* because they facilitate the exchange of electronic records between computer systems and applications. When imported by a given program, files are usually converted from nonproprietary to proprietary formats for processing or other purposes. Nonproprietary file formats may be based on published specifications prepared by cooperating software developers. Alternatively, a nonproprietary file format may be developed by a single influential software company and adopted by others. Proprietary and nonproprietary file formats are rarely exclusive options; many programs support a native file format plus additional proprietary and nonproprietary formats. Further blurring the distinction between the two format categories, files saved in proprietary formats associated with very popular software products can often be imported (read) by competing or complementary products. Similarly, a given computer program may be able to export (write) files in the proprietary formats associated with other programs. Where the importing and exporting capabilities of a given computer program are inadequate, various companies offer translator programs or services that can convert files from one format to another.

Although a comprehensive survey is beyond the scope of this book, the following sections discuss file format concepts and characteristics for the most commonly encountered types of electronic records. This subject is important because file formats have a decisive impact on the future usability of electronic records. Backward-compatibility is an obvious concern. Most software developers release new versions of, or replacements for, their products at regular intervals. Like the media formats described in Chapter Two, electronic records saved in a particular file format may be rendered unreadable by product modifications and discontinuations. As discussed in Chapter Five, retention designations for electronic records are based on the assumption of backward-compatibility with a given file format for the entire retention period, but such compatibility cannot be guaranteed.

TEXT FILES

Text files are widely associated with word processing programs. They are also created by desktop publishing and computerized typesetting programs, electronic mail systems, workgroup software, optical character recognition (OCR) products, and text editors of the type furnished as utility programs with some computer operating systems. As their name suggests, text files contain machine-readable information in character-coded form. Each character is represented by a predetermined sequence of bits, which constitute one byte of computer-processable information. Used in this context, the term *character* denotes a letter of the alphabet, a numeric digit, a punctuation mark, or any other symbol that might be encountered in a typewritten document. The symbolic content of text files is determined by the language in which documents or other textual information is created and the character-generating capabilities of specific computer systems and programs. Most new computers support multiple languages, including some non-Roman languages. Windows-based computers sold in North America, for example, support European character sets, including Cyrillic and Greek. Characters that are not represented on a keyboard can be generated by specified key-combinations or selected from displayed lists.

Coding Schemes

The bit sequences that represent individual characters in text files are determined by the digital coding scheme employed in a particular application. Since the 1960s, most text files have utilized the **American Standard Code for Information Interchange (ASCII)**. The original ASCII implementation, which dates from 1963, specified a seven-bit code capable of representing 128 different characters. Several enhanced versions, or supersets, of the ASCII coding scheme have since been introduced. An eight-bit implementation, capable of representing 256 different characters, is described as the *extended ASCII character set*. It includes accented characters associated with European languages, additional mathematical and logical symbols, and special shapes for drawing pictures. The extended ASCII character set is used by the MS-DOS operating system.

The ANSI character set, another superset of ASCII, likewise includes accented characters, as well as special punctuation marks such as bullets, em and en dashes, and ellipses; useful business symbols such as trademark, copyright, and foreign currencies; and fractions for one-quarter, one-half, and three-quarters. The ANSI character set is used by Windows 3.x and Windows 95. It omits some symbols contained in the extended ASCII character set. The ISO Latin-1 character set is an ASCII superset that is similar, but not identical, to the ANSI character set. The hypertext telecommunications protocol (HTTP) and **hypertext markup language (HTML)** are based on the ISO Latin-1 character set.

The **extended binary coded decimal interchange code (EBCDIC)**, introduced by IBM in 1964, was the first computer coding scheme to utilize eight bits to represent individual characters. Because the digits zero through nine can be represented by just four bits each, eight-bit coding formats allow two numbers to be combined in a single byte. Typically applied to data files rather than text files, that method of numeric coding is known as packed decimal representation. The EBCDIC code is utilized for text files created or processed by IBM and plug-compatible mainframe computers. Other computers, including the desktop computers that dominate word processing applications, typically employ the ASCII code in either the seven- or eight-bit implementations. The ASCII code was also utilized by some discontinued technologies, including dedicated word processors and TWX terminals.

Although the ASCII code has been widely incorporated into computing devices of all types and sizes, its continued dominance is by no means certain. **Unicode**, which can represent over 94,000 characters, was developed to support the increasingly global nature of the computer industry. The Unicode character set encompasses a variety of non-Roman scripts as well as a large repertoire of diacritical marks, currency symbols, geometric shapes, technical symbols, Braille patterns, and other nonalphanumeric characters. The Unicode character set is being expanded on a regular basis. Currently supported by Word 97 and later versions of the Windows operating system, including Windows NT, Unicode may ultimately supplant ASCII and its variants. Unicode is also supported by the latest versions of the Unix and Macintosh operating systems. Among its advantages, Unicode simplifies the development of Web sites that serve an international audience on the public Internet or organizational intranets. It permits the simultaneous display of multiple character sets within the same Web page.

Inventories of electronic records may reveal the existence of older magnetic or paper media that utilize other character coding schemes. Principally of historical interest, such coding schemes were used by defunct computers or other obsolete equipment. Seven-track magnetic tapes recorded in the binary coded decimal (BCD) code were created by IBM computers prior to the introduction of EBCDIC. The BCD code employed just six bits per character, although an extra bit was typically appended for error-checking purposes. Equipment designed to read seven-track magnetic tapes has not been manufactured for decades. Even where such devices remain in service, those aged magnetic tapes are unlikely to be readable or compatible software to process their contents does not exist. Punched paper tapes and magnetic tape cassettes created by telex machines and some telex-compatible computer terminals employed the Baudot code or its successor, the International Telegraph Code No. 2. The most widely installed punched card systems employed the Hollerith code.

Word Processing Files

Regardless of the coding scheme employed, text files store information in a relatively unstructured manner. In many word processing applications, for example, a text file contains a single record—the machine-readable equivalent of a typewritten document that contains one or more pages. Alternatively, a text file may contain several or many documents created by word processing programs, electronic messaging software, or other systems; multiple electronic messages may be downloaded to a text file during an on-line session, for example. In such cases, individual records may be separated by page break commands or other delimiting characters. Their physical sequence within a text file may be based on their order of creation or logical interrelationships. Computer software typically imposes few significant restrictions on the length of text files. File sizes may be limited by available memory or other hardware characteristics, but such constraints are rarely meaningful.

Some text file formats are specific to the computer programs that create them. Word processing programs, for example, record documents in proprietary formats. Text files created by such programs combine textual characters with embedded characters that initiate page breaks, paragraph indentations, tabs, underlining, bold printing, italics, superscripts, subscripts, and other formatting features. Although the ASCII code is typically used for both text and control characters, the control characters associated with particular formatting operations are unique to specific programs. Thus, a control character that initiates a page break or underline with one word processing program may have a completely different meaning, or no meaning at all, with competing products.

As a complicating factor, text file formats may differ among various versions of a given program. Successive releases of a word processing program may not be able to read and edit text files created by all previous versions. Usually, a word processing program can import text files created by one or two previous versions, but it may not be able to export text files in formats compatible with those versions. Software-imposed limitations on backward-compatibility pose obvious problems for retrieval of text files created in the past. They are also significant for members of project teams or other work groups who need to exchange documents with other members but have not upgraded to the latest version of a given word processing program. Incompatibility is likewise possible among versions of a given word processing program intended for different computer platforms.

To facilitate the exchange of word processing documents and other electronic records, some programs can import and export text files in proprietary formats employed by other programs, including competing products. Some word processing programs, for example, can import and export text files in the proprietary format employed by specific versions of Microsoft Word; similarly, Microsoft Word can import and export text files in the proprietary format employed by specific versions of Corel's™ WordPerfect®. As might be expected, such exchange capabilities emphasize proprietary formats employed by the most popular software packages. At the time this chapter was written, for example, the Word format, though properly considered proprietary, had become a de facto standard format for the convenient exchange of documents among many software packages, although confusion may occur concerning which version of the Word format is the appropriate one to be used for that purpose. Not surprisingly, exchange capabilities are seldom provided for proprietary file formats employed by lesser known or discontinued word processing programs. Importation of text files created by such programs must rely on one of the file exchange methods described next.

Exchange of documents in proprietary formats will prove most reliable for text files with straightforward formatting characteristics. The converted files usually retain paragraph markers and indentations, tab settings, page margins, line spacing and justification, headers and footers, and character sizes and styles. Problems can arise, however, when text files include special characters, tabular and multicolumn page formats, mathematical formulas, and embedded graphics. To address this issue, several word processing program developers have introduced file formats that promote compatibility among text files created by various competing or complementary products. Eliminating the need for multiple programs that translate to and from specific proprietary representations, they provide a canonical format in which text files can be saved and from which they can be translated. Perhaps the best-known example is Microsoft's rich text format (RTF). It records text and formatting instructions in a manner that compatible programs can correctly interpret—assuming, of course, that the target program possesses the requisite formatting capabilities. Designed to accurately reproduce the content and appearance of files during translation, the RTF format is supported by Microsoft programs and many competing and complementary products. Older canonical text file formats, such as IBM's document content architecture (DCA) format, have not been as widely adopted, and some programs that supported them have been discontinued.

Where the file exchange capabilities of a given computer program are inadequate, various utility programs can convert word processing documents and other text files from one proprietary format to another. The most versatile products can accommodate dozens of file formats, often for several computer platforms. Alternatively, computer service bureaus and consulting firms offer file conversion services for unusual situations, including the conversion of text files created by defunct programs and dedicated word processors.

Formats for Compound Documents

Text file formats are intended for alphanumeric information. Strictly defined, they cannot accommodate compound documents that combine text and graphics. Although newer word processing programs routinely support documents with embedded graphics generated by an internal drawing component or exported from other programs, the **portable document format (PDF)** is often a better choice for compound documents with complex formatting characteristics. Developed by Adobe Systems, the PDF format is compatible with character-coded text and graphics, including digitized images, which can be combined within the same page. For character-coded information, PDF preserves fonts, styles, headers, margins, and other page formatting characteristics. PDF files are viewed with the Adobe Acrobat program, which is supplied with most new personal computers or can be downloaded from Internet sites without charge. The PDF format provides excellent functionality for document display, page navigation, printing, and security. Although PDF is a proprietary format, it has been widely adopted. Among its advantages, PDF is a cross-platform file format. Software for creating and reading PDF files is available for Windows, Macintosh, and Unix computers, and PDF documents can be reliably interchanged among those platforms. PDF is compatible with distribution of documents via Web sites, e-mail attachments, or computer media such as compact disks and DVDs.

So-called markup formats provide similar support for compound documents and are compatible with a variety of computer programs. They contain embedded instructions, called *markup codes* or *tags*, which describe various document components such as chapters, titles, headings, paragraphs, lists, and tables. Compatible computer programs interpret the markup instructions and display documents accordingly. Markup codes may be inserted manually or generated by special authoring tools. The syntax and semantics of specific markup codes are defined by sets of rules called *markup languages*. Some corporations, government agencies, and other organizations utilize markup languages and formats to facilitate the exchange of computer-processable documents. One of the best-known examples, the **standard generalized markup language (SGML)**, has been adopted by the United States Department of Defense for its Computer-aided Acquisitions and Logistic Support (CALS) initiative.

The hypertext markup language (HTML), mentioned briefly earlier, and the extensible markup language (XML) are subsets of SGML. They are the markup languages used for providing information on the World Wide Web, as well as on corporate and institutional intranets and extranets. HTML and XML codes are interpreted by Web browsers that display the information as formatted text and graphics. Various software packages support the creation of Web pages with specified content and embedded formatting codes. In addition, newer word processing programs can save documents in the HTML format. They automatically insert HTML codes that correspond to specific page, line, and character formats. In addition to text, many Web pages incorporate photographs, illustrations, charts, or other graphics stored in one of the formats discussed next.

Markup languages promote the exchange of computer-processable documents by separating the content and appearance of information. Content is stored as plain text, and the embedded codes specify the appearance of pages. The encoded documents are not formatted; they contain formatting instructions that compatible software interprets. As a complication, however, different versions of a given markup language often incorporate special features and extensions that can pose compatibility problems. Some HTML extensions, for example, are incompatible with certain browsers. To increase the likelihood of compatibility of computer-processible documents with the broadest range of programs, the safest approach is to store text files with as little formatting as possible. That is the approach taken by ASCII text files, sometimes described as the text-only or plain text format.

ASCII Text Files

As their name suggests, **ASCII text files** use the ASCII code to represent the character content of word processing documents, electronic messages, or other computer-generated text, but they contain little additional information. Most word processing programs and many other software products support the ASCII text file format as an import or export option. The ASCII text file format is typically available with carriage returns at the end of each paragraph or at the end of each line of text. The user selects the desired pattern. Some computer programs support additional variations; Microsoft Word, for example, offers a choice of text-only formats based on conventional or extended ASCII character sets. These variations aside, most of the control characters that initiate formatting options are removed when files are saved in the ASCII text format. ASCII text files created by one word processing program can usually be imported and edited by others, but the absence of formatting instructions may result in loss of functionality. Paragraph indentations and tabs may be converted to spaces, but line centering, fonts, underlining, italics, and other potentially significant features are not converted. If required, they must be reinserted during document editing.

By transcending proprietary file formats, ASCII text files minimize software dependence and provide some protection against product obsolescence because computer programs will presumably accommodate the ASCII text format for the foreseeable future. Records managers should consequently consider the ASCII text format, instead of or in addition to, proprietary formats for word processing documents, electronic messages, and other textual information that must be retained for long periods of time. This recommendation is based on the assumption, of course, that special formatting information does not need to be retained for its functional value. As an additional advantage, ASCII text files are accepted as input by text storage and retrieval programs that support on-line storage and full-text retrieval of documents.

SPREADSHEET FILES

Text files store alphabetic characters and other symbols encountered in typewritten documents. If text files contain numeric digits, they are simply stored as characters, without regard to the quantities they represent. Spreadsheet files, by contrast, store numbers as quantitative values. They can also store character-coded information, but they differ from text files in their more structured formats.

Spreadsheet files are formatted as tables. They contain information stored in cells, which are formed by the intersection of rows and columns in a tabular presentation. Spreadsheet cells may contain quantitative values, formulas, textual information (labels), or even graphics, along with formatting instructions. Taking a widely encountered example, cells in the first column of a budget-planning spread-sheet typically contains labels that identify categories of expenditure such as salaries, benefits, rent, utilities, and so on. Cells in the first row of the spreadsheet contain labels that identify the months of the year or other budgetary periods. Other spread-sheet cells contain dollar amounts associated with specific expenditures for particu-lar budgetary periods. Alternatively, the cells may contain formulas that calculate those dollar amounts. The formulas may include arithmetic operators, predefined mathematical or logical functions, numeric constants, or references to other cells.

Like word processing software, all spreadsheet programs store files in a pro-prietary format as their default operating mode. With some computer operating sys-tems, these proprietary formats are identified by file extensions. With Windows, for example, the file extension *.xls* identifies Microsoft Excel spreadsheets, which are labeled as workbooks. Spreadsheets recorded in proprietary formats associated with Lotus 1-2-3 are identified by file extensions such as *.wk4*, *.wk3*, *.wk1*, and *.wks*, depending on the version used to create them. Because proprietary file formats may differ among various versions of a spreadsheet program, backward-compatibility is an obvious concern. Successive releases may not be able to read spreadsheet files in proprietary formats associated with all previous versions. Incompatible file formats are likewise possible among versions of a given spreadsheet program intended for different computer platforms.

Some spreadsheet programs can import and export files in proprietary for-mats employed by other programs, including competing products. As an example, Lotus 1-2-3 can import files recorded in the proprietary format employed by specif-ic versions of Excel; similarly, Excel can import and export text files in the proprietary format employed by specific versions of Lotus 1-2-3. Such file conversions are most reliable for quantitative values and cell labels. Formulas that contain predefined functions or user-defined macros may execute differently in Excel and Lotus 1-2-3. Several software companies have developed file formats designed specifically for exchanging spreadsheets among different, otherwise incompatible programs. Examples include the **SYLK** format introduced by Microsoft for use with its Multiplan spreadsheet program, the predecessor of Excel, and the data interchange format (DIF), which was developed and popularized by VisiCorp, a defunct compa-ny that created VisiCalc, the first spreadsheet program for microcomputers. Some older spreadsheet files, created by discontinued programs such as SuperCalc or PerfectCalc, may be stored in those formats. If so, they can be loaded for processing by newer programs that import SYLK or DIF files.

DATABASES

Databases contain records that are subdivided into one or more data elements, called **fields**, which store particular categories of information. A database for a human resources application, for example, may contain one record for each employ-ee. Within each record, such information as the employee's name, job title, office location, telephone number, and home address may be stored in designated fields. Field entries may include textual information, quantitative values, or formulas to calculate quantitative values. Within the database, records are sequenced by values contained in a designated field, which is variously described as a **key field**, *sort field*, or *sort key*. Records in a personnel database, for example, may be arranged alphabetically by employee surname, while the records in a vendor information file may be sequenced numerically by vendor number. A secondary sort field differentiates records with identical values in the primary sort field; personnel records for employees with identical names may be sequenced by date of birth, for example.

Simple database structures of this type are characteristic of the least expensive data management programs for personal computers. Sometimes described as *flat files*, they resemble spreadsheets, a fact reflected by the inclusion of straightforward database capabilities in the most popular spreadsheet programs. Individual records in a database correspond to spreadsheet rows, while fields correspond to the cells within each row. Although flat data files are often adequate for simple applications, more powerful database management programs employ elaborate data structures appropriate for complex information management operations. Available for mainframe, minicomputer, and network server implementations, they generate indexes, treelike hierarchies, relational tables, and other supporting files that permit rapid access to, and efficient processing of, data records.

Regardless of structure, database files are typically stored in proprietary formats associated with the computer programs that create and process them. Thus, Microsoft Access stores data in its native format, Oracle stores data in its native format, Informix stores data in its native format, Lotus Notes stores data in its native format, Filemaker Pro stores data in its native format, and so on. Customized programming may be necessary to import databases stored in a proprietary format. Some programs, however, include import and export components that permit the exchange of databases with other programs, including competing products. Such file exchange is particularly important when an organization changes database management software, or when a program must process archived data files that were created with discontinued software.

Among the most widely implemented nonproprietary approaches, databases can be imported and exported in the **comma separated values (CSV)** or comma-delimited format, an ASCII text format with individual records separated by carriage returns and the fields within each record separated by commas, tabs, or other delimiting characters. As with word processing and spreadsheet files, some programs can import and export data files in formats associated with other programs. As an example, many database management programs for personal computers can import and export files in the db2, db3, or db4 formats employed by the once-dominant dBASE product line. Some spreadsheet programs can also import and export files in one or more dBASE formats. With network servers and larger computers, many database products can import files in formats used by Oracle, SQL Server, Lotus Notes, or other widely installed database management programs.

IMAGE FILES

Computer-processable, digitally coded images are an increasingly common and important type of machine-readable information. They may be created by a wide variety of programs and devices. Possibilities include, but are not limited to:

- Computer-aided design (CAD) programs
- Computer painting, drawing, and other graphic arts software
- Software that produce slides, overheads, and other presentation aids
- Geographical information systems (GIS)
- Desktop publishing programs
- Spreadsheet programs that include business graphics components
- Software for statistical and demographic analysis
- Scanners that generate digitized images from paper documents or microforms
- Digital cameras
- Fax modems and related software

Depending on the application, computer-processable images may be reproduced in hard copy by printers or plotters, stored for later retrieval as an alternative to paper files, incorporated into Web pages, added to highly formatted documents by desktop publishing software, transmitted to remote devices over telecommunication facilities, or otherwise processed for specific purposes.

Computer-processable **image files** may employ vector-based or bit-mapped representation techniques. **Vector-based images** are sometimes characterized as *object-oriented* or *shape-defined representations* because they define computer-processible images as points, lines, circles, or other geometric shapes. In effect, vector-based files contain instructions that allow compatible computer programs to reconstruct the encoded shapes. **Bit-mapped image files**, by contrast, consist of dots, called *pixels*, that represent tonal values. Also known as *raster-based image files*, they are produced by computer painting programs, document scanners, and fax modems. Electronic document imaging systems, which complement, supplement, or replace paper filing systems and microfilm in many records management applications, employ bit-mapped image representations. Because they utilize different methods of representing images, object-oriented and bit-mapped files are incompatible with one another. Conversion programs exist, but they vary in their ability to reliably produce bit-mapped images from vector-based files, or vice versa.

Like text files, spreadsheet files, and databases, computer-processable images may be recorded in proprietary or nonproprietary file formats. Proprietary formats are often the default recording mode. As a previously noted complication, proprietary formats employed by previous versions of a given program may not be readable by the latest releases. Similarly, versions of a given program that operate on different computer platforms may generate incompatible image files. Because image files may need to be referenced for many years, users have a strong interest in nonproprietary formats, sometimes described as **metafile formats**, that facilitate the interchange of digitized images between different programs and computer platforms. As part of the CALS initiative, for example, the U.S. Department of Defense requires compliance with certain metafile image formats that permit file interchange. Many corporations, government agencies, and other organizations are likewise concerned about the future ability to reference mission-critical images generated by CAD programs and electronic document imaging systems; in some applications, such images replace engineering drawings, office files, and other paper records. Whether employed in the public or private sector, records managers can expect to encounter metafile formats for computer-processible images created and maintained by their organizations.

One of the most widely adopted nonproprietary formats for bit-mapped images is the **tag image file (TIF)** format, also known as the *tagged image file format* and sometimes abbreviated as *TIFF*. The TIF format was developed jointly by Microsoft and Aldus Corporation, which was subsequently acquired by Adobe Systems Incorporated. Adobe Systems, which also owns the portable document format (PDF), now publishes and maintains TIF specifications.

TIF is a flexible, multiplatform file format that is well suited to and widely supported by a variety of computer applications, including electronic document imaging, optical character recognition, desktop publishing, digitization of photographs for electronic manipulation, and PC-based facsimile transmission. A TIF image file includes a header that describes the contents, size, and other characteristics of the file. The TIF format is compatible with single- and multi-page documents and with binary, grayscale, and color scanning modes. TIF images may be stored in compressed or uncompressed form. The TIF format is compatible with the **Group 3** and **Group 4** compression algorithms. TIF images can be read by a variety of computer programs, some of which are in the public domain. Plug-ins for Web browsers allow the TIF format to be used in Internet, intranet, and extranet implementations.

Since the late 1990s, the TIF format has become the de facto standard image file format for records management applications. Some state regulations require it for electronic document imaging systems implemented by government agencies subject to their jurisdiction. With some electronic document imaging systems, TIF is the default file format; in other cases, it is an operator-selectable alternative to proprietary formats for importing, storing, and exporting document images. In theory, TIF files created by one computer program can be imported by others. In practice, however, compatibility problems are posed by permissible variations in TIF headers and by different versions of the TIF specification that have developed over time. As a further complication, some image viewer programs support a subset of the TIF specification. They may not be able to display all TIF files.

The **graphics image file (GIF) format**, also known as the *graphical interchange file format*, has become a widely utilized image format in Internet, intranet, and extranet implementations. Developed by CompuServe and supported by all Web browsers, the GIF format is designed for rapid downloading and browsing of images. Its encoding method displays an approximation of images while complete information is downloaded from a Web server. Designed to enhance the responsiveness of Web pages, this progressive display approach generates low-resolution images that are gradually improved as more detailed information arrives.

The GIF format employs the Lempel-Ziv-Welch (LZW) algorithm for image compression. Although no legal restrictions are on the creation or interchange of GIF images, developers of GIF viewers must license the LZW compression algorithm, which is patented by Unisys Corporation. To avoid this requirement and address other limitations of the GIF format, the World Wide Web Consortium (W3C) has adopted the portable network graphics (PNG) format as a GIF replacement. Like GIF, PNG provides cross-platform compatibility, good image compression, and progressive display of images. Unlike GIF, the PNG format is legally unencumbered and freely usable without licensing arrangements. Unlike TIF, GIF and PNG are single-image formats. They do not support multiple images per file. This limitation is insignificant for most of the Web pages where the GIF and PNG formats will be used, but it can prove troublesome where electronic images are produced by scanning multipage paper documents.

The JPEG file interchange format (JFIF) is the file format associated with **JPEG** compression algorithms, which were developed by the Joint Photographic Experts Group. The JFIF file format and the JPEG compression method are often confused. Many vendors and publications incorrectly describe JPEG as a file format and omit any mention of JFIF. In some cases, the combined designation JPEG/JFIF is used. JPEG compression can be used with other file formats, such as TIF, but it is rarely done. Terminology aside, the JFIF format and JPEG compression method are intended for photographs or other continuous tone images. Other examples of file formats for bit-mapped images include BMP, the Windows Bitmap image format; PCX, which was developed by Z-Soft for its PC Paintbrush program; PCD, the Photo CD format developed by Eastman Kodak; PICT, the default image format for Macintosh graphics programs; RAS, a raster image format developed by Sun Microsystems; and Targa (TGA), which is supported by some computer painting programs.

Every computer-aided design program stores data in proprietary formats, but most CAD products support one or more additional formats—so-called transfer formats—for exchanging information. The drawing (DWG) format is the proprietary vector file format developed by AutoDesk for its popular AutoCAD product line. AutoDesk also developed the **drawing interchange format (DXF)** for exchanging CAD files. All versions of the AutoCAD product line can convert DXF files to DWG files and vice versa. The DXF format is widely supported by other computer-aided design programs. DXF is one of the best-known vector-based image formats. For many users, it is the most convenient format for importing and exporting CAD drawings. Among other transfer formats for CAD files, the initial graphics exchange specification (IGES), which was developed in the early 1980s, remains in use. The HPGL/2 format was originally developed to prepare image files for output by Hewlett-Packard plotters. It is supported by many CAD software packages. The **computer graphics metafile (CGM) format** is supported by many image-oriented computer programs. It can accommodate both vector-based and bit-mapped image files. Some CAD programs can read files in the DGN format, which was developed by Bentley Systems for its Microstation line of CAD software.

Vector-based images have historically been associated with engineering drawings generated by CAD software, although they are also encountered in desktop publishing, geographical information systems (GIS), and other applications. **Encapsulated PostScript (EPS)**, for example, is a vector-based image file format based on the PostScript page description language. Many desktop publishing programs and other graphics software can import and export EPS files. Digital map files created by geographic information systems combine geographic information, which indicates the shape and position of specific map features, with display instructions that describe how a map will be plotted for display or printing. GIS users must typically import geospatial data from various sources. The DXF CAD format has become popular with some GIS products, but digital map files may include attributes, such as road names or construction dates, for specific geographic features. In this respect, GIS formats differ from CAD formats, which principally contain information about geometric objects but lack attribute data. Most GIS programs employ proprietary file formats that are optimized for efficient storage and processing, but they support transfer formats for importing and distributing information. Perhaps the best-known example is the Arc Export format, which was developed by ESRI for its popular ArcInfo and ArcView product lines. Some GIS programs can also import files in proprietary formats such as the MIF/MID formats used by MapInfo.

The foregoing discussion surveys image file formats that may be encountered in a broad range of organizations and records management environments. Special file formats have been developed for specific subject disciplines or types of information, especially in scientific fields. The following list of special file formats is a few of the many examples that might be cited:

- The flexible image transport system (FITS) is the standard data interchange and storage format for the worldwide astronomy community.
- The video image communication and retrieval (VICAR) format is used for spacecraft images generated by the Jet Propulsion Laboratory.
- The planetary data system (PDS) format is used for space mission data recorded on CD-ROM.
- The spatial archive and interchange format (SAIF) is a Canadian format for geographic data.
- The spatial data transfer standard (SDTS) is a U.S. government standard for geologic and other spatial data, while the U.S. Geological Survey uses the digital line graph (DLG) format for geographic vector data.
- The crystallographic information file (CIF) format is intended for crystallographic data.
- The topologically integrated geographic encoding and referencing (TIGER) format is used by the U.S. Census Bureau for street maps and other information.

FILE COMPRESSION

To save storage space, computer files may be stored in compressed formats. Such files are sometimes described as *packed*, and they may be identified by **extensions**, such as *.zip* or *.sit*, that indicate their compressed status. Compression is widely applied to bit-mapped image files; all electronic document imaging systems marketed for records management applications, for example, store images in compressed formats. If electronic document images were not routinely compressed, they would overwhelm available storage capacity in high-volume applications. Bit-mapped images created for desktop publishing or other low-volume applications may or may not be compressed for storage. Compression can also be applied to text, spreadsheet, and data files; the larger the file, the greater the motive for compression. Depending on information characteristics and the method selected, compression can reduce storage requirements dramatically. It also reduces bandwidth requirements when files are transmitted over computer networks.

Available compression methods, or compression algorithms, differ in their compression ratios, speed, and suitability for specific types of computer-processible information. In electronic document imaging implementations, for example, the most widely employed compression algorithms are based on specifications adopted by the International Telecommunications Union (ITU), formerly known as the Consultative Committee on International Telephony and Telegraphy (CCITT). Termed the **Group 3** and **Group 4 compression algorithms**, they take their names from the facsimile transmission standards for which they were originally developed. The Group 3 algorithm was popular in the 1980s, but it is not commonly encountered in new imaging implementations. It employs one-dimensional compression techniques. The Group 4 algorithm, by contrast, uses two-dimensional compression methodologies, which yield higher compression ratios.

The Group 3 and Group 4 algorithms are intended for bitonal documents that contain text or line art. The **JBIG** algorithm developed by the Joint Bi-Level Image Experts Group addresses the same applications. Other compression methodologies have been developed for continuous-tone images generated by grayscale and color scanners. The JPEG compression method is one of the most widely publicized examples. JPEG is actually an interrelated group of algorithms that support various combinations of image quality and compression. The possibilities range from poor quality images that are compressed by as much as 160:1 to compressed images at 11:1 that faithfully reproduce original documents. As a recent development, the Joint Photographic Experts Group has announced an improved compression method that can compress images by 200:1 without noticeable quality degradation. The previously cited Lempel-Ziv-Welch (LZW) compression algorithm, which exists in several versions, is suitable for a variety of computer applications, including character-coded text and data files as well as graphic images. Other popular compression algorithms include PKZip and StuffIt, which are encountered in Windows and Macintosh computer installations, respectively.

Specific compression techniques vary. Some algorithms rely on statistical analysis to reduce symbols to shorter codes. Others substitute short codes for predetermined bit sequences. Still others employ sophisticated mathematical compression schemes. Some compression algorithms are lossless; they achieve compression without omitting any information from computer files. Examples of *lossless compression algorithms* include Group 3, Group 4, and LZW. By contrast, *lossy compression algorithms* reduce storage requirements by omitting information from computer files. The JPEG compression algorithm, which is normally lossy, draws on studies of human perception to eliminate the least noticeable components of pictorial information. It is intended for images that will be viewed rather than processed by computer software. JPEG-LS is a lossless implementation of the JPEG compression algorithm. The MPEG format, which was developed by the Moving Picture Experts Group, employs lossy compression to reduce storage requirements for digitized video images and computer animation. Other digitized video formats, such as QuickTime, may also be implemented with lossy compression. Examples of compressed file formats for digitized audio signals include **AIFC**, a compressed implementation of the audio interchange file format (AIFF), and **MP3**, which is the audio compression component of the MPEG format.

Some compression algorithms are based on published specifications; others employ proprietary methods. Compression can reduce file sizes for efficient storage, but it should only be used when necessary. Records managers are cautioned that compressed files can pose significant problems for long-term retention of computer-processible information. In effect, compression introduces an additional layer of software dependency because future retrieval of compressed information requires access to appropriate decompression programs. Like any software, decompression programs may be discontinued. Further, software modifications over time can pose problems of backward-compatibility with files compressed by earlier versions of a given program.

VIDEO RECORDING STANDARDS

Video tape recordings, like the video signals generated by television broadcasters and other sources, contain images called *frames* that are composed of very small points of light called *picture elements* or *pixels*. The pixels are arranged in horizontal lines called *scan lines*, which are displayed in an organized pattern called a *raster*. The illusion of moving images is created by slight differences in successively displayed frames.

To ensure compatibility among video signals and devices, the number of scan lines per frame and the frequency of frame changes are specified by television standards. Such standards affect the design and operation of video tape recorders, video cameras, and other devices that generate television signals. Although they are all based on the raster-scanning method of image formation, prevailing television standards differ in the number of scan lines provided per frame and in the frequency with which frames are changed. Three different and incompatible television standards are currently employed by video equipment in various parts of the world. Video recordings produced in one television standard can only be played by devices that adhere to the same standard. This incompatibility complicates the exchange of video tapes in multinational corporations and other international organizations.

The U.S. standard for television broadcasting was developed in 1941 by the National Television Systems Committee. Termed the **NTSC standard**, it specifies a television frame with 525 scan lines and 30 complete frame changes per second. The NTSC standard has been adopted by Canada, Mexico, Japan, the Caribbean, much of Latin America, Saudi Arabia, and a few other countries. Video cameras, video cassette recorders, video disk players, prerecorded video tapes and video disks, and other video components sold in those countries conform to the NTSC standard.

The two major European video standards provide more horizontal scan lines and higher quality images than their NTSC counterpart. The United Kingdom, Germany, some other European countries, and parts of South America, Asia, and

Africa adhere to the **phase alternation line (PAL)** television standard. It provides for 625 scan lines per television frame with 25 complete frame changes per second. France, Russia, and some Middle Eastern countries employ the **Sequential Couleur a Memoire (SECAM)** television standard, which likewise provides for 625 scan lines per frame and 25 frame changes per second. The SECAM and PAL standards differ, however, in other characteristics, which render them incompatible. Slight differences in national implementations of the SECAM and PAL standards also pose compatibility problems, even within the same standard.

The three prevailing television standards were developed at a time when electronic technologies in general, and video technology in particular, were new and, by current standards, primitive. **High-definition television (HDTV)** formats take advantage of the significant technological advances that have occurred over the last half-century. The definition, or amount of detail, visible in television images is determined by the number of scan lines that form the image. With 1,000 or more scan lines per frame, HDTV images are noticeably sharper than their NTSC, PAL, and SECAM counterparts. Prototype HDTV systems have been demonstrated since the 1970s, and HDTV broadcasting has been operational in Japan since the 1980s. HDTV-compatible video cameras, video tape recorders, and related equipment have likewise been in use for some time. Like conventional television standards, early Japanese HDTV technology employed analog coding of video images. HDTV broadcasting based on digital rather than analog coding began in the United States in late 1998. HDTV signals are incompatible with television receivers, video tape recorders, camcorders, and other devices that conform to the NTSC standard, which it is expected to eventually supplant.

As one of their most important advantages, digitally coded HDTV signals are compressed to conserve transmission bandwidth and, more pertinent to this discussion, for efficient storage. HDTV compression is based on the **MPEG-2** standard, which was developed by the Moving Picture Experts Group (MPEG) and approved by the International Organization for Standardization (ISO). MPEG is the collective designation for a group of standards for recording digitally coded audio-visual information in a compressed format. The MPEG format is also used to record video information on DVDs, compact disks, and the digital video tape media described in Chapter Two; by digital satellite television systems; and for digital audio recording.

AUDIO FILE FORMATS

Like video signals, audio information may be recorded on analog or digital media. As described in the preceding chapter, voice and music are widely recorded on magnetic tape cassettes and, in some cases, magnetic tape reels. These media store information in an analog-coded format that is supported by audio tape recorders and players. Product-compatibility is rarely an issue. Analog-coded voice or music information can be played by any devices that accept specific media such as C-type cassettes or microcassettes.

Compact disks store digitally coded audio information in the compact disk-audio (CDA) format, which is supported by CD-ROM and DVD-ROM drives as well as by audio compact disk and DVD players. As with analog tape recording systems, compatibility of equipment with recorded information is rarely an issue, although some CD-R and CD-ROM drives may have problems playing specific compact disks. DVD-Audio is a high-capacity, high-quality audio format based on DVD-Video technology. Principally intended for music, DVD-Audio disks can also store a limited amount of video information or graphic still images.

Web pages on the Internet or institutional intranets and extranets increasingly incorporate digitally coded sound clips that contain voice, music, or other audio information. These sound clips are usually posted to Web pages in the file formats in which they were digitized. Sound clips may be downloaded from Web pages to desktop computers, where they are stored on hard drives, optical disks, or other media. Apart from Web pages, digitized audio information may be incorporated into multimedia presentations, databases, or other electronic records.

As with all electronic records, digitized audio information is distributed and stored in formats determined by computer programs that create the information. These audio file formats differ in their technical characteristics, including file size and audio quality, which affect their suitability for specific applications. Whatever file format is employed, appropriate software is required to play digitized audio information. The required programs are termed *audio players*. In some cases, digitized audio information is compressed for efficient distribution or storage, in which case the audio player must include decompression capabilities. Although dozens of formats are available for computer storage of digitized audio information, the following file formats are widely encountered:

- The **waveform audio file (WAV) format** was developed by Microsoft and IBM for Windows-based computers, which are routinely equipped with appropriate software to play WAV files. Web browsers also incorporate the required audio player. The WAV format stores uncompressed audio files that must be downloaded then opened for playback.

- The Motion Picture Experts Group (MPEG) Audio Layer III (MP3) format is an outgrowth of digital audio technologies developed by Fraunhofer Institut Integrierte Schaultungen (Fraunhofer II-S) in Germany. It was approved by the International Organization for Standardization (ISO) and integrated into the MPEG specification in 1992. The MP3 format uses compression algorithms that drastically reduce the size of audio files while retaining a high level of sound quality. Two other MPEG formats (MP1 and MP2) support lower levels of audio quality.

- The Real Audio (RA) format, created by Progressive Networks, is compatible with streaming audio, which is played in real-time from Web servers subject to bandwidth considerations that limit audio fidelity. Real Audio files can also be downloaded for playback. Real Audio players are incorporated into Web browsers.

- VQF, developed in Japan by the NTT Human Interface Laboratories and Yamaha Corporation, is a file format for compressed audio. Intended for Windows-based computers, it is not as widely encountered as the MP3 format.

- The AU file format, developed by Sun Microsystems, is an uncompressed file format used by Unix computers.

- The audio interchange file format (AIFF) was developed by Apple Computer for Macintosh applications. An uncompressed file format, it has since been adopted by some other companies. The AIFC version supports compression.

SUMMARY

Computer files are customarily categorized by the type of information they contain. Text files, which may be produced by word processing programs or other software, contain character-coded information. The ASCII coding scheme, or one of its super-sets, is typically used to represent individual characters. Various utility programs facilitate the interchange of text files in proprietary formats. Alternatively, the ASCII text format provides broad compatibility for file importing and exporting.

Spreadsheet files may contain quantitative values, mathematical formulas, and predefined functions, in addition to textual information. Data files contain records that are subdivided into fields. Spreadsheet and data file formats are typically specific to the programs that created them, but utility programs and ASCII-delimited formats facilitate the interchange of information between different programs.

Computer-processible image files may be vector-based or bit-mapped. The former describes images in terms of geometric shapes such as points, lines, or circles. Bit-mapped images, in contrast, consist of dots that represent tonal values. Various image file formats have been developed for specific purposes. Commonly implemented formats, such as TIF and GIF, facilitate the exchange of computer-processible images. Image files be may recorded in compressed or uncompressed formats on magnetic or optical media. Compression is the rule in electronic document imaging implementations. Other computer files may be compressed to save space or reduce bandwidth requirements during file transfers, but compression can complicate the long-term retention of computer-processible information.

Television recording standards specify the characteristics of video images and, by implication, the devices that produce and play them. The NTSC standard is employed in North America, much of Latin America, Japan, and some other countries. The PAL television standard is employed in the United Kingdom, Germany, other European countries, and parts of South America, Asia, and Africa. The SECAM standard is employed in France, Russia, and parts of the Middle East. HDTV formats, which record video images in a digital compressed format, are incompatible with existing television standards.

Like video signals, audio information may be recorded on analog or digital media. Analog-coded voice or music information can be played by any devices that accept specific media such as C-type cassettes or microcassettes. Digitized audio information is distributed and stored in formats determined by computer programs that create the information. Audio file formats differ in their technical characteristics, including file size and audio quality. Appropriate software is required to play digitized audio information, which may be compressed for efficient distribution or storage.

CHAPTER FOUR

INVENTORYING
ELECTRONIC RECORDS

Broadly defined, a *records inventory* is a fact-finding survey used to identify and describe the characteristics of records created or received by all or part of a business, government agency, or other organization. The purpose of conducting an inventory is to gather information about the nature and number of records that an organization maintains. By conducting a records inventory, a records manager can obtain a detailed listing that could include the types, locations, dates, volumes, equipment, classification systems, and usage date of an organization's records. Records management, as previously noted, is a problem-solving activity. An organization's records management problems cannot be successfully addressed until those problems are clearly delineated and fully understood. The characteristics of an organization's records cannot be determined by intuition or anecdotal evidence; empirical methods are necessary. Conducting a thorough inventory is the initial step in a scientific approach to systematic control of recorded information. Whether records are in paper, photographic, or electronic format, a thorough inventory is an essential component of an effective records management program.

Properly conducted, a records inventory provides comprehensive information about the nature and number of records maintained by a corporation, government agency, educational institution, or other organization. It describes the purpose and characteristics of the organization's records, the conditions under which they are stored, and the ways in which they are used. A records inventory is a means to an end rather than an end in itself. Information collected during the inventory is used to prepare records retention schedules, which, as discussed in Chapter Five, indicate the lengths of time that specific types of records are to be kept. In particular, a records inventory will identify inactive records that might be discarded or transferred from office locations to off-site storage. A comprehensive records inventory will also identify vital records and provide potentially valuable information about the quantity, arrangement, and use of an organization's active records.

A comprehensive inventory, by definition, encompasses records of all types. It must include machine-readable electronic records as well as human-readable information recorded on paper or photographic media. The following discussion is limited to inventories of electronic records. Inventory strategies and procedures for human-readable records have been defined and refined by five decades of records management experience. Well developed and widely accepted, they are explained in various records management textbooks and other publications. Inventory methodologies for electronic records are similar to, and adapted from, methods for inventorying paper and photographic records, but the distinctive characteristics of electronic records—especially their machine-readable content and dependence on specific configurations of hardware and/or software for continued utility—warrant special consideration. In particular, certain descriptive information collected during an inventory of electronic records will differ from information gathered when inventorying human-readable paper or photographic media.

As with human-readable paper or photographic records, an inventory of electronic records consists of four work steps:

1. Develop an inventory strategy—that is, a plan for conducting the records inventory.
2. Prepare a survey instrument for collection of inventory information.
3. Conduct the inventory according to plan.
4. Tabulate or otherwise write up the inventory results, gathering additional information and performing other follow-up work as necessary.

The following sections explain and discuss these work steps, emphasizing practical considerations for records managers who must plan and conduct inventories of electronic records. Much of the discussion is also applicable to human-readable paper and photographic records, but those information resources are outside the scope of this book. However, inventories of electronic records may also collect information about computer printouts, computer-output microfilm (COM), data entry source documents, or other human-readable records that are related to electronic records. Once an inventory of electronic records is completed, its results must be analyzed. That activity, which leads to the preparation of retention schedules, is considered in Chapter Five.

INVENTORY STRATEGY

The purpose of an inventory is to identify and describe records maintained by all or part of an organization. At a minimum, an inventory strategy must address the scope of the inventory and the procedures to be used to identify electronic records within a given organization. To accomplish its intended purpose in a reasonable amount of time with usable results, an inventory must have a manageable scope, where *scope* denotes the specific parts of an organization and/or the types of records to be included in the inventory. To be comprehensive, as discussed in Chapter One, a records management program must encompass all information created, maintained, and used by a business, government agency, or other organization, regardless of the format. Ultimately, inventories must cover all records, whether electronic or nonelectronic, in every division, department, or other unit of an organization. Enterprise-wide inventories may be possible in small-to-medium-size work environments—a company or government agency with fewer than 100 departments, for example. Ambitious inventory strategies pose significant logistic and analytical complications, however, in large corporations, government agencies, or other organizations with complex administrative structures.

Inventorying electronic records is a labor-intensive activity that requires painstaking attention to detail. In large organizations, enterprise-wide inventories that attempt to cover all electronic records in a single initiative can take a long time to complete; multiyear inventorying projects are not unheard of. Preparation of retention schedules and other tasks that depend on inventory data—and are the rationale for conducting an inventory—will be correspondingly delayed. Data gathering can be accelerated by hiring temporary workers, forming special project teams, or otherwise augmenting personnel resources, but data gathering is only one part of an inventory initiative. The inventory results must be analyzed by records management staff, an intellectual activity that can rarely be expedited. If useful results are to be obtained, an inventory cannot be rushed. Further, some information collected during early stages of a lengthy enterprise-wide inventory may become obsolete before the inventory is completed. Computer, audio, and video systems that generate electronic records may be modified, replaced, or taken out of service, with a resulting impact on the reference value or other characteristics of electronic records. Departments or other organizational units may merge, expand, or be dissolved. Recordkeeping practices will be affected, and inventory work must be redone.

A manageable scope is critical to the success of an inventorying initiative. For best results, an inventory's scope should be limited initially to a single division or other part of a large organization or to one organizational function that crosses departmental boundaries. In a pharmaceutical company, for example, an inventory of electronic records might begin in the research and development division. When that inventory is completed, and results have been analyzed, inventory work can proceed to marketing, manufacturing, and other organizational units. In a hospital, an inventory of electronic records may be initially limited to accounting, human resources, and other administrative departments, with patient records to follow in a second stage. Alternatively—and, often, less successfully—an inventory might be limited to a specific type of electronic records such as financial records in a corporation or government agency, case files in a law firm, engineering project records in a manufacturing company, or student records in an academic institution. Limitations on record type can be combined with organizational limitations; as an example, an inventory might be limited to the research and development division of a pharmaceutical company and, initially, to regulatory records within that division.

Under the best circumstances, inventorying electronic records is a difficult and time-consuming task. Meetings must be scheduled. Information must be collected and analyzed for completeness and usability. Follow-up discussions may be necessary to verify information or clarify specific points. The invisible nature of electronic records complicates matters. Limiting the scope of an inventory will make it more manageable and permit faster completion. Results and benefits will be obtained more quickly, although the results will admittedly impact only a segment of the organization.

Regardless of scope, inventories of electronic records are typically conducted on a program unit basis. This approach was developed for nonelectronic records, and it is applicable to electronic records as well. For purposes of this discussion, a *program unit* is broadly defined as a division, department, section, or other administrative unit of a corporation, government agency, or other organization. As a generic designation, *program unit* avoids confusion associated with differing hierarchical relationships among administrative units. In some organizations, departments are subordinate to divisions; in other cases, the reverse is true. A department may be divided into offices, branches, or sections; alternatively, a section, branch, or office may be the highest level in an organization's administrative hierarchy.

Within a corporation, government agency, educational institution, or other organization, program units vary in size, complexity, and hierarchical interrelationships, as well as in the number and types of records they create, maintain, and use. Some program units may be large departments with hundreds of employees and huge quantities of electronic and nonelectronic records; others may be small offices staffed by one or two persons who maintain a few paper files and a small quantity of electronic records. When planning an inventory of electronic records, the program units to be included must be identified. Identification is typically done by consulting organization charts, directories, or administrative handbooks. In many cases, however, such documents are out-of-date, and additional program units may be discovered while the inventory is in progress or after it has been completed.

Program units are typically distinguished by their specific missions and responsibilities, which are presumably related to and supported by the electronic records they create or maintain. For each program unit, inventorying, retention scheduling, and related operations are applied to records at the series level. For purposes of this discussion, a *records series* is a group of logically related records that support one or more business operations performed by a given program unit. Records in a series are normally used, indexed, and/or filed together. A records inventory seeks to identify and describe the individual records series maintained by and in each program unit. Examples of records series might include a file of open purchase orders in a corporate purchasing department, a file of construction contracts in an engineering project management office, a file of employee resumes in a human resources department, a file of unresolved claims in an insurance company, a master accounts payable file in an accounting department, a file of property records in a municipal building department, or an applications pending file in a college admissions department. Records in any of these series might be maintained in electronic or nonelectronic formats. Often, they exist in both formats.

Many records series are readily identified and inventoried in the program units where they are physically maintained or in other locations, such as off-site storage, that a program unit may employ. If desired, inventories of paper, photographic, and electronic records can be integrated and performed at the same time. If systematic records management is a new activity for a given organization, inventories should cover all types of records. Combined (integrated) inventories are also recommended for organizations that need to update retention schedules prepared in the past for nonelectronic records. Among its advantages, the integrated approach can simplify the logistics of inventorying by reducing the number of required site visits and meetings when compared with separate inventories of electronic and nonelectronic records. Integrated inventories can also provide useful insights into the interrelationship and redundancy of information maintained in various formats. Often, electronic records series are related to nonelectronic records series. For example, many computer-processible records series, including word processing files from which correspondence and other documents are printed, databases from which paper or COM reports are generated, and CAD files from which engineering drawings are produced, are related to the printed nonelectronic documents. Similarly, audio recordings created by dictation equipment are usually transcribed to produce paper copies.

Whether inventories of electronic records are combined with paper and photographic records or performed separately, the identification of electronic records is complicated by the fact that such records are invisible. They may be maintained on magnetic tapes, diskettes, optical disks, or other removable media described in Chapter Two, but many are stored, out of view, on nonremovable hard drives. Electronic records may contain unique information, or their contents may coexist with records in nonelectronic formats. When inventorying individual program units, the existence of electronic records can be determined by inquiring about electronic counterparts whenever paper or photographic records are identified. That approach, however, will not identify electronic records that have no paper or photographic counterparts. Some records managers consequently recommend that electronic records be inventoried by identifying and analyzing the automated information systems with which they are associated.

Broadly defined, an *automated information system* consists of hardware and/or software components designed to perform one or more information processing operations. To identify electronic records associated with computer-based information systems, a records manager must first identify the application software utilized by a given department, office, or other program unit. Both custom-developed computer programs and prewritten software packages must be considered. Data files, text files, or other electronic records series associated with such programs are then identified and inventoried in a manner described later in this chapter. This method is easiest to implement for electronic records created and maintained by timeshared minicomputers, network servers, and personal computers installed in and operated by a given program unit. It can also be used for electronic records associated with information processing applications that run on mainframes, minicomputers, and network servers installed outside the program unit. Such computers, which create and maintain electronic records for a program unit, may be operated by a centralized information technology department or by a commercial computer service bureau.

The same methodology can be used to inventory electronic records created and/or used by audio and video recording and playback equipment, as well as by data recorders and other specialized instrumentation encountered in certain scientific, engineering, and medical applications. As with computer-based information systems, the records manager must first determine the types of devices employed by a given program unit, then identify the electronic records associated with such devices. If a program unit has camcorders or other video recording equipment, for example, the records manager should inquire about video tapes or other media produced by such equipment. Similarly, records managers should inquire about video records produced for the program unit by centralized video departments or video service companies.

As a potentially significant limitation, inventories conducted on a program unit basis may fail to identify electronic records shared by two or more program units. Such records are often associated with enterprise-wide information systems that support interdepartmental communications, budget preparation, multidepartmental transaction processing, and such analytical activities as knowledge management, data mining, and decision support. Examples include electronic mail, Web pages posted on the public Internet or organizational intranets and extranets, computerized document repositories created by electronic document imaging and document management software, and centralized databases and data warehouses of financial, personnel, customer, product, and other information. Although electronic mail systems, database management systems, and other centralized information resources serve multiple program units, they are not the property of any single program unit. The records they create and maintain usually reside on mainframes, minicomputers, or network servers operated and administered by centralized information technology departments. Program units access these enterprise-wide electronic records, but they are not responsible for storing, protecting, or otherwise managing them. The records are not stored locally. Consequently, they may not be mentioned during program unit inventories.

In some respects, records associated with enterprise-wide information resources are the electronic counterparts of central files of paper documents or microfilm maintained by some organizations. Although the existence of centralized information systems may be revealed when individual program units are inventoried, program unit personnel may not be able to answer detailed questions about the scope, formats, technical attributes, or other characteristics of the electronic records stored in enterprise-wide repositories. To obtain this information, electronic records must be inventoried at their centralized locations. As a complication, however, information technology departments that operate the computer systems on which electronic records reside may know little about the role of recorded information in specific business operations. Their principal concern is the implementation and operation of computer hardware and software for records creation, storage, and backup. Information about the use of and retention requirements for electronic records stored in enterprise-wide repositories must usually be obtained from program unit personnel who retrieve or otherwise work with the records. Often, multiple program units must be consulted to obtain a complete picture of the various uses of the records.

Identifying electronic records in their program units and identifying electronic records by the automated information systems that produce them are not mutually exclusive inventorying strategies. Both methods are usually necessary to identify all electronic records maintained by a given organization.

INVENTORY METHODOLOGY

An inventory of electronic records cannot succeed without top management support and the cooperation of individual program units. To encourage support, the objective of the inventory and its relationship to the systematic control of electronic records, must be explained to, and appreciated by, appropriate levels of management. To demonstrate its support, top management should send a directive to all program units that will be affected by an inventory of electronic records. The directive should announce that an inventory of electronic records has been authorized and that the cooperation of program unit personnel is expected. Presented as a management memorandum, the directive is typically drafted by the records management staff for signature by the top managers. At a minimum, the memorandum should:

- Acknowledge the value of electronic records as information resources;
- Emphasize the importance of managing electronic records in a systematic manner;
- Explain the role of the records inventory as an essential data gathering activity and the critical first step in the systematic control of electronic records;
- Indicate when the inventory will begin, who will conduct it, and approximately how long it will take; and
- Instruct each program unit to designate a liaison person who will assist the records manager in inventorying electronic records.

Liaison persons, sometimes described as *records coordinators* or *program unit records officers*, are crucial to the success of records inventories and other records management initiatives. Liaison persons are the principal contact persons for all records management activities within their program units. They will assist the records manager in conducting inventories of electronic records and in formulating retention and disposition recommendations for their program units. Once schedules are finalized, the liaison persons will be responsible for implementing them.

To be useful, an inventory of electronic records must collect certain information about the physical and application characteristics of such records. The information will be used to prepare retention schedules for electronic records; an inventory's effectiveness is entirely judged by its suitability for that purpose. Inventories of electronic records must be conducted systematically and efficiently, using well-planned inventory procedures. A formalized survey instrument will ensure the usefulness, uniformity, and completeness of information collected during the inventory process. The survey instrument delineates the descriptive data and other items of information that must be collected for each electronic records series.

The survey instrument may be distributed as a questionnaire to liaison persons in individual program units. Completed questionnaires are to be returned to the records management unit by a specified date. Alternatively, records management staff can consult with individual program units to conduct physical surveys of electronic records series. Assisted by the program unit's liaison person, records managers will personally collect the information required by the survey instrument. The questionnaire and consultative methods are equally applicable to electronic and nonelectronic records. Five decades of records management theory and practice involving paper documents and microfilm have identified the advantages and limitations of each approach.

The principal advantage of the *questionnaire method* is shorter elapsed time for the data collection phase of a records inventory. A short timeframe is achieved through distribution of the inventory workload among liaison persons. Multiple program units can consequently be inventoried simultaneously. The *consultation method*, in contrast, relies on the records management staff or, in many cases, a records manager as solo practitioner who must inventory program units sequentially. As an obvious shortcoming, the questionnaire method provides limited opportunities for direct interaction between program unit personnel who conduct the inventory and the records management staff who must prepare retention recommendations based on inventory data. Even under the best circumstances, obtaining information sufficiently clear and detailed for analysis by others is difficult. Misinterpretations, discrepancies in calculations, and some marginally useful responses are to be expected. For best results, records management staff should provide orientation sessions for liaison persons, supplemented by detailed written instructions, to explain the questionnaire's purpose and content. The orientation sessions should review the data elements to be collected and provide examples of appropriate responses to specific questions. Records management staff must also be available, in person or by telephone, to answer questions or clarify issues that may arise during the inventorying process.

Although it takes longer than the questionnaire method and involves a greater commitment of time and resources by the records management department, the *consultation method* usually yields more accurate, reliable, and immediately usable information about electronic records. It produces more detailed responses and minimizes the potential for misinterpretation; confusing points can often be clarified during the inventory itself. The consultation method relies on two techniques that are well established in information systems analysis: direct observation by the records manager of electronic recordkeeping practices and interviews with persons who create, maintain, and use electronic records. The records management staff works directly with liaison persons in each program unit to identify and describe electronic records. Presumably, liaison persons are knowledgeable about the way in which electronic records series are created, stored, and used in their program units. During the inventory, the records manager interviews the liaison person to determine the characteristics of electronic records series maintained by a given program unit. The formalized survey instrument serves as an interview script. Where more detailed information about specific records series is required, liaison persons will arrange interviews with other program unit employees. The records manager also has the opportunity to retrieve samples of electronic records for display or printing. Electronic storage media can likewise be examined.

The questionnaire and consultation methods are not mutually exclusive. As a potentially effective combination of the two approaches, records management staff may distribute survey instruments to individual program units for completion, then conduct site visits and interviews with liaison persons to review, clarify, or expand the responses from program units. In some cases, the questionnaire method is the only practical approach to inventorying electronic records. Because of time or economic constraints, for example, records management staff may be unable to conduct site visits and interviews at field offices, branch locations, international subsidiaries, or other geographically remote program units. If an organization has multiple field offices or branch locations with similar recordkeeping practices, a site visit and interviews may be conducted at several locations, and the remainder surveyed by the questionnaire method.

Regardless of the method employed, sufficient time must be allotted to complete the inventory. Although a sense of urgency may stimulate productivity, unrealistic deadlines are not compatible with quality work. If the consultation method is used, site visits and interviews will require at least one-half day per program unit, exclusive of preparation, travel time to the program unit location, and follow-up work. These tasks can double or triple the time required to inventory a given program unit. Several days and multiple site visits may be required to inventory electronic records in large program units. As discussed at the end of this chapter, additional time will be required to tabulate or otherwise write up the inventory's findings from notes taken during interviews and site visits. Follow-up interviews or telephone calls will often be necessary to clarify specific points raised during interviews.

Thus, an inventory of electronic records in a corporation or government agency with 100 program units will require at least 200 to 250 working days (about one calendar year), exclusive of the time required to analyze inventory results and draft retention schedules, as discussed in Chapter Five. That estimate may be optimistic. Some site visits may be difficult to schedule. Cancellations and rescheduling are inevitable and will delay the work. Follow-up requirements are unpredictable and can be time-consuming. Inventories that combine electronic and nonelectronic records will take longer to complete. Even when the questionnaire method is used, inventorying electronic records is a time-consuming process. Some responses will be late. Repeated telephone calls may be necessary to obtain the completed questionnaires. Responses prepared by liaison persons must be reviewed and, where necessary, clarified by records management staff. Systematic, thorough inventories cannot be rushed. Top management must understand that time spent obtaining reliable, detailed information about electronic records will facilitate the preparation of appropriate retention recommendations, the identification of vital electronic records, and other records management activities that depend on accurate, complete inventory data.

THE SURVEY INSTRUMENT

Electronic records are typically inventoried at the series level, where a *records series* is a group of logically related records that support one or more operations performed by a given program unit. Presumably, liaison persons are familiar with the major electronic records series maintained by their program units. Major electronic records series are notable for both their quantity and importance to program unit operations. They are readily identifiable. Records managers will usually have to work harder during interviews and site visits to identify minor electronic records series, which are less important and less voluminous. No matter how diligent the inventory procedures, some minor series may be overlooked.

A survey instrument specifies the descriptive data and other items of information to be collected for each electronic records series maintained by a given program unit. Depending on the inventory method employed, the survey instrument may be formatted as a questionnaire to be distributed to individual program units. Alternatively, it may simply be a checklist of questions to be asked by records management staff, a script to be used when conducting site visits and interviewing program unit personnel. The checklist shown in Figure 4-1 may be used to assure that all necessary information is collected during an inventory.

Regardless of approach, the following discussion lists and explains the types of information to be collected about each series during an inventory of electronic records. Typically, an inventory begins with general information about the scope, purpose, and quantity of an electronic records series. Other information describes the physical and technical characteristics of electronic media, their storage locations, and reference requirements for electronic records series.

Series Title

The series title is the name by which an electronic record is known to the program unit that creates or maintains it. The title will identify the electronic records series in retention schedules, reports, and other documents prepared from inventory data. Consequently, it should be as descriptive as possible. At a minimum, the title must clearly distinguish a given electronic records series from others maintained by the program unit. Examples of acceptably descriptive series titles for electron-

Figure 4-1:
Electronic Records Series Inventory Checklist

CHECKLIST FOR INVENTORYING ELECTRONIC RECORDS SERIES

- ❑ Series title
- ❑ Summary description
- ❑ Copy type(s)
  - ❑ Storage copy
  - ❑ Working copy
  - ❑ Security copy
- ❑ File type
- ❑ Dates covered
- ❑ Arrangement
- ❑ Quantity
  - ❑ Item count
  - ❑ Bytes
  - ❑ Recording time
- ❑ Estimated growth
- ❑ Physical storage requirements
- ❑ Storage location(s)

- ❑ Media characteristics
  - ❑ Type and size of medium
  - ❑ Brand and model
  - ❑ Recording format
  - ❑ Special features
- ❑ Media manufacturing date
- ❑ Hardware environment
- ❑ Software environment
  - ❑ Systems software
  - ❑ Application software
- ❑ Reference activity
- ❑ Retention requirements
- ❑ Relationship to human-readable records
- ❑ Supporting files
- ❑ Vital record status

---

ic records include "Technical Reports Catalog," for a data file of bibliographic citations pertaining to research reports created by a pharmaceutical laboratory; "Construction Cost Estimates," for spreadsheet files pertaining to projects undertaken by a construction company; "Standard Clauses," for word processing files that contain clauses to be incorporated into contracts prepared by a law firm; "Building Site Inspections," for video tapes that provide visual records of field inspections undertaken by a municipal building department; and "Liability Case Depositions," for audio recordings of legal depositions.

Summary Description

A brief (approximately one paragraph) description of the contents of the electronic records series should summarize the business purpose, scope, and content of the series. With some records series, such as the "Construction Cost Estimates" example, the title describes the series' content, but additional details can clarify the business purpose and scope of such a series. The additional details might indicate the specific construction projects for which costs are estimated, the types of estimates provided, the circumstances under which the estimates are prepared, or the relationship of a series to other records series maintained in the program unit or elsewhere in the organization. Similarly, a brief descriptive paragraph for the "Building Site Inspections" series of video tapes might indicate the specific buildings covered by the videotaped inspection reports and describe the circumstances under which the video tapes were created. In every case, a statement of purpose should indicate the relationship of the electronic records series to the mission of the program unit, administrative activities, or business operations.

Copy Type(s)

An electronic records series may be a unique accumulation of information or one of several copies. In the latter case, which is more likely where appropriate back-up procedures are implemented, the type of copy should be indicated. A given electronic records series may be a storage copy, a working copy, or a security copy kept off-site. Multiple copies of electronic records series should be inventoried separately, and their intended purposes should be reflected in their series titles. For example, a descriptive title such as "General Ledger—Backup" could be used for a security copy of an electronic records series recorded on magnetic tape; a title such as "General Ledger—Archival" might denote a copy that contains older, inactive electronic records intended for long-term storage.

File Type

Electronic records series are usually categorized by file type, where a file broadly denotes a collection of electronic information. Electronic file types, as discussed in Chapter Three, include computer files, video files, and audio files. Electronic files may be further categorized by the type of information they contain and by the format in which the information is recorded. Examples of descriptive categories for computer-processable information include text files, spreadsheet files, data files, or image files. For each category, further subdivision provides additional description.

Text files, for example, might be categorized as ASCII text, ASCII text with line breaks, or native word processing formats. Image files might be categorized as TIF, GIF, or proprietary formats. Video recordings may be described by the television standard employed. Audio recordings may be categorized as music or spoken word.

Dates Covered

During inventories, records managers must determine the inclusive (beginning and ending) dates for information contained in each electronic records series. Compared with paper documents and microfilm maintained by a given program unit, electronic records series will usually have more recent beginning dates. Computer-processible records series rarely predate the mid-1960s for information generated by mainframe computers, the mid-1970s for information generated by minicomputers, and the mid-1980s for information generated by personal computers. In most organizations, video recordings date from the mid-1980s, when video cassette recorders and portable video cameras became widely available and affordable. Often, audio recordings are the oldest types of electronic records maintained by an organization. Voice dictation equipment has been used in office applications since the early twentieth century. Regardless of type, electronic records series that support ongoing business operations will have open ending dates. Closed electronic records series are typically characterized by obsolete media, defunct equipment, or discontinued business operations.

Arrangement

The arrangement is the physical sequence of electronic records within a series. It denotes both the sequencing of information within a given medium—the arrangement of files within a magnetic tape, for example, and the sequencing of individual media within a collection—the arrangement of multiple tapes in relation to one another. Arrangement concepts are borrowed from paper filing systems, where alphabetic, numeric, or other arrangements are easily identified and reflect users' reference requirements. In paper filing systems, documents are usually arranged by their principal retrieval parameter. If patient records are requested by patient name, for example, they are filed in that sequence. Similarly, legal files retrieved by case number are filed by that identifier.

Arrangement concepts are applicable to some electronic records, particularly audio and video recordings. In a series of videotaped building inspections, for example, one tape may be made per inspection, and the tapes may be arranged by building number or project number. Similarly, dictated correspondence and other office documents may be arranged chronologically within a series of audio tapes. In an oral history collection, interviews may be recorded on separate audio tapes, which are arranged alphabetically by the name of the interviewee.

Arrangements are more difficult to determine and less meaningful when inventorying computer records series. Within a given magnetic or optical disk, electronic records are invisible; record sequences cannot be determined by observation, as they can with paper files. Further, the arrangement of word processing documents, spreadsheet files, database records, document images, or other information within a magnetic or optical disk is usually beyond the user's control. The computer's operating system determines where electronic records will be stored, often on a space available basis. Access is provided by directories and indexes; users are unaware of the physical sequence in which information is recorded within a given medium. In many cases, unrelated documents and files are intermingled within a disk, and a given file may be fragmented among several disk locations.

Within magnetic tapes, information is often recorded in the sequence in which it will be processed. Back-up tapes usually mirror the sequence of the media they copy. For removable computer media, such as magnetic tapes, diskettes, and optical disks, arrangement is often synonymous with the shelving sequence in off-line storage. Such media may be arranged on shelves by control number, application, program unit, or other parameters.

Quantity

For each records series, the inventory must collect information about the quantity of electronic records and the locations and conditions in which the records are stored. The quantity of a given electronic records series should be expressed in one or more measures appropriate to the type of records being inventoried. For video and audio records, quantity is easily measured by the number of tapes or other media the series occupies. It may also be measured by recording time in minutes or hours. If an electronic records series does not fill a given medium, the percentage occupied should be indicated. If other records series are stored on the same medium, they should be described briefly. For word processing documents, databases, image files, or other computer-processible records series, quantity is customarily measured in bytes or multiples thereof (megabytes, gigabytes, etc.). That measure may be supplemented by an item count in the case of magnetic tapes, diskettes, or other removable media.

Estimated Growth

Information about the annual growth of electronic records is essential for planning future storage requirements. When presented to management in an appropriately alarmist manner, growth estimates can also encourage a sense of urgency about records management initiatives. Unless the operations they support are discontinued, the quantity of electronic records created and maintained by a corporation, government agency, or other organization will increase over time. Anticipated annual growth rates for a given electronic records series are most easily and conveniently determined when the series is subdivided by year. In such cases, the number of media, byte totals, or other quantity measures can be compared for different years.

Where a given series is not subdivided by year, annual growth must be estimated in other ways, such as relating the growth of records to some measurable factor. As with paper documents, the creation of electronic records is typically linked to events or transactions, such as the receipt of new orders in a sales application, the issuance of new policies or receipt of new claims in an insurance application, the acceptance of new clients in a social services application, the hiring of new employees in a personnel application, or the initiation of new projects in an engineering application. If such events or transactions are increasing at a specific annual rate, electronic records associated with such transactions will grow at a corresponding rate. Thus, if a database record is created each time an order is received from a customer and if new orders are increasing by 10 percent per year, the number of database records pertaining to customer orders should also increase by 10 percent. If 5,000 order records were created this year, 5,500 order records will be created next year.

Where the foregoing methods are inapplicable, dates for database entries, word processing documents, video recordings, or other items from one or more segments of an electronic records series can be tabulated and the totals compared. As an aid to such tabulations, media directories, described in Chapter Seven, often indicate creation dates for specific files.

Physical Storage Requirements

Quantity estimates, measured in linear feet occupied by removable magnetic or optical media, provide useful information about the amount of physical storage space required by a given electronic records series. In particular, such measurements alert the records manager to potential storage space problems posed by voluminous electronic records series. The approximate number of linear feet occupied by commonly encountered types of media can be calculated from the following measurements:

- Nine-track magnetic tape reels: one linear inch per reel, 12 reels per linear foot.
- Half-inch magnetic tape cartridges: one linear inch per cartridge, 12 cartridges per linear foot.
- Digital linear tape (DLT) cartridges: one linear inch per cartridge, 12 cartridges per linear foot.
- QIC magnetic tape cartridges: 1.5 linear inches per QIC data cartridge, eight cartridges per linear foot; one linear inch per QIC minicartridge, 12 cartridges per linear foot.
- Eight-millimeter data cartridges: 0.75 linear inch per cartridge, 16 cartridges per linear foot.
- Digital audio tape (DAT) cartridges: 0.5 linear inch per cartridge, 24 cartridges per linear foot.
- Diskettes, 3.5-inch: 0.14 linear inch per diskette, 85 diskettes per linear foot.
- Audio tape cassettes: 0.75 linear inch per boxed cassette, 16 cassettes per linear foot.
- Video cassettes: one linear inch per unboxed cassette, 12 cassettes per linear foot; 1.25 linear inches per cassette in a plastic box, 9 cassettes per linear foot.
- Optical disk cartridges, 5.25-inch: 0.75 linear inches per cartridge, 16 cartridges per linear foot.
- Compact disks and DVDs: 0.5 linear inch per compact disk or DVD in a plastic box, 24 compact disks or DVDs per linear foot.

Storage Location(s)

Electronic records series may be housed in an office, a computing center, an off-site warehouse, or another facility. Records from a given series may be stored on different types of media and in multiple locations; active records may be kept on a hard drive, for example, while older records are transferred to magnetic tape for off-site storage. The inventory should indicate all storage locations for each electronic records series and for all copies of a given series. If storage facilities have special security or environmental attributes, whether suitable or unsuitable, they should be noted.

Media Characteristics

The inventory must include a detailed description of the physical and technical characteristics of the media on which particular electronic records series are stored. As discussed in Chapter Two, magnetic disks, magnetic tapes, and optical disks are the most important media for electronic records, but punched cards, punched paper tape, or other obsolete media may also be encountered, particularly when inventorying off-site storage locations. The description of physical and technical characteristics should include the type and size of medium (5.25-inch rewritable optical disk, 3.5-inch diskettes, 200-foot 3480-type cartridge, etc.), the brand and model (the manufacturers' product designation, such as 3M DC2000 data cartridges or Maxell XL II audio cassettes), the recording format (such as double-sided, high-density for 3.5-inch diskettes or 9.4 gigabytes for double-sided DVD-R media), and any special attributes or enhancements (such as backcoating) that may affect performance. This information can be used to evaluate the suitability and quality of media on which electronic records are stored.

Media Manufacturing Date

Information about media stability and hardware or software dependencies is necessary to estimate the remaining service lives of specific media that contain electronic records. As discussed in Chapter Five, magnetic and optical media are subject to time-dependent degradation that will ultimately affect their utility for recording and retrieving information. If the remaining stable life of a given medium is shorter than the retention period for the electronic records the medium contains, the records must eventually be recopied onto new media. The stability of magnetic and optical media is measured from the media manufacturing date, not the date when information was recorded.

Unfortunately, media manufacturing dates can be difficult to determine. Occasionally, manufacturing dates are printed on media packaging or shipping documents. If the manufacturing date is not indicated, the procurement date or the date when the medium was first put into service is often a satisfactory substitute. Presumably, the media in question were recently manufactured when purchased or initially used. Including the manufacturing date, or an estimate thereof, is helpful when preparing media labels.

Hardware Environment

Electronic records, as discussed in Chapter One, depend on specific hardware components for reference or other uses. An inventory must consequently include a list and description of all equipment required to retrieve or otherwise process a given electronic records series. In some cases, a generic hardware description will suffice. Examples of acceptable generic descriptions include "a Macintosh computer system with CD-RW drive," "a video cassette recorder with Super-VHS playback capabilities," or "an audio cassette deck with Type IV tape compatibility." Some electronic records can only be utilized with specific equipment, however. Certain computer-processible electronic records require specific brands and/or models of computers and storage peripherals. Hard disk cartridges and high-capacity diskettes, for example, require proprietary storage peripherals. Further, inventories may encounter older electronic records that require discontinued equipment such as nonstandard 5.25-inch write-once optical disk drives or U-Matic videocassette players. Electronic records may also require computer configurations an organization has replaced with different models.

Software Environment

Computer-processible electronic records are used with specific programs. The inventory must include a list, with brief descriptions, of all computer programs required to reference or otherwise process electronic records. The list must include systems software (operating systems, compilers, interpreters, and utility programs), as well as application software (word processing programs, spreadsheet programs, database management systems, electronic document imaging programs, etc.). Program names and version numbers must be provided because electronic records created by one version of a given computer program may not be compatible with other versions. For custom-developed software, the programming language should be determined and a brief developmental history obtained. For prewritten software packages, the publisher or procurement source should be indicated. As with hardware components, some organizations may maintain electronic records that require obsolete software components such as discontinued software packages or custom-developed programs that have been removed from service.

As a potential complication discussed in Chapter Three, some computer applications employ compression algorithms to reduce storage requirements for data, text, or image files. Such algorithms can have an impact on the future utility of electronic records because compressed information must be decompressed by compatible programs for reference or other processing. When inventorying compressed records, specific compression algorithms and software requirements should be determined. Compression adds another layer of software dependency to the management of electronic records. To minimize future problems, compression should be used sparingly for electronic records intended for long-term storage. With some computer-processible information, such as electronic document images or multimedia presentations, compression is necessary for efficient storage. Compression is rarely necessary with word processing documents, database records, or other character-coded information.

Reference Activity

An analysis of reference activity should consider the functions an electronic records series supports, the method and frequency of reference, the departments or other organizational units that use the records, and access privileges or restrictions associated with specific users and/or business operations. This information is best obtained by interviewing representative users of an electronic records series. For electronic records series, as with most information, frequency of reference usually diminishes over time. During interviews with program unit personnel, the records manager should determine the point in time when reference activity begins to decline and, where applicable, the point in time when all or part of a given electronic records series is no longer referenced.

The records manager should also determine the users' speed expectations when retrieving information from specific electronic records series; such requirements will dictate the devices and media to be used for records storage. Four levels of information retrieval requirements can be distinguished:

- **On-line:** Certain information processing applications require that electronic records be continuously available for immediate reference. In such applications, reference activity is frequent and, more often than not, unpredictable. To satisfy such reference requirements, electronic records are stored on hard disk drives for on-line access in fractions of a second.

- **Near-line:** Some computer applications, such as electronic document imaging, may be satisfied by slightly longer retrieval times. Near-line storage devices, such as optical disk autochangers, provide unattended access to large amounts of information with retrieval times of 20 seconds or less. Near-line access may also satisfy reference requirements for multimedia applications that involve combinations of computer, video, and audio information. Although a bit slower than their on-line counterparts, near-line storage devices may better satisfy voluminous storage requirements. Magnetic tape autochangers are sometimes categorized as *near-line devices*, but the serial-access characteristics of magnetic tape limit retrieval responsiveness. Access times with such devices are measured in minutes rather than seconds.

- **Off-line:** Removable electronic media, such as floppy disks, optical disk cartridges, and magnetic tapes, can be stored in desktop trays, in cabinets, on shelves, or in other containers until required for specific information processing operations. Retrieval times with off-line media may be measured in minutes or fractions of an hour. Manual intervention is required for media retrieval, mounting, and reshelving.

- **Off-site:** Removable magnetic and optical media may be stored in records centers, warehouses, or other off-site locations. Off-site storage is best suited to inactive electronic records or to security copies. Depending on the off-site storage location, retrieval times may be measured in hours or days.

Retention Requirements

A records inventory is a means to an end, rather than an end in itself. Its principal purpose is to provide information necessary to prepare retention schedules for electronic records. As discussed in Chapter Five, most retention recommendations rely on the perceived requirements of program units that create, maintain, and use electronic records. Such requirements are typically based on operational experience with specific electronic records series. A program unit contends that it must retain a specific electronic records series for seven years, for example, because it has referenced records from that series that were seven years old. During the inventory, records managers should ask about the program unit's operational retention requirements. Records managers should also determine events, such as the end of a fiscal year, expiration of a contract, or completion of a project, that may cause electronic records within a given series to become less active and, ultimately, inactive.

Relationship to Human-Readable Records

Many electronic records are related to, and often duplicate, human-readable information recorded on paper or microfilm. In most word processing applications, for example, paper file copies are printed from computer-processible files. Electronic mail may be printed for reference purposes. Databases are used to print paper reports that provide a "snapshot" of database records at a particular point in time or for a particular set of variables. Whenever paper or microfilm records are encountered during an inventory, records managers should inquire about any electronic records with identical or similar contents. Whenever electronic records are encountered, records managers should inquire about corresponding paper and microfilm records.

Supporting Files

The inventory should include a brief description of any electronic or other files that support the creation, maintenance, or use of a given electronic records series. As an example, some databases and other computer files rely on indexes that contain pointers to specified field values. Such indexes are essential to effective and efficient processing of database records or other information. Similarly, electronic document imaging systems are linked to a computer database that serves as an index to digitized images. If the database is discarded or damaged, image retrieval will be difficult or impossible.

Vital Record Status

As discussed more fully in Chapter Six, vital records contain information essential to an organization's mission-critical operations. They are essential for the continuation or survival of an organization if a disaster strikes. To eliminate the need for a separate survey of vital records, identify potentially vital records during a records inventory.

INVENTORY FOLLOW-UP

As previously explained, inventory information will be used to prepare retention recommendations for specific electronic records series. Responses to questions contained in the survey instrument need to be both accurate in content and correctly interpreted by the records manager. If the questionnaire method is utilized, the records manager should review the responses with liaison persons or others responsible for completing the questionnaire in each program unit. To avoid misunderstandings that can lead to inappropriate retention recommendations, the records manager's interpretation of major points should be confirmed by program unit staff. Clarification should always be requested for vague or incomplete responses.

If the consultation method is used, the records manager should prepare a written summary of information obtained during each interview with liaison persons or other program unit representatives. The summary can be written as if it were the minutes of a meeting. The written summary should be submitted to the interviewee for examination and, where necessary, correction or clarification. Such follow-up work steps will necessarily increase the time required to complete inventories of electronic records; but, although admittedly difficult to implement, they are highly advisable. The time and effort required to conduct thorough inventories of electronic records will be repaid in appropriate retention recommendations that are less likely to require time-consuming negotiation and revision.

SUMMARY

The purpose of a records inventory is to gather information about the number and characteristics of an organization's electronic records. Conducting a thorough inventory is the critical initial step in a systematic approach to the management of electronic records.

Electronic records are inventoried at the series level, where a series is defined as a group of logically related records that support one or more business operations. Adapting a technique widely utilized for paper documents, electronic records are often inventoried on a program unit basis. As a potential shortcoming, such inventories may fail to identify electronic recordkeeping systems shared by multiple program units. To address this problem, electronic records may be inventoried by identifying and analyzing automated information systems with which they are associated.

To demonstrate its support for records management initiatives, an organization's top management should send a directive to all program units. The directive should announce that an inventory of electronic records has been authorized and solicit the cooperation of individual program units. Liaison persons, to be designated by each program unit, will serve as principal points of contact for inventorying and related records management activities.

To formalize working procedures, a specially designed survey instrument must be developed to collect information about specific characteristics of electronic records. The survey instrument may be distributed as a questionnaire to program unit liaisons; alternatively, it can be used as an interview guide by records management staff who will determine records characteristics in consultation with liaison persons or other program unit personnel. The questionnaire method typically shortens the completion time required for a records inventory, but misinterpretations, discrepancies, and some marginally useful responses can be expected. The consultation method, which relies on interviews and observation, can minimize these problems, but it is often more time-consuming.

Regardless of approach, the survey instrument should collect information about the title and purpose of each electronic records series; the physical and technical characteristics of the media on which the series is recorded; the locations where such media are stored; the types of hardware and software with which the media must be utilized; the current volume and anticipated growth of records contained in a given series; the records' reference characteristics and retention requirements; and the relationship of particular electronic records series to other machine-readable and human-readable information created, maintained, and used by the organization. Because the information gathered during an inventory of electronic records will ultimately be used to formulate retention recommendations, accuracy is critical. To avoid misinterpretations, information obtained through consultations or questionnaires should be carefully reviewed with liaison persons or other program unit representatives.

CHAPTER FIVE

RETENTION SCHEDULES FOR ELECTRONIC RECORDS

As discussed in Chapter Four, a records inventory is a means to an end. Its principal purpose is to obtain information required to formulate retention schedules for electronic records. Broadly defined, a *retention schedule*—variously described as a *retention and disposition schedule* or, simply, a *disposition schedule*—is a list of records series maintained by all or part of an organization, together with the period of time each series is to be kept. Some retention schedules also include information about the reasons records are kept for specified time periods, as well as instructions regarding the locations and conditions under which records are to be retained. Retention schedules may be maintained as paper copies or computer files. In the latter case, they may be printed for reference purposes, although corporations, government agencies, and other organizations are increasingly posting Web-based versions of retention schedules on intranets as alternatives to printed copies.

Retention schedules may be general or program-specific in scope. A *general retention schedule*, sometimes described as a *master schedule*, specifies retention periods for designated records series, regardless of the particular program units where the series are maintained. General retention schedules are often characterized as *functional schedules* because they categorize records series by the business functions to which they pertain. Examples of functional categories include administrative records, financial records, human resources records, and product development records. An organization may issue separate general schedules for specific functional categories or prepare a single general schedule that groups records by functional categories.

Functional categories aside, a general schedule provides one set of retention guidelines for all program units in an organization. A given program unit will maintain some, but not all, records series enumerated in a general schedule. A *program-specific retention schedule*, by contrast, is limited to those records series actually maintained by a specific department, office, or other program unit. Sometimes described as *activity-oriented* or *departmental retention schedules*, program-specific retention schedules are custom-prepared for each program unit within an organization.

As their principal advantage, program-specific retention schedules are highly prescriptive. They list only those records series that a given program unit maintains, with unequivocal retention designations for each. Each program unit has direct input into the formulation of retention periods. Being tailored to the requirements of individual program units, program-specific retention schedules are easy to understand and can include detailed implementation instructions. General schedules, by contrast, can be difficult to interpret. To determine retention requirements, a given program unit must first locate its records series among the many listed in a general schedule. In some cases, program units identify records series by different titles than those listed in the general schedule. An exact match is further complicated by slight variations in the scope and content of records series maintained by different program units. Offsetting these potential problems, proponents of functional retention schedules claim that they are easier and faster to create than program-specific schedules and that they promote consistent retention practices across departments. They also note that program-specific schedules can be difficult to update, given the increasing incidence of reorganizations, mergers, divestitures, and other changes that realign or eliminate departments.

General schedules present retention guidelines for multiple program units. The retention designations are based on input from some, but not necessarily all, program units that maintain a given records series. Presumably, the retention designations reflect the longest retention requirements for the listed series. For records that exist in multiple copies, however, a program unit may want to discard its copies of a given records series before the generalized retention period has elapsed. To address this requirement, a general schedule may designate an office of record responsible for retaining specific records series for the entire designated time period. Other program units can discard their copies of that series when local need has expired, but they must not retain them longer than the designated retention period.

General and program-specific schedules are not mutually exclusive options. They can, and often do, coexist in a given organization. Both types are equally applicable to electronic and nonelectronic records. General schedules can prove particularly useful for commonly encountered types of electronic records, such as e-mail or draft versions of word processing documents, or for enterprise-wide information resources referenced by many program units. The latter include centralized databases, data warehouses, and Web pages on organizational intranets or the Internet. An organization may issue general retention guidelines for its commonly held or enterprise-wide records series and prepare customized program-specific schedules for electronic records unique to particular departments, offices, or other program units.

Whether they are general or program-specific in scope, retention schedules must cover all records maintained by a corporation, government agency, or other organization regardless of format. An *integrated schedule* combines retention designations for electronic and nonelectronic records series. That approach is particularly recommended for organizations that have no formalized retention schedules. In that case, electronic and nonelectronic records can be inventoried and scheduled in the same initiative. The integrated approach is likewise suitable where existing schedules for nonelectronic records require updating, additions, or other revisions. Organizations that have acceptable schedules for nonelectronic records may prefer to issue separate schedules for electronic records. Alternatively, an organization's existing schedules can be modified to incorporate electronic records series without altering retention designations for nonelectronic records.

With respect to content, a retention schedule must list electronic records series and indicate the period of time each series is to be retained. Other useful information includes the physical storage media to be used, the location(s) where the records are to be stored, the date and method of records destruction where applicable, and the storage or records transfer instructions if destruction is not authorized. If this information is not contained in a retention schedule itself, a separate procedure or other supporting documentation must provide it.

A retention schedule may specify more than one physical storage medium and location for an electronic records series. As an example, computerized customer order records maintained by a mainframe or minicomputer system may be stored on a hard drive for several months to support frequent inquiries during the period of order fulfillment and for a brief amount of time thereafter. As orders are processed and shipments completed, however, certain records will be referenced less frequently. Those records may then be transferred to magnetic tapes, optical disks, or other removable media for off-line storage. This approach to information management is sometimes described as data archiving. The removable media may initially be retained in office locations, then transferred to off-site storage after a specified period of time. As used in this context, data archiving denotes the transfer of information from on-line to off-line media, presumably for more economical storage. It does not imply permanent preservation, as is the case with so-called archival records. Records subject to data archiving may ultimately be discarded.

RETENTION CONCEPTS

The preparation of retention schedules is a defining characteristic of records management work. No other information management discipline can properly claim responsibility for retention-related activities. Retention schedules are the core component in a systematic electronic records management program. They provide a foundation upon which other records management activities are based. Electronic records, like their nonelectronic counterparts, are the property of the corporation, government agency, university, or other organization that creates and maintains such records. By preparing retention schedules, an organization acknowledges that systematic disposition of its electronic records is a critical information management activity to be governed by formalized operating procedures rather than the discretion of individual employees.

The business benefits of formalized retention schedules for paper records have been widely acknowledged for over half a century. With slight variations, those benefits apply to electronic records as well. When properly formulated, implemented, and enforced, retention schedules will:

- Ensure the availability and utility of specific electronic records series for appropriate periods of time, allowing such records to be referenced or reprocessed, as required, in the future;

- Ensure compliance with recordkeeping requirements specified in legal statutes and government regulations;

- Ensure that electronic records needed for evidentiary purposes will be available for and facilitate compliance with discovery requests and other judicial orders;

- Prevent the unwarranted accumulation and inappropriate reference use of obsolete electronic records;

- Prevent the unauthorized or arbitrary destruction of electronic records, thereby avoiding potential legal problems associated with such actions;

- Make the most effective use of available storage devices and media for electronic records by identifying records series appropriate to on-line and off-line storage;

- Minimize storage requirements by destroying (deleting or discarding) electronic records no longer needed; and

- Release magnetic disks, magnetic tapes, rewritable optical disks, and other recording media for reuse, thereby minimizing expenditures for new media.

A comprehensive inventory will identify the electronic records series to be included in retention schedules. The inventory provides information about the relationship of the records series to the missions of the program units that create and maintain them. The inventory survey instrument solicits descriptions of the physical characteristics of electronic storage media, the types and volume of records that each electronic records series contains, the ways in which electronic records are organized and referenced, and the relationship between electronic records series and other records maintained by a given program unit or other parts of an organization. The records manager, in consultation with program unit personnel and others, will use the inventory information, supplemented in some cases by additional research, to determine appropriate retention periods for specific electronic records series.

A retention period places a value on an electronic records series. The value is an estimate of the future usefulness or lack thereof of the series. Because retention periods are estimates, uncertainty and risk are unavoidable; but a careful analysis of retention requirements, based on an understanding of the purpose and characteristics of a given records series, will increase the likelihood of a satisfactory determination.

Retention Criteria

Retention concepts developed over the last half century for paper documents are applicable to electronic records. Retention decisions are principally based on the content of records rather than their format, although format considerations can prove significant in some circumstances. Like their nonelectronic counterparts, retention periods for electronic records are determined by legal, administrative, and research (scholarly) criteria. Legal criteria may be defined by laws or government regulations that mandate the retention of records for specific periods of time. A broader group of legal considerations is concerned with the admissibility of electronic records as evidence in trials and other legal proceedings. Some records managers consider fiscal and tax-oriented retention criteria, which are concerned with the management and expenditure of public or corporate funds, to be distinct from legal parameters. Many fiscal and tax retention criteria, however, are embodied in laws and regulations; for purposes of this discussion, they are considered a subset of legal criteria.

Administrative (operational) retention criteria are based on the continued need for specific records series to support an organization's mission, the public interest (in the case of government records), and stockholders' interest (for records of publicly held companies). Such criteria are concerned with the availability of electronic records for long-term administrative consistency and continuity, as well as for day-to-day operations of individual program units. Administrative criteria are the most important considerations when determining retention periods for many, if not most, electronic records. (This statement does not denigrate the importance of legal criteria; it merely recognizes that many records are not subject to legally mandated recordkeeping requirements and have no evidentiary significance.)

Legal and administrative significance aside, electronic records maintained by corporations, government agencies, and other organizations may contain information of interest to historians, political scientists, sociologists, economists, demographers, or other scholars. Some electronic records are also of interest to genealogists, private investigators, market trends analysts, and others who are not necessarily scholars but are nonetheless involved in research. Research-oriented retention criteria are sometimes characterized as secondary value to distinguish them from the primary business purposes for which electronic records were created.

This chapter discusses legal and administrative criteria for retention of electronic records. (As noted previously, legal criteria include fiscal and tax considerations.) Research-oriented retention criteria are beyond the scope of this book. This book emphasizes business rather than scholarly uses of electronic records, although portions of the discussion of administrative criteria may be relevant for research applications as well. Determination of secondary value is principally the concern of archivists and librarians rather than records managers. It requires specialized knowledge about the scholarly disciplines and research activities for which particular electronic records may be relevant. Many archivists and librarians have advanced academic degrees in a subject specialty as well as training in archival management or library science.

Electronic Records as Official Copies

Whether legal, administrative, or research criteria apply, records managers must consider the relationship between electronic and nonelectronic records when preparing retention schedules. Much information maintained by corporations, government agencies, and other organizations exists in both electronic and nonelectronic formats. Some electronic records are the originating sources for paper documents that fully replicate the content of electronic records in printed form. For example, word processing documents are usually printed for distribution, reference, filing, or other purposes. CAD files are another common example; they are often used to print copies of engineering drawings for reference, filing, or incorporation into bid packets. Electronic records that produce printed documents of identical content and functionality are referred to as *electronic source records*.

Electronic source records precede paper documents of identical content and functionality; but in many situations, the opposite scenario applies. Information contained in paper documents, such as invoices or employee time sheets, is converted to computer-processible form by key-entry, scanning, or other means in order to create electronic records. In such cases, the paper document is considered the source record. Often, however, the resulting electronic records are augmented through calculations or key-entry of additional information from other documents so that a given electronic record and its associated nonelectronic source record cannot be considered identical copies.

In the presence of multiple copies of a given record, the copy that will satisfy an organization's legal and administrative retention requirements is called the *official copy*. The program unit that maintains that copy is the designated *office of record* for retention purposes. Copies maintained by other program units are considered duplicate records. Where information is unique to an electronic records series, that series is necessarily an official copy. Where the same information exists in electronic and nonelectronic records, however, a corporation, government agency, or other organization may designate either the electronic record or the nonelectronic record as the official copy for retention purposes.

Although these concepts are straightforward, they can be applied in several different ways. In some organizations, retention schedules separately enumerate and specify retention periods for all copies of a given records series in all formats, electronic and nonelectronic. Alternatively, one electronic or nonelectronic copy may be designated as the official copy for retention purposes and the others treated as duplicate records to be kept as long as the official copy or discarded sooner if no longer needed. Taking another approach, many organizations designate retention periods and an office of record for specific types of information, such as accounts receivable records or product specification sheets, without prescribing the format in which the information is to be retained. In such cases, the office of record determines the retention format for the official copy.

Official copy determinations are based on the assumption that electronic and nonelectronic records are equivalent in content and functionality, but variations may be encountered within a given record type. As an example, a Web page on an organization's intranet or the public Internet may contain unique information not available in other information resources, in which case the Web page is considered an official copy for retention purposes. Some Web pages, however, replicate information fully available in paper documents. If a Web page lacks unique content but employs a distinctive presentation format or has other attributes with informational or evidentiary value lacking in its paper counterpart, it is to be treated as a unique record and an official copy. If the Web page lacks such distinctive attributes, it could be treated as an official copy or as a duplicate record for retention purposes.

LEGALLY MANDATED RETENTION PERIODS

Various laws and government regulations contain recordkeeping requirements that specify minimum retention periods for certain types of records. Such laws and regulations apply to all private and public organizations operating within a specific governmental jurisdiction. U.S. corporations, for example, are subject to record-keeping requirements contained in federal laws and in the laws of every state or locality where they do business. An organization is considered to be doing business in a location if it maintains an office, employees, or property there. When scheduling records, legally mandated recordkeeping requirements are the first retention criteria to be considered. Compliance with legally mandated recordkeeping requirements is an important benefit of formalized retention schedules. If such recordkeeping requirements exist, they establish minimum retention periods for the records series to which they pertain. Retention periods determined by other criteria discussed in this chapter may be longer than those defined by legally mandated recordkeeping requirements, but they can never be shorter.

In the United States, recordkeeping requirements can be found in the **Code of Federal Regulations (CFR)**, which is updated by the Federal Register, as well as in various state codes and local government statutes and regulations. Similar provisions apply in other countries. Canadian corporations, for example, must comply with Canadian federal, provincial, and local laws and regulations that specify retention periods for certain records. International companies must observe recordkeeping requirements in all countries where they do business. In some countries, however, such requirements can be difficult to determine. Advice from local legal counsel will usually be necessary.

The purpose of legally mandated recordkeeping requirements and their associated retention specifications is to enable government agencies to monitor compliance with laws and regulations. As might be expected, various legally mandated retention periods apply to financial records pertinent to tax assessments. Such retention requirements ensure that government agencies will have sufficient information to determine taxes owed and paid. Retention of specific personnel and payroll records are likewise mandated by laws and government regulations. They ensure the availability of information about hiring procedures, proper payment of wages, and other fair labor practices, as well as the health and safety of employees. A widely publicized group of recordkeeping requirements applies to business activities or industries regulated by government agencies. Examples include banking, food processing, insurance, pharmaceuticals, and utilities. Some legally mandated retention requirements apply to government agencies as well as private companies. Government agencies are subject to laws that specify the retention authority of archival agencies over public records. The National Archives and Records Administration (NARA), for example, has retention authority over records maintained by U.S. government agencies. State archival agencies have similar retention authority over state government records and, in many cases, records maintained by local governments, school districts, quasi-governmental authorities, public benefit corporations, and other entities.

As a group, recordkeeping laws and regulations require the creation of information and its retention for designated time periods. In some cases, acceptable records storage formats and media are specified, but many recordkeeping requirements predate widespread computerization of business operations. They are written in a manner based on an assumption that the required information will be contained in paper documents. As an example, the Uniform Preservation of Business Records

Act uses the terms *records* and *business papers* synonymously. As discussed in Chapter One, corporations, government agencies, and other organizations rely on computer, video, and audio records for rapid, convenient information creation and retrieval. Increasingly, such organizations prefer to use electronic records, in lieu of paper documents, to satisfy certain legally mandated retention requirements.

Compared with paper documents, electronic records can store large quantities of information more compactly and retrieve it more quickly for government audits or other purposes. In many cases, electronic records contain more information than their hardcopy counterparts. Word processing files, for example, typically include multiple drafts of documents, some of which may never have been printed. Some data files contain a superset of information that appears in printed reports. Others contain original information that never existed in paper documents. In order processing applications, for example, customers and vendors may utilize electronic data interchange (EDI) to enter information directly into data files maintained by each other's computers. Although Web pages often contain information extracted from paper documents, their contents may be augmented with additional material or innovative formats that have no paper counterparts. Many video and audio recordings likewise contain original information. Video tapes, for example, may provide the only detailed record of a scientific experiment or a building inspection. Audio tapes may contain interviews or speeches that will never be transcribed.

Although electronic records enjoy unquestioned functional advantages over paper documents in certain information management applications, their ability to satisfy legally mandated recordkeeping requirements has been the subject of much discussion and uncertainty. U.S. law permits the retention of records in any form provided that a particular form is not specifically mandated or prohibited by legal statutes or government regulations. Some records managers, however, want a clear affirmation that electronic records are acceptable for retention purposes. As a complicating factor, an organization's legal department, which often has approval authority over retention schedules, may interpret the mention of specific media to mean nonacceptance of others for retention purposes.

Many recordkeeping requirements were formulated at a time when paper documents—or photographic reproductions such as microfilm—were the only available recordkeeping media; electronic records were not an option. Increasingly, however, recordkeeping laws and regulations are being revised to accept electronic records for retention. The following items are among the hundreds of examples that might be cited:

- 12 CFR 12.3 specifies a minimum retention period of three years for records pertaining to security transactions executed by banks for their customers. The records may be retained in electronic form.
- As specified in 21 CFR 1304.04, the Drug Enforcement Administration will accept computer media for storage of records and inventories pertaining to controlled substances.
- According to 15 CFR 762.5, the Bureau of Export Administration of the Department of Commerce will accept "electronic digital storage" as a substitute for paper records.

- 29 CFR 516.1 does not prescribe specific formats for recordkeeping as long as retention requirements are met. It indicates that "automatic word or data processing memory" is acceptable for retention of information required by the Fair Labor Standards Act.

- According to 49 CFR 1220.3, the Surface Transportation Board of the Department of Transportation permits preservation of records by "any technology that is immune to alteration, modification, or erasure," a requirement that limits electronic recordkeeping to certain media. The Department of Transportation accepts machine-readable media to satisfy recordkeeping requirements for railroads, freight carriers, and other companies subject to the Interstate Commerce Act. Such media must be accompanied by a statement indicating the type of information they contain.

- According to Section 1795.28 of the California Health and Safety Code, health service providers can retain patient records in electronic form and discard paper versions. The providers must implement safeguards for security and confidentiality of the electronic records.

- 29 CFR 1904.2 permits the use of "data processing equipment" to maintain a log of occupational injuries and illnesses required by the Occupational Safety and Health Administration (OSHA).

- As specified in 48 CFR 4.7, Federal Acquisitions Regulations allows government contractors to store records in computer-processible form, provided that a reliable storage medium is used.

- 21 CFR 11 indicates the conditions under which the Food and Drug Administration (FDA) considers electronic records to be reliable equivalents of paper documents for regulatory submissions and other purposes. Public Docket No. 92S-0251 specifies the type of regulatory submissions the FDA will accept in electronic form under the Federal Food, Drug, and Cosmetic Act and the Public Health Services Act. In other cases, paper records are considered official records and must accompany electronic submissions. The FDA also considers electronic records acceptable for information that must be maintained but not submitted to the agency.

Although these examples apply to the United States, the passage or revision of laws and government regulations to accept electronic records for retention of information is occurring internationally. A comprehensive survey is beyond the scope of this book; however, many countries allow corporations to maintain accounting and tax-related records in electronic form. The Australian Securities and Investment Commission, for instance, permits electronic recordkeeping for accounting information as provided in the Corporations Act of 2001. Similarly, the Australian Tax Commissioner will accept electronic records for transaction-related information pertinent to tax law, provided the records are readily accessible and convertible to human-readable form. In its Model Law on Electronic Commerce, the United Nations Commission on International Trade Law (UNCITRAL) specifies that retention requirements for documents, records, or information can be satisfied by "data messages." The Model Law, which was adopted by resolution of the United Nations General Assembly in December 1996, has influenced legislation in many countries. This law is discussed in detail in the section dealing with electronic signatures.

Regardless of the countries in which they apply, most laws and regulations that accept electronic records for retention purposes stipulate that the records must be complete, readily available, and appropriately indexed for convenient retrieval; that required retrieval equipment and software must be available; and that paper copies must be produced in a reasonable amount of time on demand for audits or other purposes. Further, the laws and regulations typically require complete descriptive documentation for electronic records and the computer systems that create and maintain them.

Unfortunately, the examples cited previously do not permit generalizations; laws and regulations must be individually and thoroughly examined to determine the acceptability of electronic records for retention purposes in particular circumstances. Some recordkeeping laws and regulations specifically disavow restrictions on record formats for retention, but exceptions may be noted. As cited in 29 CFR 1910.20, for example, OSHA permits retention of employee exposure and medical records in any retrievable form, but it requires that X-rays be "preserved in their original state." Section 1500 of the California Corporations Code requires that minutes of board and shareholder meetings be maintained in "written form." Other corporate records may be kept in any form capable of being converted to written form. Section 224 of the Delaware Code allows corporate records to be maintained in various machine-readable formats, provided that such records can be converted to "clearly legible written form" within a reasonable time upon request of any person entitled to inspect the records. The State of Vermont's Insurance Division Regulation 99-1 states that computer records "shall be archival in nature only, so as to preclude the possibility of alteration."

At the time of this writing, no laws or government regulations required the creation and retention of electronic records as the sole method of satisfying legally mandated retention requirements. Paper records are always an option. Some laws and government regulations, however, specify retention periods for electronic records where such records exist. Over the past three decades, for example, the U.S. Internal Revenue Service has required the retention of computer-processable accounting records for as long as their contents may be pertinent to the administration of federal tax law. Section 6001 of the Internal Revenue Code specifies that taxpayers must keep records to establish income, deductions, credits, or other matters relating to tax assessments. IRS Revenue Ruling 71-20 defines computer-processable accounting data as records within the meaning of Section 6001. As specified in IRS Revenue Procedure 98-25, computer-processable records must be maintained in a retrievable format that provides information necessary to determine tax liability. At a minimum, the records must be retained until the expiration of the limitation period for assessment, including extensions, for each tax year, although records pertaining to fixed assets, inventories, and certain losses may need to be retained longer.

Computer-processable records must be accompanied by documentation that describes the electronic records and the computerized accounting system that produced them, including procedures and controls that prevent simple mistakes and preclude fraud. If electronic data interchange (EDI) is used for accounting transactions, EDI records must provide the same level of detail as an acceptable paper record. Media that contain electronic records must be labeled clearly and stored safely. The IRS recommends that taxpayers follow procedures defined by the National Archives and Records Administration for storage and inspection of electronic records. Those procedures are described in Chapter Seven. At the time of an IRS audit, taxpayers must furnish all computer resources required to access electronic records.

IRS Revenue Procedure 98-25 applies to all taxpayers with assets of ten million dollars or more, to insurance companies that use computer-processible records to determine losses, and to foreign corporations that do business within the United States. Because most medium-size and larger corporations, partnerships, and other businesses have implemented computerized accounting systems, these electronic recordkeeping requirements have broad impact. IRS Revenue Procedure 98-25 also applies to taxpayers with fewer assets where records are kept exclusively in electronic form rather than hardcopy, or where electronic records are used for calculations that require a computer for verification. Retention of computer-processible records does not supercede long-standing IRS retention requirements for human-readable accounting records. Taxpayers must also retain copies of such records, in paper or microfilm form, as long as their contents are pertinent to tax law.

Some other countries have adopted similar regulations regarding computerized recordkeeping systems for tax information. As an example, Revenue Canada's Information Circular IC78-10R3, issued in 1998, requires the retention of computerized tax records for time periods specified in income tax regulations, even if paper documents contain the same information. Taxpayers' retention practices must be appropriate to the medium on which electronic records are stored, and information must be reliably preserved when electronic records are converted to new formats. Procedure manuals, flowcharts, and other documentation must describe controls that prevent unauthorized alteration or loss of electronic records. The electronic records must also show an audit trail from source documents to financial accounts.

LEGAL STATUS OF DOCUMENT IMAGES

Electronic document images, as a type of electronic record, are often singled out for special treatment in recordkeeping laws and regulations. *Electronic document imaging systems* record digitized reproductions of documents on magnetic media or optical disks. In most cases, the electronic images are produced by scanning paper records. Microfilm scanners are also available. Since the mid-1980s, all published discussions of the legal status of electronic document images have been based on the following premise: *Electronic document images are true copies of the documents from which they were made, a true copy being one that accurately reproduces an original document.* Consequently, electronic document images have the same legal status as duplicate records produced by other reprographic processes such as photocopying and microfilming. In the United States, the Uniform Photographic Copies of Business and Public Records as Evidence Act—commonly abbreviated as the Uniform Photographic Copies Act or, simply, the UPA—permits the substitution of photographic copies for original documents in all judicial or administrative proceedings. As its title indicates, the UPA applies to copies of public records maintained by federal, state, and local government agencies. It also applies to business records maintained by corporations, partnerships, sole proprietorships, nonprofit institutions, and other nongovernmental organizations.

The UPA applies to records retention as an administrative activity. It does not override any legal statutes or governmental regulations that require the retention of original documents, however. Statutes and regulations must be examined individually and thoroughly to determine whether such requirements apply. Other UPA conditions are also pertinent: The copies must be accurate reproductions of the original documents, and they must have been produced in the regular course of business. This copying should be done in conformity with formally established retention schedules that specify that original documents from specified records series will be copied at predetermined intervals. Similar provisions are contained in the Uniform Preservation of Private Business Records Act, which allows recordkeeping requirements to be satisfied by copies.

The UPA permits, but does not mandate, the destruction of original documents, thereby allowing organizations to rely solely on copies for whatever purpose the originals were intended. Destruction is prohibited, however, where preservation of the original documents is specifically required by law. Some states have added a clause to the UPA that prohibits destruction of original documents held in a custodial or fiduciary capacity. In such situations, their owners' permission is required prior to destruction.

Written in 1949, the Uniform Photographic Copies Act predates the introduction of electronic document imaging systems. Although it specifically mentions photocopying and microfilming, it does not provide an exhaustive list of acceptable reprographic technologies, nor does it exclude technologies that are not mentioned. The UPA applies to any copying process that "accurately reproduces or forms a durable medium for so reproducing" original documents. It might be argued, however, that the application of data compression and/or enhancement algorithms to electronic document images prior to recording affects the accuracy of reproduction. Application of the UPA to electronic document images would be complicated if compressed or enhanced document images do not constitute exact reproductions of original documents. Fortunately, the most common compression methods utilized by electronic document imaging systems are *lossless*—that is, they achieve compression without omitting any information from document images. Lossless methods produce accurate reproductions. Few electronic document imaging systems employ enhancement algorithms. In any case, such algorithms affect only the quality of reproduction, not the content of information.

The Uniform Photographic Copies Act applies only in those legal jurisdictions where it has been adopted. At the time of this writing, it had been adopted by the U.S. federal government and approximately two-thirds of the state governments. Some states have developed and passed their own laws that address the substitution of copies for original documents. The scope and content of such laws is typically similar to that of the Uniform Photographic Copies Act.

Government regulations that apply to specific business activities or industries often permit the substitution of copies for original documents to satisfy records retention requirements. Because such regulations usually predate the commercial availability of electronic document imaging technology, they do not mention it specifically. Several regulating agencies have recently revised their retention requirements to incorporate guidelines or opinions concerning the acceptability of electronic document images for certain types of records. The Nuclear Regulatory Commission was the first regulating agency to accept electronic document images for records storage by organizations within its scope of authority. The Securities and Exchange Commission authorizes the use of electronic document images for records retention by brokerage firms, subject to certain conditions. Brokerages must provide prior notice to the examining authority of their intent to use electronic document imaging technology, and their systems must include appropriate indexing, display, and printing capabilities. Brokerages must have an audit system for accountability regarding input of records to the electronic document imaging system. Federal Acquisition Regulations allow contractors to substitute electronic document images for paper records, provided that the images are accurate reproductions of the original records and that they are conveniently indexed. Contractors must retain the original records for one year following scanning for periodic validation.

Retention practices of government agencies are subject to policies promulgated by archival authorities. At the time of this writing, the National Archives and Records Administration, which has retention authority over U.S. government agencies, did not accept electronic images recorded on optical disks or other media for permanent records to be transferred to the National Archives. Paper and microfilm are the only acceptable media for such permanent retention, although electronic imaging systems may be implemented for business process improvement or other reasons. Some state archives limit electronic document imaging technology and optical disk storage to records that will be retained for less than 10 years. If electronic document imaging systems are used for records with longer retention periods, the paper documents must be retained or microfilmed.

ADMISSIBILITY INTO EVIDENCE

The preceding section addressed the ability of electronic records, including electronic document images, to satisfy recordkeeping requirements specified in legal statutes and governmental regulations. A different, much discussed group of legal considerations involves the admissibility of electronic records as evidence in courts cases or administrative proceedings and the retention of specific electronic records series for that purpose. Compared with legally mandated retention periods, admissibility issues will typically affect a greater number and variety of electronic records. Although they are critical for retention scheduling, statutes and government regulations that specify retention periods affect a subset of an organization's electronic records. In contrast, any electronic record might prove useful as evidence.

Broadly defined, *evidence* consists of testimony, documentation, or physical items submitted that are pertinent to alleged facts in judicial or quasi-judicial proceedings such as court trials or administrative hearings. The purpose of evidence is to prove or clarify a point at issue in a legal proceeding. Evidence that a judge or jury can properly consider is referred to as *admissible*. Records managers, corporate and institutional attorneys, and others responsible for planning and implementing recordkeeping systems that will effectively support legal actions are understandably concerned about the admissibility of electronic records.

In court trials, the admissibility of records is determined by rules of evidence, which are embodied in legal statutes and court decisions (common law). Such rules apply equally to electronic and nonelectronic records. To be admissible as evidence, any records, regardless of form, must satisfy two foundation requirements that apply to all evidence:

1. The content of the records must be relevant to the matter at issue.
2. The records' authenticity must be firmly established; that is, the court must be convinced that the records are what their proponents claim them to be.

Relevance determinations are case-specific and typically fall outside the scope of records management responsibilities. Authentication of electronic records, however, is a direct concern of records managers.

The purpose of authentication is to demonstrate the reliability of records to a court's satisfaction. General authentication considerations apply equally to electronic and nonelectronic records. To be considered reliable, a record, regardless of form, must meet the following three criteria:

1. The record must have been created at or near the time of the event that is the subject of litigation.
2. The record must have been created by a person with knowledge of the event.
3. The record must have been maintained in the regular course of an organization's business.

Questions and concerns about the reliability of electronic records relate to the operation of hardware and software that generates such records, and to the potential for erasure, editing, or other alteration of contents. Various judicial opinions have raised questions about inaccurate information attributable to hardware malfunctions or software errors. Hardware-related concerns are most commonly associated with emerging technologies of questionable or unproven reliability. During the 1960s, for example, a high incidence of equipment downtime raised doubts about the ability of computer systems to maintain accurate records. Continuing improvements in hardware reliability since that time has dispelled such doubts, but software defects remain notoriously widespread.

Concerns about the improper alteration of electronic records have been widely publicized in discussions of computer crime. In nonelectronic recordkeeping systems, such modifications are often difficult to make and easy to detect. The alteration of an organization's paper-based financial records, for example, may require tampering with various ledgers, balance sheets, invoices, and other source documents, some of which may be inaccessible to the perpetrator. As a further impediment, alterations to paper records involve physical changes, which may be detectable by specialists or even casual observers. Forensic scientists have decades of experience with the examination of suspect documents. Where records are stored on microfilm, undetectable alterations can prove particularly difficult to make.

By contrast, records stored on rewritable electronic media, such as magnetic disks, magnetic tapes, or certain optical disks, may be changed, erased, or otherwise manipulated with little or no trace. Character-coded text and quantitative values can be easily overwritten with new information. Recent advances in computer technology permit the undetected manipulation of electronic document images, digital photographs, computer-aided design files, video recordings, and audio recordings. In the case of electronic records maintained by networked computer systems, such alternations may be performed by a remote perpetrator, thereby circumventing physical accessibility requirements associated with the alteration of paper records.

To successfully address these formidable concerns, records managers must develop and implement electronic recordkeeping systems and procedures that will facilitate authentication and dispel any doubts about the reliability of electronic records. According to the **Federal Rules of Evidence (FRE)** and **Uniform Rules of Evidence (URE)**, authentication requirements for computer-generated business records can be satisfied by describing the system or process used to produce a given electronic record and by showing that the system or process produces an accurate result. Similar authentication provisions are contained in the Canadian Uniform Electronic Evidence Act. To demonstrate the accuracy and trustworthiness of electronic records created and maintained by a given computer, video, or audio system, records managers may be expected to provide testimony and/or documentation pertaining to system administration, input procedures, equipment, software, security, and the competency of employees who operate the system. The following records management procedures can facilitate compliance with such authentication requirements:

- An administrator should be designated for each system that creates or maintains electronic records. The system administrator should be identified by job title rather than by personal name. The system administrator will typically be a management-level employee who is involved with one or more aspects of the system's operation such as the supervision of data entry or records retrieval. To be able to give the knowledgeable testimony required for authentication purposes, the administrator should become familiar with the entire system, including its technical and operating characteristics. The system administrator may also be given other responsibilities with legal implications such as control over the release or expungement of electronic records.

- The system's hardware and software characteristics must be documented in a manner that fully describes the role of each component in the creation and maintenance of electronic records being submitted as evidence. Hardware documentation should indicate the types, brand names, and model numbers of all hardware components and recording media used in the system, together with the dates that specific components were put into or taken out of service. Technical specification sheets provided by vendors will typically provide sufficiently detailed information to satisfy documentation requirements for hardware and recording media. To confirm that hardware is being maintained in proper working condition, records should be kept of equipment inspections and repairs.

- Software documentation should also include descriptions of all systems and application programs involved in the creation and maintenance of electronic records. For custom-developed application software, flowcharts, source code, program debugging procedures, and other developmental documentation should be included. Descriptions of prewritten software packages should include version numbers and implementation dates for all software upgrades.

- The accuracy and trustworthiness of electronic records can be affirmed by thorough documentation of records creation procedures, as well as by descriptions of training given to data entry clerks, video camera operators, or other personnel responsible for creating electronic records. Business processes that create electronic records must be documented through written procedures and work flow diagrams. Detailed written instructions should be prepared for operators of data entry terminals, document scanners, video cameras, audio recorders, and other input devices. They should delineate the records creation work steps to be followed in specific situations. Descriptions of input verification procedures—such as double-keying of data entries, computer-based validation of specified field values, or visual inspection of digitized images—should also be included. The written instructions should be used when training personnel who create electronic records. The nature and amount of such training should likewise be documented, and the training should emphasize compliance with established records creation procedures. Logbooks, employee time sheets, or other records should indicate the names of persons who operated input equipment on specific dates.

- Electronic records must be protected from physical damage or tampering that could impair their accuracy or raise questions about their trustworthiness. Specific protection measures employed by a given electronic record-keeping system should be fully documented. Detailed descriptions of media handling procedures and storage conditions, which are discussed in Chapter Seven, will affirm the physical integrity of electronic records. Access control procedures for electronic records and security provisions, such as password protection and privilege controls in computer-based systems, should be documented. A list of all authorized users and their access privileges should be maintained. The list should differentiate those users who are authorized to create or edit electronic records from those who are restricted to retrieval of previously created records from specific files.

- All aspects of system operation should be audited regularly for compliance with established procedures. Audit findings and the implementation of corrective actions should be fully documented.

These procedures and documentation requirements will increase the likelihood that electronic records will be admissible into evidence over objections that might be raised by an opposing party in a legal action. Historically, such objections have been based on the rule against hearsay and/or the best evidence rule. Typically, authentication questions are raised in the context of a hearsay objection. *Hearsay* is a statement made out of court that pertains to some matter that is raised in court. Because hearsay is not subject to cross-examination by the opposing party in a legal action, it is generally inadmissible under the rules of evidence that apply in federal and state courts. Because electronic records, like their nonelectronic counterparts, are usually created out of court, they are considered hearsay and will not be admitted into evidence unless they fall within one of the several exceptions to the rule against hearsay. Such exceptions exist for business and public records.

In U.S. federal courts, electronic records are admissible into evidence under Rule 803(6) of the Federal Rules of Evidence (FRE), the so-called business records exception to the hearsay rule. The exception is based on the premise that records created in the normal course of business activities possess a circumstantial probability of trustworthiness; because organizations that create such records must rely on them, their accuracy is presumed. The business records exception to the hearsay rule covers records "in any form." It interprets business records broadly to include those created and maintained by institutions, associations, and non-profit organizations. At the state level, an identical business records exception is included in the Uniform Rules of Evidence (URE), which have been adopted by approximately 60 percent of the states. A business records exception to the hearsay rule is similarly included in the Uniform Business Records as Evidence Act (UBREA) and in various state-specific statutes, as well as in common law.

Explicitly or through judicial interpretations, these business records exceptions to the hearsay rule have delineated certain requirements for authentication of electronic records. A qualified witness must provide foundation testimony concerning the reliability of the records. The witness is sometimes referred to as a *custodian*, although that description is not elaborated. The witness's qualifications have been variously defined. In general, the witness must be familiar with the organization and understand the procedures and circumstances under which the electronic records are created, maintained, and retrieved. Courts have held that the witness need not be personally familiar with the subject of electronic records, but he or she must know how the records are processed and used. The witness need not have been employed by the organization at the time the electronic records in question were created, nor personally involved with the actual recording of information on magnetic or optical media.

Technical knowledge requirements vary; some state courts, for example, have required that a qualified witness be a supervisor of computing activities. Where detailed technical knowledge is required, a consultant or industry analyst can provide expert testimony. Regardless of technical expertise, the witness must establish that electronic records were made in the regular course of business and testify to the method and circumstances of records creation and maintenance. In the absence of a qualified witness, these foundation requirements may be satisfied by other means such as examination of the electronic records themselves plus surrounding circumstances.

Business records exceptions to the hearsay rule require that electronic records be made within a reasonable time after the transaction, business activity, or other event to which they pertain. Data entry should occur soon after the event, and records should not be retained in main memory or on interim media for long periods of time. Courts and legal authorities have generally treated computer-generated printouts as electronic records, even though they are paper documents that

contain human-readable information. Several authorities contend that the requirement for timely creation of electronic records applies primarily to the entry and
recording of information rather than to the interval between input and printing.
Although a long delay prior to creating computer printouts may increase the
potential for tampering or errors, such delay alone should not impede admissibility. In several cases, computer printouts have been judged admissible even though
they were produced long after entry of the data they contain.

Several early court cases required proof of a computer's mechanical accuracy;
however, such issues are seldom raised today. Courts have likewise rejected the con-
tention that admissibility depends on a demonstration that a given computer system
was operating properly at the specific time when an electronic record was created.

If authentication requirements are satisfied, the business records exceptions
described previously will overcome most hearsay objections to the admissibility of
electronic records into evidence. Because they define business records broadly, such
exceptions have also been applied to records created by government agencies. Rule
803(8) of the Federal Rules of Evidence and Uniform Rules of Evidence provide an
additional exception, however, for public records. The relationship between the two
exceptions has not been fully delineated. For records created by government agencies, the public records exception provides an additional method of overcoming
hearsay objections. The Federal Rules of Evidence, Uniform Rules of Evidence, and
various state-specific statutes also include residual exceptions to the hearsay rule.
They can conceivably be used to admit electronic records that cannot satisfy the
requirements of other exceptions.

Objections to the admissibility of electronic records into evidence may also
be raised under the best evidence rule, which requires the introduction of an "original writing" into evidence unless its absence can be satisfactorily explained. If the
original record is unavailable, a trustworthy copy may be received into evidence.
An original record may be unavailable for various acceptable reasons. It may, for
example, have been destroyed in conformity with an organization's established
business practices, as embodied in formally approved retention schedules. In some
cases, an original record is in the possession of a third party who is beyond the
court's subpoena power. Alternatively, an adversary in a legal proceeding may fail
to produce an original record, despite notice. The best evidence rule precludes
admission of a copy into evidence if the original record is available.

Application of the best evidence rule to electronic records poses certain con-
ceptual problems. The rule appears most obviously and directly relevant to electronic document images that are recorded on optical disks or magnetic media. Such
images are considered copies of the documents from which they were made. The best
evidence rule has also been applied to computer printouts, which may be considered
copies of original information stored on other media; but Rule 1001(3) of the Federal
Rules of Evidence and Uniform Rules of Evidence treats printouts as original
records, thereby precluding an objection to their admissibility under the best evidence rule. Other provisions of the FRE and URE, however, suggest that computer
printouts are duplicate records.

Where that view is sustained, best evidence objections to the admissibility of electronic records can be overcome in various ways. The Uniform Photographic Copies of Business and Public Records as Evidence Act and various state-specific statutes of similar scope permit the substitution of copies for original records to satisfy judicial and administrative requirements. They give copies and originals equivalent legal status, provided that the copies are accurate reproductions of the originals, that they are produced in the regular course of business, and that retention of the original records is not required by law. Rule 1003 of the FRE and URE permits the admission of duplicate records into evidence as substitutes for originals unless serious questions are raised about the authenticity of the original records or, in specific circumstances, admitting a copy in lieu of the original is judged unfair. By recognizing the admissibility of copies, Rule 1003 places the burden of argument on the party seeking to exclude a copy rather than the party seeking to admit it. Under Rule 1003, the availability of an original record does preclude the admissibility of a copy. If computer printouts are considered copies, they may be admissible into evidence under FRE and URE Rule 1006, the voluminous writings rule. That provision allows admission of summaries, such as computer-generated tabulations or graphic depictions, for voluminous records that are judged too unwieldy to produce in court.

The foregoing discussion examined the rules of evidence that determine the admissibility of electronic records in federal and state courts. Many legal proceedings, however, are held before federal and state administrative agencies where court-oriented rules of evidence do not apply. Generalizing about the admissibility of electronic records in such situations is impossible. Federal administrative agencies are bound by the Administrative Procedures Act, which gives such agencies considerable discretion in determining the admissibility of records. Some federal administrative agencies have informal rules of evidence that must be evaluated on a case-by-case basis to determine their application to electronic records. At the state government level, the admissibility of evidence into administrative proceedings is typically governed by state administrative procedures acts and agency procedural rules. Significant variations in admissibility rules may be encountered from one state to another and, within a given state, from one agency to another.

Retention periods appropriate to the use of records in evidence are influenced by statutes of limitations that prescribe the time periods within which lawsuits or other legal actions must be initiated. Statutes of limitations define the time period when a person or organization can sue or be sued for personal injury or breach of contract, for example. Limitations of assessment periods are the fiscal counterparts of statutes of limitations. They prescribe the period of time that a tax agency can determine taxes owed. Once the period defined by a given statute of limitations or limitation of assessment has elapsed, no legal action can be brought for a specific matter; if the statute of limitations on personal injury lawsuits is three years in a given state, the injured party loses the legal right to sue after that time. As a complicating factor for retention decisions, statutes of limitations begin when an event such as personal injury or breach of contract occurs, not when records relating to that event are created. Electronic records pertaining to products manufactured today may be relevant for legal actions several decades in the future.

Although they can have a significant impact on a given agency's records retention practices, statutes of limitations do not mandate retention periods. They simply define the maximum period of time during which records that are being retained in support of an actual or possible legal action can be used for that purpose. If electronic records are being retained specifically and exclusively to support legal actions, retention periods longer than pertinent statutes of limitations serve no purpose. Electronic records can be destroyed in conformity with retention schedules while statutes of limitations are in effect, provided that no laws or government regulations mandate the retention of such records. If litigation is pending or imminent, however, no records can be destroyed, even if their retention periods elapse.

LEGAL STATUS OF ELECTRONIC SIGNATURES

Signatures are used to authenticate documents, to signify intent or approval, and to prevent repudiation. To be considered valid, certain business documents must be signed. Contracts, leases, purchase orders, and payment authorizations are obvious, commonplace examples. In many applications, such documents are printed from databases, word processing files, or other computer-processible sources for the sole purpose of creating a signed file copy to satisfy retention and evidentiary requirements. The substitution of electronic records for such purposes depends on the acceptability of electronic signatures.

Broadly defined, the phrase *electronic signature* denotes any electronic method of signing a computer-processible record. An electronic signature need not resemble a handwritten signature. The possibilities range from straightforward typing of the author's name at the end of an electronic message or document created by word processing software to sophisticated biometric identifiers based on a signer's physical characteristics such as hand geometry or fingerprint recognition. Other approaches include a personal identification number (PIN), a digitized image of a handwritten signature, or user selection of an icon in a dialog box possibly supplemented by a password or other verification. The phrase *digital signature* denotes a specific type of electronic signature that employs signer verification and encryption technology.

In the United States, the Electronic Signatures in Global and National Commerce Act (15 U.S. Code §7001-7031), also known as the E-Sign bill, became law on October 1, 2000. It clarifies the legal status of electronic signatures and records in the context of signing requirements imposed by law. It provides that agreements, contracts, or other transactions cannot be rendered invalid solely because they are signed electronically. The law defines an electronic signature broadly as "an electronic sound, symbol, or process attached to or logically associated with a contract or record and executed or adopted by a person with the intent to sign the record." Exclusions are limited to wills and other testamentary instruments, matters relating to family law, certain sections of the Uniform Commercial Code, court orders and other judicial documents, insurance cancellation notices, certain records relating to product recalls, and records relating to the transportation of hazardous substances.

State laws may modify, limit, or supercede the E-Sign bill under certain conditions. The Uniform Electronic Transactions Act (UETA), approved in 1999 National Conference of Commissioners on Uniform State Laws, facilitates and promotes e-commerce and other electronic transactions by eliminating uncertainties about the legal status of electronic signatures and records associated with such transactions. According to the UETA, the legal significance of a record or signature is not affected by its format. Like the E-Sign bill, the UETA affirms the equivalency of manual and electronic signatures for authenticating records in business transactions where the parties have agreed to conduct the transactions by electronic means. The UETA addresses some issues such as the attribution of electronic signatures and records that are not covered in the E-Sign bill. It also states that electronic signatures and records satisfy evidentiary and audit requirements, although it allows individual states to limit the acceptability of electronic records and signatures for audit purposes. Like the E-Sign bill, the UETA excludes testamentary documents, which are unlikely to be subject to electronic transactions, but it permits electronic signatures and records for certain family law matters such as property settlements and post-nuptial agreements. At the time of this writing, the UETA had been adopted by over half the states and was under consideration in more than half a dozen others.

Some states have enacted their own laws regarding electronic signatures. Such laws resemble the UETA in concept, but they may differ in scope and detail. As an example, the New York Electronic Signatures and Records Act (I NYCRR Part 540), also known as the NYESRA, establishes standards and procedures for the use and authentication of electronic signatures by government entities in New York State. Generally, the NYESRA provides that an electronic signature has the same validity as a conventional hand signature. It defines an electronic signature broadly as an electronic identifier "that is unique to the person using it, capable of verification, under the sole control of the person using it, attached to or associated with data in such a manner that authenticates the attachment of the signature to particular data and the integrity of the data transmitted, and intended by the party using it to have the same force and effect as the use of a signature affixed by hand." Exclusions include wills, trusts, powers of attorney, deeds, mortgages, and negotiable instruments.

In the United States and elsewhere, electronic commerce initiatives and projects for electronic delivery of government services are important motivators for electronic signature legislation. Internationally, the UNCITRAL Model Law on Electronic Commerce allows for a variety of electronic signature technologies, provided that they identify the signer and are appropriately reliable for their intended purposes. At the time of this writing, UNCITRAL was preparing rules to determine the reliability of specific electronic signature methods such as encrypted digital signatures. The UNCITRAL Model Law has influenced electronic signature legislation in several countries. The Canadian Uniform Electronic Commerce Act, for example, extends the UNCITRAL Model Law to any business transaction or legal relationship that involves documentation. Like the similar U.S. laws, it equates electronic and handwritten signatures for many purposes, as does the United Kingdom Electronic Communications Act of 2000, the Australian Electronic Transaction Act of 2000, and the Singapore Electronic Transaction Act of 1998.

ADMINISTRATIVE RETENTION REQUIREMENTS

Laws and government regulations can have a significant impact on records retention practices; however, legally mandated recordkeeping requirements affect a
small percentage of most electronic records. In some organizations, large numbers
of records may be retained for possible use in evidence. For many electronic
records series, however, retention decisions are based on administrative rather
than legal considerations.

Administrative retention parameters are variously described as *operational
retention parameters* or *user retention parameters*. As their name suggests, they are
determined by the administrative requirements of users who reference records to
support a program unit's daily business operations or long-term goals. As with
paper documents, administrative retention decisions for electronic records are
based on their content and business purpose rather than their format. Electronic
mail (e-mail) is a case in point. E-mail technology is a means of transmitting written
messages. Depending on the circumstances of creation or receipt, e-mail messages
are the electronic counterparts of interoffice memoranda or of conventional mail.
Some corporations, government agencies, and other organizations have developed
retention guidelines for correspondence based on its content and business value. As
an example, correspondence that documents significant policies, decisions, actions,
events, or business relationships may be retained permanently, while correspondence that deals with routine administrative matters may be discarded within a few
years if it is saved at all. Such guidelines apply to e-mail messages. The mere fact
that a message is transmitted by e-mail rather than conventional delivery methods
is irrelevant for retention decisions.

Although content and business purpose are determining factors in every
case, some electronic records have special attributes that complicate retention
decisions. Significant differences exist, for example, between Web pages and other
types of records, including other electronic records. The dynamic content of Web
pages makes version control critical and raises questions about retention of
superceded information. Given the interrelationships among pages at a given Web
site, retention actions can have a ripple effect throughout a Web site. In particular,
modification or deletion of one or more Web pages can adversely impact site navigation on an intranet or the Internet. Similarly, some Web pages contain links to
external sites, which may be modified or deleted by their originators.

Administrative retention parameters should not be confused with legal
retention requirements. Even where laws or regulations mandate specific retention
periods for particular records series, administrative requirements must also be considered. Often, such requirements exceed legally mandated retention periods. For
each electronic records series, administrative and legal requirements should be
defined separately; the applicable retention period is determined by the longer of
the two requirements. In some organizations, research-oriented retention criteria
are also considered. Scholarly considerations may lead to retention periods that
exceed legal or administrative requirements. Electronic records that have no continuing administrative value may be significant to historians or other scholars.

Like their legal counterparts, administrative retention periods are usually measured in years following the occurrence of a specified event such as the end of a fiscal year or calendar year, the completion of an audit, the fulfillment of a contract, the completion of a project, or the termination of employment. Administrative retention periods for electronic records are typically negotiated through meetings or other consultations with persons who must use the records to fulfill their assigned work responsibilities. A fundamental records management assumption is that users of records are uniquely qualified to determine their reference value, based on their experience with a given records series and their knowledge of the business operations and objectives the records support. Through questions and discussion, records managers can help users clarify the relationship between reference value and retention requirements.

Meetings about administrative retention requirements are attended by one or more representatives of the departments or other program units that create and maintain electronic records. Often, the department's records management liaison person takes the lead in explaining the program unit's operational requirements at such meetings. Other interested parties, including administrative and managerial employees who maintain and use specific records series, may also be involved. Electronic records maintained by one program unit are often referenced by other program units. In the case of computer-processible records, for example, such information sharing is encouraged by the implementation of databases, data warehouses, intranets, and other centralized information resources that serve the needs of multiple departments. It is facilitated by the widespread implementation of computer networks that provide convenient remote access to electronically stored information.

As discussed in Chapter Four, a thorough inventory of electronic records includes questions about reference activity and retention practices associated with specific records series. A program unit's responses to such questions provide a useful starting point for determining administrative retention periods, which should be based on the reasonable probability that a given electronic records series will be needed in the future to support specific business objectives or activities. Administrative retention designations are based on the concept of an information life cycle. Decades of records management theory and practice indicate that the operational utility of many, if not most, records varies inversely with the age of the records. Typically, records maintained by corporations, government agencies, and other organizations are most valuable and are referenced frequently for a relatively brief period of time following their creation or receipt. As the records age, their business value and reference activity diminish, either gradually or abruptly. When, and if, their business value falls to or approaches zero, the records can be discarded. This life cycle applies equally to records in electronic and nonelectronic formats.

Operational retention periods are essentially estimates of life cycle duration for specific records series. Certain electronic records, such as e-mail distributed by list services, have very short life cycles; they are often discarded after an initial reading. Others, such as drafts of word processing documents and reminder files stored by personal digital assistants, are updated by replacement at similarly brief intervals. Some electronic records, such as routine office documents created by word processing programs and financial planning documents stored as spreadsheet files, may be retained for a brief period then discarded, usually within several years of creation. Many transaction-oriented records, such as database records pertaining to purchase orders and insurance claims, are referenced frequently for several weeks or months following their creation or receipt but only occasionally after the matters to which they pertain are resolved. Total retention periods for such electronic records may range from 6 to 10 years.

Certain electronic records are retained for much longer periods. Their retention parameters may be determined by the life cycles of objects to which the records pertain. As an example, CAD files and digitized engineering drawings pertaining to facilities or equipment are retained as long as the facilities or equipment remain in service. Test results, statistical data, and other electronic records that relate to pharmaceutical products are retained as long as the products are marketed and often longer as continuing proof of safety or efficacy. Finally, some electronic records have continuing administrative value that warrants permanent retention.

In some cases, the time-dependent operational utility of electronic records can be established with confidence. Past experience with a particular records series is usually a reliable basis for retention determinations. Experience may confirm, for example, that mechanical and electrical drawings stored as CAD files contain information essential to future building repairs and must be retained as long as the building remains in service. Similarly, word processing files pertaining to closed contracts may have been used in the past to prepare subsequent contracts or contract amendments; consequently, they will likely be useful in the future for that purpose.

As a helpful feature, some computer programs keep track of the frequency or last date of reference activity for specific types of records. Certain word processing programs, for example, indicate the dates when a text file was created and last edited. Similarly, accounting and database management programs may create an audit trail by recording the dates of file entries and revisions. Whenever possible, similar features should be incorporated into the design plan for new or updated computer applications. As a complicating factor, many electronic records series are relatively new entities; organizations may consequently have little long-term reference experience to guide their retention decisions. Often, however, electronic records are replacements or adjuncts for paper files for which reference patterns are well understood.

Because the future utility of specific electronic records series cannot be predicted with certainty, some risk is inevitably associated with administrative retention decisions. Because destruction is irreversible, some program units may be reluctant to discard electronic records, and long retention periods are often established by default to allow for improbable contingencies. Such conservative retention practices entail their own risks, however. When an organization is involved in litigation or government investigations, electronic records—like their paper counterparts—are subject to discovery actions that may ultimately prove harmful. The opposing party in a legal action often builds its case on information obtained through such discovery actions. In particular, draft word processing files and poorly worded or ill-informed e-mail messages are subject to misinterpretation that can pose significant problems. Even where electronic records contain no damaging information, the organization that maintains them must bear the often substantial cost of locating the required information and providing copies in response to a subpoena or other court order.

Discovery considerations aside, unneeded electronic records can be expensive to maintain. Proper storage conditions and handling precautions must be observed. Where rewritable media are involved, unneeded electronic records will occupy disk or tape space that might be used for new information. Additional media must be purchased to accommodate records growth. On-line retention of large quantities of unneeded information also increases the time and effort required for data backup and other computer operations.

MEDIA STABILITY AND SYSTEM DEPENDENCE

Long administrative retention periods for electronic records are complicated by the limited storage stability of certain electronic recordkeeping media and their dependence on specific configurations of computer, video, or audio hardware and/or software. Limited media stability and hardware/software dependence also have obvious and significant implications for research-oriented retention criteria, many of which involve the permanent preservation of records. Used in this context, *stability* denotes the extent to which an information storage medium retains physical characteristics and chemical properties appropriate to its intended purpose. The stable life of a given medium is the period of time during which it can be used for reliable recording or playback of information. With electronic media, reliability is determined by the preservation of signal strength and the absence of permanent read/write errors. In the computer industry, for example, the de facto standard of error-free operation specifies that media must contain less than one permanent read/write error per trillion recorded bits. Because most commercially available magnetic and optical media contain fewer than one trillion bits (approximately 120 gigabytes) of recording capacity, any given medium should be free of errors during the claimed stability period. Another measure of media stability specifies that the error rate for a given medium must not exceed the error correction capabilities of the device in which the medium will be recorded or read.

In their product specifications, media manufacturers may differentiate recording stability from playback stability. *Recording stability* denotes the period of time that a given magnetic or optical storage medium permits reliable recording of new information. *Playback stability*—the ability to retrieve previously recorded information—is more significant for this discussion of records retention; retention periods for specific electronic records series are obviously limited by the playback life of the media on which the records series are stored.

Discussions of stability are most relevant for electronic records stored on removable media such as magnetic tapes, diskettes, or optical disks. Although hard drives are the storage devices of choice in high-performance computing applications, information recorded on them is continuously vulnerable to damage from head crashes or other equipment malfunctions. Electronic records stored on hard drives must be copied onto removable media for back-up protection. Removable hard disks, like their fixed counterparts, are vulnerable to crashes when mounted into their drives. In many computer applications, database records, word processing documents, and other information stored on hard disks will be replaced or overwritten with new information or updated versions at regular intervals. In such situations, media stability is of limited concern, because the information—being changeable—has a relatively short useful life.

The stability of a given information storage medium depends on various factors, including the medium's chemical composition and the conditions under which it is stored and used. Although magnetic tapes and optical disks are sometimes described in product advertisements and other promotional literature as archival media, they do not offer the permanence implied in that description. As applied to magnetic and optical media, the term *archival* is employed in the data processing sense, where *to archive* means to transfer inactive information from relatively expensive on-line storage devices, such as hard drives, to presumably less expensive removable media for off-line storage. This process is the data archiving activity defined previously.

Although national and international standards provide lifetime estimates for specific paper and photographic records media, no comparable published standards address the stability of electronic records stored on magnetic or optical media. In the case of magnetic tapes, however, anecdotal evidence based on operational experience with older media suggests the possibility of long life. For example, some audio and video tapes created several decades ago remain playable today. Computing facilities have likewise successfully retrieved information from magnetic tapes that have been in storage for more than a decade. Various journal articles, technical reports, and other scientific publications suggest that magnetic media will retain their utility for one to three decades, depending on media composition.

On the other hand, audible and visible distortions attest to the deterioration of many older audio and video recordings on magnetic tape reels and cassettes, although such media may remain playable despite impaired quality. In the case of computer-processible information, however, physical or chemical changes in magnetic media can render information unretrievable. Many personal computer users, for example, have had the disturbing experience of being unable to retrieve information recorded onto diskettes, even though the recording was performed just a few weeks or months before the attempted retrieval. Serious concerns have been voiced about the integrity of information stored on magnetic tapes in large data archives. In a widely reported development, a study by the General Accounting Office questioned the integrity of magnetic tapes maintained by the National Aeronautics and Space Administration. The tapes, which contain data generated by unmanned space missions undertaken since the late 1950s, were judged to have undergone significant deterioration in storage, making their continued utility suspect.

Factors that influence the stability of electronic media are documented in many publications. Computer, video, and audio information recorded on magnetic media are vulnerable to accidental erasure by magnetic fields of sufficient strength. Information recorded on magnetic tapes can be damaged by print-through effects; that is, the migration of recorded signals from one layer of tape to another. Magnetic recordings are also imperiled by changes in the physical and chemical characteristics of a given medium. The most significant physical changes result from media wear and improper media handling. The physical and chemical characteristics of magnetic tapes and diskettes are adversely affected by improper storage environments. These effects can be minimized, and media stability extended, by implementing storage and handling procedures and precautions discussed in Chapter Seven.

Stability claims for optical media are based on accelerated aging tests rather than on operational experience. Because most optical media have been in existence for less than two decades, direct observation of media in prolonged storage is impossible. Among optical media, compact disk–recordable (CD-R) is the most stable. Manufacturers claim playback stabilities of 75 to 200 years for their CD-R media. These claims are based on accelerated aging tests. Stability periods for other optical disks range from 10 to 40 years, with 30 years being a typical claim for magneto-optical disks, which are widely utilized for data and image recording.

Even if the stability of magnetic and optical media were to improve to levels comparable to those of high rag content papers or silver gelatin microfilm, retention periods for electronic records would still be limited by complications resulting from the interdependence of media, recorded information hardware, and software. Media stability is rarely the limiting factor for long-term storage of computer-processible information, audio recordings, or video images. The service lives of magnetic and optical storage devices is typically shorter than that of media intended for use in such devices. Although magnetic tapes and optical disks may remain stable for several decades, few magnetic recording and playback devices are engineered for a useful life longer than 10 years, and most will be removed from service within a shorter time. Computer storage peripherals are usually replaced with newer equipment within five years. Audio and video recorders may have longer service lives, but the enhanced capabilities and attractive cost-performance characteristics of new models provide a powerful motive for replacement at relatively short intervals.

New magnetic and optical storage devices typically support higher-density recording formats than their predecessors. For example, successive generations of magnetic tape and optical disk drives intended for computer applications have higher-density recording formats. To preserve the utility of previously recorded information, successor products may offer backward-compatibility; that is, they can read media recorded by older models. However, such backward-compatibility is not guaranteed to be continued in all future products. In fact, the history of magnetic and optical storage technology suggests that backward-compatibility provides a bridge between two or, at most, three generations of equipment. Eventually support for older formats is phased out. As an example, magnetic tape units available at the time of this writing do not support low-density recording formats such as 200 and 550 bits per inch. Even nine-track magnetic tapes recorded at 800 bits per inch, which were widely encountered in the 1970s, are no longer supported by some newer tape drives, most of which operate at 1,600 or 6,250 bits per inch.

As an additional complication, backward-compatibility does little, if anything, to address problems of discontinued media. Diskettes in the 8-inch and

5.25-inch sizes, for example, have been supplanted by the 3.5-inch size. The eight-track magnetic tape cassette is an obvious example of an obsolete audio recording medium for which playback equipment is difficult to obtain. U-matic video cassettes have been driven from the market by half-inch video tape formats. Since the early 1980s, manufacturers of optical disk drives and media have discontinued certain models or entire product lines without providing replacements. As an example, none of the 5.25-inch write-once optical disks manufactured before 1988 could be read by optical disk drives that were available for sale 10 years later.

In computer applications, problems of hardware dependence are compounded by software considerations. Electronic records are intended for retrieval or other processing by specific application programs which, in turn, operate in a specific systems software environment. Even more than equipment, software is subject to changes that can render previously recorded information unusable. Successor versions of a given program may not be able to read data, text, or images recorded by earlier versions. Customized software is particularly susceptible to changes in recording media or hardware characteristics.

Many computer, audio, and video records exist only in electronic formats. They cannot be converted to human-readable representations without prohibitively high cost or significant loss of functionality. In such cases, media stability and hardware/software considerations pose formidable, but not necessarily insurmountable, obstacles to long-term retention. *Data migration*, the process of periodically converting electronic records to new file formats and/or new storage media, can satisfy long retention requirements. Conversion of electronic records to new file formats will maintain the usability of recorded information when computer systems and/or software are upgraded or replaced. Conversion of electronic records to new storage media will maintain the usability of recorded information where the stable life span of a given storage medium is shorter than the retention period for recorded information or where product modifications or discontinuations render a given storage medium unusable.

Data migration requirements should be determined when retention periods are defined for electronic records. The longer the retention period for recorded information, the greater the need for data migration to ensure the future usability of electronic records. A data migration plan is essential where the destruction date for electronic records is greater than five years from the implementation date of the computer system or software that maintains the records, or where the total retention period for electronic records is 10 years or longer.

At a minimum, a data migration plan should specify the electronic records to be included, the migration method, the anticipated migration interval, the program unit responsible for performing the migration, and the resources required to implement the plan. Data migration plans should be reviewed periodically and revised, as necessary, based on experience or other considerations. At a minimum, data migration plans should be re-evaluated whenever computer systems and/or software are upgraded or replaced, or whenever recorded information is transferred to new storage media.

Where electronic records are subject to long retention periods, data migration plans will involve a significant future commitment of personnel and technological resources through multiple iterations of file format conversion and/or storage media conversion. Where electronic records are designated for permanent retention, the commitment is perpetual. The practicality of such data migration commitments must be carefully considered when designating electronic records as official copies for retention purposes. Where the same information exists in electronic and non-electronic formats, or where information can be converted easily and reliably to nonelectronic formats through printing or transcription, records managers may prefer paper or microfilm for information designated for long-term retention. Although conceptually unattractive, this method is easily implemented and minimizes the risk that required information will be unreadable in the future. Compared with most magnetic and optical media, paper and microfilm are more stable. Because paper and microfilm records contain human-readable information, problems of hardware and software dependence are minimized or eliminated. The conversion of electronic records to human-readable formats is unacceptable, however, where future reprocessing of the records in machine-readable form is anticipated.

SUMMARY

Retention schedules establish the infrastructure on which many other records management activities are based. They enumerate electronic records series and indicate the period of time that each is to be retained. They may also indicate the physical storage media to be used, the locations where electronic records are to be stored, and the disposition of electronic records when their retention periods have elapsed. Retention schedules vary in scope and content. They may be prepared for electronic records maintained by individual program units within a given organization or for electronic records maintained by the organization as a whole. The same retention schedules may cover electronic and nonelectronic records. Properly formulated, retention schedules will ensure the availability and utility of electronic records for appropriate periods of time, while preventing the unwarranted accumulation of obsolete records. Retention schedules also promote the efficient use of electronic storage media and devices.

Retention periods for electronic records are determined by legal, administrative, and research criteria. Recordkeeping requirements presented in various laws and government regulations specify minimum retention periods for certain information. Some laws and regulations permit the retention of electronic records to satisfy such requirements. Although no laws or regulations require the creation and retention of electronic records as the sole method of satisfying legally mandated recordkeeping requirements, certain laws do specify retention periods for electronic records where they exist.

A broader group of legal considerations involves the admissibility of electronic records as evidence in court trials, administrative hearings, or other legal proceedings. To be admissible, electronic records must satisfy authentication requirements. The purpose of such authentication is to demonstrate the reliability of electronic records to the court's satisfaction. Records managers must develop and implement electronic recordkeeping systems and procedures that will facilitate authentication and enable organizations to overcome objections to the admissibility of electronic records. An administrator capable of providing knowledgeable testimony for authentication purposes should be designated for each system that creates or maintains electronic records. All system characteristics and operating procedures should be fully documented. Security provisions must be implemented to protect electronic records from tampering or other modifications that may impair their trustworthiness.

Operational retention parameters for electronic records are determined by administrative reference requirements. They are typically negotiated through meetings or other consultation with persons who must use the records to fulfill their assigned work responsibilities. The limited storage stability and hardware/software dependence of electronic media generally argue against long operational retention periods. Lifetime estimates for most magnetic and optical storage media are typically shorter than for paper records and photographic films. The future utility of electronic records is further limited by the interdependence of media, information, hardware, and software. Electronic media are designed to be recorded and read by specific devices. In most cases, the service lives of such devices are much shorter than that of electronic recording media. The continued utility of electronic records is consequently imperiled by equipment obsolescence and product discontinuations. In computer applications, problems of hardware dependence are compounded by software dependence. Even more than equipment, computer software is subject to changes that can render electronic records unusable. Data migration plans can address these complications, but records managers may prefer paper or microfilm for long-term retention of information in some situations.

CHAPTER SIX

MANAGING VITAL ELECTRONIC RECORDS

Vital records, as briefly defined in preceding chapters, contain information essential to an organization's mission. Put another way, vital records contain information needed for mission-critical business operations; that is, for operations an organization must perform. Such records are necessary to re-create the organization's legal and financial status and to determine the rights and obligations of employees, customers, stockholders, and citizens. If a vital record is lost, damaged, destroyed, or otherwise rendered unavailable or unusable, such operations will be curtailed or discontinued, with a resulting adverse impact on the organization. Without vital records, an equipment manufacturer will be unable to build, ship, or repair its products. A pharmaceutical company will be unable to develop, test, or prove the safety and efficacy of chemical compounds. A government agency will be unable to provide essential services to citizens. A hospital will be unable to render effective medical care. A school or college will be unable to document the academic achievements of students. A law, accounting, or architectural firm will be unable to serve its clients.

Vital records are considered vital specifically and exclusively for the information they contain. Vital record status is not necessarily related to other record attributes. Format is immaterial; vital records may be paper documents, photographic films, or electronic media. They may be active or inactive records, originals, or copies. Vital record status is independent of retention designations. Vital records need not be permanent records; they may, in fact, be retained for brief periods of time and replaced at frequent intervals. Furthermore, some records may be considered vital for only a portion of their designated retention periods. Records in an accounts receivable database, for example, are vital until paid, but they are often retained for several years following receipt of payment for legal reasons, internal audits, or other purposes.

Specific record attributes aside, a *vital records program* is a set of policies and procedures for the systematic, comprehensive, and economical control of losses associated with vital records. Traditionally, records management has emphasized the protection of vital records against accidental or willful damage, destruction, or misplacement; the last of these encompasses a spectrum of events ranging from misfiling to theft of records. An organization may also be harmed by misuse of, alteration of, or unauthorized access to vital records. In the case of computer-stored electronic records, such considerations have been widely discussed by public policy analysts, legal scholars, and others.

The development, implementation, and operation of policies, programs, and procedures to protect vital records have traditionally been considered records management responsibilities. In most organizations, however, vital records protection is closely related to other loss-control activities. Many corporations, government agencies, and other organizations, for example, have developed contingency plans for the protection of personnel, buildings, machinery, inventory, and other assets in the event of a disaster such as a fire or flood. Properly implemented, such contingency plans can reduce exposure to loss and increase the likelihood of an organization's survival. They provide formalized procedures to help an organization withstand and limit the impact of adverse events, enabling it to continue operations—though possibly at a reduced level—following a disaster. Vital records protection is an indispensable aspect of contingency planning. For U.S. government agencies, for example, 36 CFR 1236 states that the management of vital records must be part of each agency's plan for continuity of business operations in the event of emergencies. For many organizations, information contained in vital records is their most important asset. In some cases, the loss of information can have more devastating consequences for continuation of business operations than the loss of physical plant or inventory.

In computer installations, vital records protection is often viewed as a facet of the broader, much publicized field of computer security and disaster recovery. In the typical organization, planning for computer security is the responsibility of a centralized information systems department. Often, committees of information systems staff and user departments are formed to address issues of loss control, including the replacement of computing equipment and restoration of computer operations following a disaster, the protection of computer resources against electronic intrusion, and the detection and prevention of computer fraud. Computer security committees may also include internal auditors, security personnel, legal counsel, and risk management specialists.

Records management participation in such contingency planning activities is essential to facilitate the coordination of vital records protection with other aspects of computer security. Vital records protection is a critical element in any disaster recovery plan. The rapid restoration of computing operations following a disaster serves little purpose if the information needed to support specific applications is unavailable. In a given organization, the records manager is the employee most likely to have a broad understanding of the nature and importance of vital electronic records and the ways in which they relate to other information resources that support an organization's mission.

A vital records protection program for electronic records includes the following components:

- Formal establishment of the program by senior management with responsibility and authority for protection of vital electronic records assigned to the records management activity—to be coordinated, where appropriate, with related contingency planning activities;

- Identification and enumeration of vital electronic records;
- Risk analysis to determine the extent to which specific vital records are threatened by hazards and to calculate exposures;
- Selection and implementation of appropriate loss prevention and records protection methods; and
- Employee training and compliance auditing.

The following sections explain and discuss these program components. Although the discussion emphasizes vital electronic records, many of the concepts and methods presented here also apply to vital nonelectronic records in paper or photographic formats. A comprehensive disaster recovery plan must encompass such nonelectronic information resources.

ESTABLISHING THE PROGRAM

Citizens have a reasonable expectation that government agencies will safeguard essential records. Similar expectations apply to corporate shareholders, to clients of professional services firms, to medical patients, and to any other persons who may be affected by the recordkeeping practices of others. These expectations are based on the legal concept of "standard of care," which is the degree of care that a reasonable person would exercise to prevent injury to another. An organization's electronic records are assets that contain potentially valuable, sometimes vital information. In any organization, senior management has ultimate responsibility for protection of assets, including the formulation of effective loss-control plans. Information contained in vital electronic records is an asset. Therefore, senior management is ultimately responsible for the protection of vital electronic records. If the destruction or misuse of vital electronic records results in the interruption of critical business operations, senior management must accept responsibility for the ensuing financial losses or other consequences.

Protection of vital records is not merely a good idea; it is a statutory obligation in some cases. In the United States, senior management's responsibility and obligation to protect vital electronic records is implied or explicitly stated in several laws and government regulations. Within the U.S. government, for example, 36 CFR 1236.12 makes agency heads responsible for protecting vital records, which are defined as records needed to meet operational responsibilities under emergency conditions or to protect the legal and financial rights of the government and those affected by government activities. For corporations, partnerships, and other private businesses, the most frequently cited legal statute is the Foreign Corrupt Practices Act (FCPA) of 1977 (as amended in 1988 and 1998). It imposes significant penalties for failure to keep accounting records and other information pertaining to certain assets. The FCPA applies to all domestic companies and their employees.

Among laws and regulations that specifically address the protection of computer-stored records, the Computer Security Act of 1987 (40 U.S. Code 759) requires the development and implementation of security plans for "sensitive" information maintained by computers operated by U.S. federal government agencies and federal government contractors. Sensitive information is defined as "any unclassified information, the loss, misuse, or unauthorized access or modification of which could adversely affect the national interest or the conduct of a federal program or the privacy to which individuals are entitled under the Privacy Act." This definition conforms closely to that given previously for vital records. The Computer Security Act gives the National Institute of Standards and Technology (NIST) responsibility for establishing security standards and guidelines for federal computer systems and mandates security training for personnel involved with sensitive information. Required training topics, as outlined in 5 CFR 930, include disaster recovery and hazard protection.

OMB Circular A-130, issued by the Office of Management and Budget (OMB), defines policies to secure information, including electronic records, maintained by federal government agencies. Although many of its provisions concern privacy protection and prevention of unauthorized access to computer systems, Circular A-130 also requires contingency plans to ensure continuity of operations for automated information systems. It specifies that U.S. government agencies must implement safeguards to protect information commensurate with the "risk and magnitude of the harm that would result from the loss, misuse, or unauthorized access to or modification of such information." In its original version, Circular A-130 concentrated on securing centralized data processing facilities and large custom-developed computer applications that involved sensitive information. Subsequent revisions, issued in 1993 and 2000, do not differentiate sensitive and nonsensitive computer systems. As delineated in Appendix III to Circular A-130, security and contingency planning requirements extend to "general support systems," which are defined as personal computers, local area networks, and wide area networks that run a variety of prewritten computer programs. Circular A-130 is based on the recognition that all general support systems operated by federal government agencies store some sensitive information.

Circular A-130 makes computer security the responsibility of agency heads and chief information officers, who must develop and implement security plans encompassing personnel controls and accountability for their general support systems. The security plans must be consistent with guidelines established by the National Institute of Standards and Technology. Contingency planning is recognized as a critical component of computer security. For each general support system, a single individual must be assigned operational responsibility for security. That individual must be knowledgeable about the information resources processed by the system. Security provisions for each major computer application must be audited at three-year intervals.

Organizations in specific industries are subject to records protection and computer security requirements promulgated by regulating agencies. As an example, financial institutions insured by the Federal Deposit Insurance Corporation (FDIC) are required to develop disaster recovery plans for their computer installations. Specific requirements for contingency plans for depository institutions are presented in the Comptroller of the Currency Bank Circular 177, the Federal Home Loan Bank Board Thrift Bulletin 30, the National Credit Union Administration Letter 109, and a joint policy statement by the Federal Financial Institutions Examination

Council (FFIEC). As part of the administrative simplification provisions of the Health Insurance Portability and Accountability Act of 1996 (45 CFR 142), the Department of Health and Human Services makes data backup and disaster recovery planning mandatory components for security standards for information maintained by healthcare providers and plans. IRS Revenue Procedure 86-19 required off-site protection of computer-processible tax records. It has been supplanted by IRS Revenue Procedure 98-25, which recommends but does not require off-site storage.

Protection against unauthorized disclosure of computer-stored records is maintained by various privacy statutes. Among U.S. laws, the Privacy Act of 1974 (5 U.S. Code 552A) is the best known example. Other federal statutes with privacy provisions for recorded information include the Fair Credit Billing Act (15 U.S. Code 1637), the Fair Credit Reporting Act (15 U.S. Code 1681), the Family Educational Rights and Privacy Act (20 U.S. Code 1232), the Right to Financial Privacy Act (12 U.S. Code 3401), the Electronic Communications Privacy Act of 1986 (18 U.S. Code 1367), the Drivers Privacy Protection Act of 1994 (18 U.S. Code 2721), the National Information Infrastructure Protection Act of 1996 (18 U.S. Code 1030), and the Children's On-line Privacy Protection Act of 1998 (16 CFR 312). Similar privacy laws have been passed by various states. Medical records and adoption records, in particular, are subject to state-specific privacy legislation. Privacy legislation with restrictions on access to recorded information has also been passed in certain other countries. Examples include the Canadian Privacy Act of 1983 and Canadian Personal Information Protection and Electronic Document Act of 2000, the United Kingdom Data Protection Act of 1998, the Swiss Federal Law on Data Protection of 1992, the Australian Privacy Act of 1998, the New Zealand Privacy Act of 1993, and the New Zealand Health Information Privacy Code of 1994.

Organizations have been held liable for damages associated with inadequate provisions for the security of electronic records. Reported cases have dealt with the failure to prevent unauthorized disclosure of computer information such as consumer credit records or medical records. Comparable civil liability could conceivably result from an organization's failure to protect specific operating records from accidental or willful loss or destruction. Accidental deletion of computer-stored medical records, for example, could complicate treatment and damage a patient's health. Similarly, a university's failure to implement a disaster recovery plan could render it unable to provide academic transcripts should such computer-stored records be destroyed, thereby placing its graduates at a disadvantage when competing for employment or seeking further education. A corporation's failure to protect its personnel records could make determining retirement eligibility or other benefits impossible. Destruction of birth, death, marital, or land records maintained by state or local government agencies can have widespread adverse consequences for individuals and organizations.

Quite possibly, legal actions related to incidents of this type have occurred but gone unreported, having been settled out of court in favor of the injured party to avoid publicizing an organization's computer security problems. The legal outcome in such situations is far from certain, however. Arguments in favor of liability are based on the previously discussed concept of standard of care, with its presumed duty to secure electronic records against destruction or misuse, including unauthorized access; but the nature and scope of such a duty have not been firmly established in statutory provisions or case law. Until recently, the lack of industry-wide standards for computer security has complicated agreement about reasonable measures to protect electronic records. Addressing this problem, the publication in 2000 of the ISO/IEC 17799 standard, *Information Technology—Code of Practice for Information Security Management* provides a starting point for the development of computer security policies by corporations, government agencies, and other organizations. Similarly, guidelines developed for federal government computers by the National Institute of Standards and Technology under authority of the Computer Security Act of 1987 are applicable to nongovernmental organizations as well.

Legal requirements and liabilities aside, a vital records protection program is, in effect, an insurance policy for essential information. Like any insurance policy, vital records protection may be difficult to sell to decision makers. Vital records protection is costly but makes no direct contribution to revenues, product development, or the delivery of services. It provides no benefits unless and until a disaster occurs. Many threats to vital records have a low probability of occurrence. Senior management may consequently ignore them in favor of more pressing business concerns, but vital records protection is justified by the intolerable consequences that follow an adverse but improbable event. Senior management must appreciate the potential for tangible and intangible damages associated with the loss, destruction, or misuse of vital electronic records, however unlikely that loss, destruction, or misuse may seem. The damages may include, but are by no means limited to, the loss of customers; interruption of cash flow; lawsuits associated with dereliction of duties, fines, or other penalties for failure to provide records needed for government investigation or tax audits; lack of needed documentation for litigation support; inability to document insurance claims or other transactions; longer completion times for information-dependent business operations; high reconstruction costs for recorded information; and a tarnished public image. By initiating and supporting a program to protect vital electronic records, senior management acknowledges that these consequences are intolerable.

Although an organization's senior management bears ultimate responsibility for safeguarding vital electronic records, its involvement is typically and properly limited to delegating authority for the creation, implementation, and operation of a systematic vital records program. To formalize a protection program for vital electronic records maintained by a corporation, government agency, or other organization, senior management should issue a written directive that:

- Acknowledges the importance of protecting vital electronic records as a component in the organization's contingency planning efforts;
- Establishes a program for the systematic, comprehensive, and economical protection of vital electronic records; and
- Solicits the cooperation of personnel in all program units where vital electronic records are maintained.

If an organization does not have a program to protect its nonelectronic vital records, or if an existing program for such records is in need of revision, the scope of the management directive should be broadened to include information resources in paper and photographic formats.

As with other records management activities, the development and implementation of a successful vital records program depends on the knowledge and active participation of program unit personnel who are familiar with the nature and use of vital electronic records in specific work environments. An advisory committee of program unit representatives provides a formal structure for such participation. The committee will support the records management department in planning, implementing, and operating a program to protect vital electronic records.

IDENTIFYING VITAL RECORDS

Vital electronic records are typically identified by surveying individual program units to determine which, if any, vital records they create and maintain. The end product of such a survey is a list of the vital electronic records created and maintained by each program unit. For those electronic records series identified as vital, the list should include the following data elements:

- The series title;
- A brief description of the series' purpose, scope, and operational and physical characteristics;
- The reason the series is considered vital;
- The name of the program unit responsible for protecting the vital records series; and
- The method of protection to be implemented.

Lists prepared for individual program units may be combined to form a master list of vital electronic records maintained by an entire organization or by a specific administrative entity such as a division, subsidiary, or field office. As with retention schedules, electronic and nonelectronic vital records may be integrated into a single listing, and that approach is often advisable. At a minimum, vital record designations for electronic and nonelectronic records series should be coordinated. If exactly the same information exists in electronic and nonelectronic records, one format should be selected for vital records protection. If purposeful duplication and off-site storage will be used, protecting electronic records will typically prove faster and more economical than protecting paper or photographic records that contain the same information. Compared with their nonelectronic counterparts, electronic records are more compact and easier to duplicate.

As noted in Chapter Four, a vital records survey may be combined with an inventory of electronic records performed to assist in preparing retention schedules. That approach is recommended where practical. A combined records inventory/vital records survey will minimize duplication of effort; vital record status can be evaluated for each series identified during a records inventory. Vital records protection measures can also be coordinated with retention-oriented management actions such as off-site storage of specific machine-readable media.

Where a separate vital records survey must be conducted, the procedures are similar to those employed in a conventional records inventory. Based on interviews with program unit personnel, a records manager prepares a tentative list of vital electronic records for consideration and comment by interested parties, both within and outside the program unit that maintains the records. A series of meetings or other consultations will resolve concerns and disagreements, leading eventually to a final approved list of vital electronic records for each program unit or, if desired, a master list. Several drafts may be required before a final version is obtained, however. As with retention scheduling, the records manager coordinates the meetings, directs the discussion, redrafts the vital records lists, and provides a broad perspective on information management issues that transcend the responsibilities and requirements of specific program units.

In corporations, government agencies, or other organizations, most program units maintain one or more electronic records series that contain useful information. Program unit personnel rely on such records to perform specific tasks. When asked to identify vital electronic records, they will include most, if not all, of the records they routinely utilize. Program unit personnel value records information they reference frequently and would not want to lose any of it. A given series of electronic records may be important but not truly essential, however. Records managers must help program unit employees distinguish vital records from important ones.

Important records support a program unit's business operations and help it fulfill its assigned responsibilities. Unavailability of such records may cause delays or confusion, but it will not render a program unit inoperative. The loss of important records may impede a program unit's work, but it will not prevent it. Some important records are replaceable; their contents may be reconstructed from other records, although such reconstruction may involve considerable time, inconvenience, and expense. In some computer applications, operations supported by important electronic records may be performed—though, admittedly, less quickly or efficiently—by reversion to manual procedures. Truly vital electronic records, by contrast, are essential and irreplaceable. Their contents cannot be reconstructed, and the operations they support cannot be performed without them. Reversion to manual procedures is impossible.

Vital records are always associated with mission-critical operations; that is, operations that pertain to an organization's fundamental responsibilities and most essential activities. For records to be considered vital, the business operations they support must be essential. In most organizations, a small percentage of nonelectronic records are properly considered vital. By contrast, a somewhat higher, but not necessarily large, percentage of an organization's electronic records may be vital records. In corporations, government agencies, and other organizations, mission-critical operations have historically been priority candidates for computerization or other forms of automation. Certain mission-critical operations, such as accounts payroll, accounts receivable, and payroll processing, are encountered in a broad range of work environments. Those activities have been computerized for decades. Other mission-critical operations are associated with specific types of organizations or industries. Examples include claims processing and policy management in an insurance company; maintenance of customer accounts in a bank or other financial institution; inventory control in a retail organization; development and testing of drugs in a pharmaceutical company; creation and maintenance of patient records in a hospital; and creation and maintenance of student records in a school, college, or university.

Electronic records that are essential to mission-critical operations are, by definition, vital records, because the operations cannot be performed without them. The identification of vital electronic records consequently begins with the identification of an organization's mission-critical operations. Once mission-critical operations are identified by program unit personnel or others, records managers must determine which electronic records are required by those operations. Although all vital records are associated with mission-critical operations, nonvital records may be employed in those operations as well. When determining that a given electronic records series is vital, the records manager must be able to clearly and convincingly state which mission-critical operations would be prevented by loss, destruction, or other unavailability of the indicated records series. That determination is the ultimate test of a vital record.

As a complicating factor, the records manager must differentiate those electronic records vital to a corporation, government agency, or other organization as a whole from those records vital to a specific program unit within that organization. Records series in the former group support operations that are truly mission-critical, while those in the latter group support valuable but not mission-critical activities. In many organizations, certain program units perform useful functions that are not critical to the organization's mission. Loss or destruction of electronic records may cause a temporary or permanent disruption of business operations in such program units, but the organization's mission will not be imperiled. Such records cannot be considered vital, because the activities they support are not vital to the organization as a whole. As an example, a hospital's community relations department may maintain a database of information about community groups with which it is involved. If the database is damaged, the department's work will be impeded or rendered impossible, but patient care—the hospital's mission—will not be affected.

RISK ANALYSIS

As an important part of vital records planning, records managers must consider the risks to which specific electronic records are subject. The purpose of *risk analysis*, sometimes called *risk assessment*, is to determine and evaluate exposure to particular risks. It is an evaluation of the probabilities of an adverse event occurring and the possible extent of the damage in order to help minimize the exposure. Its outcome provides the basis for protection planning and other records management decisions.

Threats to Vital Electronic Records
- Malicious or accidental destruction
- Loss through theft or misplacement
- Corruption through unauthorized modification
- Unauthorized disclosure

Identifying Risks

A thorough risk analysis begins with the identification of threats and vulnerabilities. Threats to vital electronic records can be divided into four broad groups: destruction, loss, corruption, and disclosure. Protection of essential information against malicious or accidental destruction is a well-established component of vital records planning. Malicious destruction of electronic records may result from warfare or warfare-related activities such as terrorism, civil insurrections, purposeful sabotage, or seemingly aimless vandalism. Obvious, potentially catastrophic agents of accidental destruction include natural disasters such as violent weather, floods, and earthquakes. Electronic records can also be damaged or destroyed by human-induced events such as fire or explosions that result from carelessness, negligence, or lack of knowledge about the consequences of specific actions.

Various other causes of accidental records destruction are less dramatic but no less catastrophic. Magnetic and optical media may be damaged by improper environmental conditions and careless handling. Information recorded on magnetic media and certain optical disks can be erased by exposure to strong magnetic fields. Careless work procedures, such as mounting tapes or diskettes without write protection, can expose vital electronic records to accidental erasure by overwriting. Mislabeled media may be inadvertently marked for reuse, their contents being inappropriately replaced by new information. Head crashes or other hardware failures can destroy valuable information. Improperly adjusted equipment, such as misaligned tape guides, can cause scratches or other media damage. Malfunctioning software is likewise a potentially significant cause of damage to electronic records. When a computer program locks up or terminates abnormally, for example, information may not be properly recorded. Similarly, computer records may be accidentally deleted during database reorganizations or by utility programs that consolidate disk space.

Removable magnetic or optical media may be misplaced, misfiled, or stolen. The potential for misplacement or theft is increased by the widespread storage of electronic records in users' work areas where systematic handling procedures are seldom implemented and security provisions may be weak or absent. The use of compact, easily concealed electronic media, such as removable hard disk cartridges and high-density magnetic tapes, facilitates theft, while the high capacity of such media increases the amount of information affected by a single incident of theft. In fact, the inherent and continually improving compactness and high storage density of all electronic media, when compared with paper documents, exposes more information to loss-related incidents.

The potential for unauthorized tampering with electronic records has been widely discussed in publications and at professional meetings. Records stored on rewritable media, such as magnetic disks, magnetic tapes, and certain optical disks, are subject to modification by unauthorized persons in a manner that can be very difficult to detect. Such unauthorized modification may involve deleting, editing, or replacing information. Viruses and other malicious software are much publicized causes of corruption of computer-stored records. Broadly defined, a **virus** is a computer program that replicates itself into other programs that are shared among systems with the intention of causing damage. The virus then performs operations specified by its developer. The operations often involve modifying or destroying information stored by the computer the virus infiltrates. Viruses can also prevent the recording of information, consume system resources required by other programs, cause software failures, and damage hardware components. Depending on the virus, such effects may be immediate or delayed. Because they replicate themselves, computer viruses can spread in a geometric progression through a computer system or network. A related type of malicious software, called a *worm*, travels through a computer installation or network without replicating itself, while a *Trojan horse* is a program that performs a desirable task and some unexpected functions. The latter programs are often destructive.

Dangers associated with improper disclosure of electronic records have been the subject of considerable discussion by a variety of interested parties, including records managers, computer specialists, lawyers, public policy analysts, and civil rights advocates. Although such discussions have typically warned against the unauthorized disclosure of sensitive personal information protected by privacy legislation, electronic records may also store business plans; pricing information; trade secrets; or other proprietary technical, strategic, or financial information of interest to an organization's competitors. Certain government computers similarly store electronic records with national security implications. Improper disclosure of vital electronic records may result from espionage-related activities such as unauthorized access to computer systems, electronic eavesdropping, or bribery of employees who have access to desired information. Computer networks are vulnerable to intrusion by hackers. Accidental disclosure is also possible when computer output is routed to the wrong device in a local or wide area network, when electronic messages are incorrectly addressed or distributed, or when incompletely erased rewritable media are distributed for reuse.

Qualitative Risk Assessment

Regardless of the specific threats involved, risk assessment may be based on intuitive, relatively informal qualitative approaches or more structured, formalized quantitative methods. Qualitative approaches rely principally on group discussions. They are particularly useful for identifying and categorizing physical security problems and other vulnerabilities. A risk assessment team or committee, preferably lead by a records manager, evaluates the dangers to specific vital electronic records series from catastrophic events, theft, and other threats. The team typically produces a prioritized list of vital electronic records judged to be at risk and for which protective measures are recommended.

A *qualitative risk assessment* is usually based on a physical survey of locations where electronic records are stored, combined with an examination of reference activity and patterns that may increase vulnerability and a review of security procedures already in place. Geophysical and political factors, such as the likelihood of destructive weather or the possibility of warfare or civil unrest, are also considered. In the case of electronic records stored on hard drives in centralized or decentralized computing installations, the team may examine the following factors:

- Physical security in the computer area;
- Number and types of employees who have access to the computer area;
- Number and locations of on-line workstations;
- Password protection or other precautions against unauthorized access;
- Network security arrangements;
- Use of surge protectors or uninterruptible power supplies to prevent electrical damage;
- Availability of fire control apparatus;
- Implementation of back-up procedures and off-site storage arrangements for recorded information; and
- Frequency of hardware or software malfunctions that can damage electronic records.

Similarly, a risk analysis of magnetic tapes or other removable media stored off-line will be concerned with the appropriateness of environmental conditions, security provisions to prevent unauthorized access to storage areas, and the proximity of the storage areas to flammable materials or other hazardous substances.

Qualitative risk assessments do not estimate the statistical probabilities associated with destructive events or the financial impact of the resulting losses. Typically, vulnerabilities and probabilities are evaluated in general terms, although the nature and frequency of adverse historical events, such as power outages, network security breaches, or reported theft of computer storage media, are considered. The vulnerabilities of specific records series, for example, may be categorized as acceptable risk, immediate risk, short-term risk, or long-term risk. Similarly, the likelihood of loss associated with specific threats may be described as very low, low, medium, high, or very high. In the project team's report, these evaluative designations should be accompanied by definitions or clarifying narrative. The greatest concern is for those vital electronic records with high vulnerabilities to threats that have a high probability of occurrence with sudden, unpredictable onset—magnetic tapes containing vital information stored in laboratory areas where flammable materials are used in scientific experiments, for example, or confidential product specifications and pricing information stored in desktop computers in unsecured areas.

Quantitative Risk Assessment

Quantitative risk assessment is based on concepts and methods originally developed for product safety analysis and subsequently adapted for computer security applications. Like its qualitative counterpart, quantitative risk assessment relies on site visits, discussions, and other systems analysis methodologies to identify vulnerabilities, but it uses numeric calculations to estimate the likelihood and impact of losses associated with specific vital records series. The effects are expressed as dollar amounts, which can be related to the cost of proposed protection methods. As an additional advantage, quantitative risk assessments provide a useful framework for comparing exposures for different vital records series and prioritizing vital records protection recommendations.

Although various quantitative assessment techniques have been proposed by risk analysts and others, all are based on the following general formula:

$$R = P \times C$$

where:

R = the risk, sometimes called the *annualized loss expectancy (ALE)* associated with the loss of a specific vital records series due to a catastrophic event or other threat;

P = the probability that such a threat will occur in any given year; and

C = the cost of the loss if the threat occurs.

This formula measures risk as the probable annual dollar loss associated with a specific vital electronic records series. The total annual expected loss to an organization is the sum of the annualized losses calculated for each vital electronic records series.

Quantitative risk assessment begins with the determination of probabilities associated with specific events and the calculation of annualized loss multipliers based on those probabilities. Quantitative risk assessment has a subjective component: The qualitative risk assessment approach is typically used to determine the probabilities. Information systems specialists, program unit personnel, or others familiar with a given electronic records series are asked to estimate the likelihood of occurrence for specific threats. Whenever possible, their estimates should be based on the historical incidence of adverse events. Reliable probability estimates are easiest and most conveniently obtained for events such as power outages, equipment malfunctions, software failures, network security breaches, and virus attacks for which maintenance statistics or other documentation exists. The frequency of potentially destructive geophysical or political events, such as hurricanes or terrorist attacks, may likewise be documented in books, newspapers, or other published sources.

In the absence of written evidence or experience, probability estimates must be based on informed speculation by persons familiar with the broad information management environment within which a given vital records series is maintained and used. Often, the records manager must ask a series of probing questions, followed by lengthy discussion, to obtain usable probability estimates. As an example, the records manager may ask a data processing manager or user whether file damage resulting from hardware malfunctions is likely to occur once per year. If the answer is yes, the records manger should ask whether such an event is likely to occur once every half year, once per quarter, once per month, and so on. This procedure can be repeated until a satisfactorily specific response is obtained.

Once probabilities are estimated, annual loss multipliers can be calculated in any of several ways. Using one method, a calamitous threat to vital electronic records with a given probability of occurrence is assigned a probability value of 1. Other threats are assigned higher or lower values, based on their relative probability of occurrence. As an example, a threat estimated to occur once per year is assigned a probability value of 1, which serves as a base line for other probability estimates. An event estimated to occur once every three months (four times per year) is assigned a probability value of 4, while an event with an estimated frequency of once every four years is assigned the probability value of 0.25.

Applying the quantitative assessment formula, the probability value is multiplied by the estimated cost of the loss if the event occurs. Factors that might be considered when determining costs associated with the loss of vital electronic records include, but are by no means limited to, the following:

- The cost of file reconstruction, assuming that source documents or other input materials remain available;
- The value of canceled customer orders, unbillable accounts, or other business losses resulting from the inability to perform specific business operations because needed electronic records are unavailable;
- Labor costs associated with reversion to manual operations, assuming that such reversion is possible;
- The cost of defending against or otherwise settling legal actions associated with the loss of vital electronic records.

Quantitative risk assessment is an aid to judgment not a substitute for it. The risk assessment formula is an analytical tool that can help records managers clarify their thinking and define protection priorities for vital electronic records. Assume, for example, that a hospital executive estimates that one chance exists per year that a database of patient records essential to mission-critical medical care will be corrupted, though not extensively damaged, by unauthorized modification, defective software, minor hardware malfunction, or infiltration by computer viruses. A probability (P) of 1 is assigned to that risk. The adverse event will affect a subset of patient records. The cost (C) to reconstruct the corrupted records by rekeying information from paper documents is estimated at $2,000 when the adverse event occurs. Applying the formula, the risk (annualized loss expectancy) is 1 times $2,000, or $2,000.

Assume further that one chance exists in ten years that the same database of patient records will be extensively damaged by a catastrophic hardware or software failure. A probability (P) of 0.1 is assigned to that risk; it is one-tenth as likely to occur as the base case cited previously. If the cost (C) to reconstruct the database following hardware failure is estimated at $40,000, the risk is 0.1 times $40,000, or $4,000. These calculations indicate that catastrophic hardware failure, while having a much lower probability of occurrence, poses a more significant risk than unauthorized modification or computer viruses. Consequently, it should be made a higher priority for vital records protection.

RISK CONTROL

Risk control is an important component of any vital records program. The purpose of risk control is to safeguard vital electronic records. Where vital records protection is part of a broader computer security, business continuity, and disaster recovery plan, risk control measures may also safeguard equipment, software, and networking components necessary to retrieve or process vital electronic records. Regardless of scope, risk control encompasses preventive and protective measures.

Although some recorded information may be reconstructable in the event of a disaster, the high cost of such reconstruction makes it a last-resort component of risk control. Prevention is the first line of defense against risk. Preventive measures are designed to minimize the likelihood of damage to vital electronic records from one or more threats. Preventive measures apply to both working copies and security copies of vital electronic records. For purposes of this discussion, protective measures are designed to facilitate the reconstruction of files and the restoration of business operations if one or more vital records series is damaged. Protective measures typically apply to security copies, sometimes described as *back-up copies*, of vital electronic records.

Whether prevention or protection is involved, risk control begins with heightened security awareness formalized in organizational policy and procedures, which must be communicated to every employee who works with vital electronic records. Security of automated systems and the information they store is the responsibility of every employee. A directive from senior management, in the form of a memorandum sent to managers of program units, should acknowledge the critical nature of vital electronic records and emphasize the need to safeguard them. Risk control guidelines should be conspicuously posted in areas where vital electronic records are stored or used. One person in each program unit should be assigned specific responsibility for the implementation of risk control guidelines; ideally, that person will also serve as the program unit's records management liaison. Program unit managers should review risk control policies and procedures at staff meetings. The records manager should be available as a resource person to address such meetings and clarify risk control policies and procedures. To publicize the vital records initiative, the records manager can prepare articles on vital electronic records and the importance of risk control for employee newsletters, intranet Web pages, or other in-house publications.

Preventive Measures

Preventive risk control measures address the physical environment where electronic records are stored and used. To the greatest extent possible, storage facilities for vital electronic records should be located in areas where floods and destructive weather are unlikely. Locations near chemical manufacturing facilities, airport landing patterns, and other potential hazards should also be avoided. Often, records managers have little control over the geographic locations where working copies of vital records are maintained, but they can specify the locations of storage copies. Because electrical system failures can lead to equipment failures that may damage vital electronic records, electrical outlets should be protected by circuit breakers and surge suppressers. Although such controls are routinely encountered in mainframe and minicomputer installations, they may not be implemented at all personal computer sites. Storage areas for vital electronic records should contain zone-controlled smoke detection and fire-extinguishing equipment that conforms to requirements outlined in local fire codes. Environmental controls and media handling precautions also apply to vital electronic records.

Elements of an Effective Risk Control Program for Vital Electronic Records

- Heightened awareness of risks formalized in policy and procedures
- Risk Control guidelines widely promulgated
- Secure storage environment for vital records copies
  - Physical and climatological hazards avoided
  - Unauthorized entry prevented
  - Storage area locked when unattended
  - Safeguards implemented against electrical failures
- Supervision of working copies
- Protection against electronic intrusion
  - Access to computer equipment restricted
  - Equipment turned off and locked when not in use
  - Access controlled by passwords and personal identifiers
  - Virus protection implemented

Certain preventive risk control measures promote the physical security of vital records against malicious destruction, corruption, theft, or access by unauthorized persons. One storage location is easier to secure than many. Whenever possible, centralized filing repositories should be designated for off-line storage of working copies of vital electronic records contained on removable magnetic or optical media. Commonly encountered examples of such filing repositories include the magnetic tape libraries associated with mainframe and minicomputer installations and the video tape libraries associated with corporate or institutional television studio facilities. Media filing repositories should be situated away from high traffic locations, preferably in areas without windows. Access to media filing repositories should be restricted to authorized individuals who have a specific business reason for entering such areas. Badges should identify authorized individuals. Employees in the vicinity of a media filing area should be instructed to challenge and report suspect persons who enter the area. Media filing areas should not be included in building tours designed to impress visitors.

Access to media filing repositories should be limited to a single supervised entrance. Other doors should be configured as emergency exits with strike bars and audible alarms. All media containing vital records should be stored in the designated filing repository when not in use. Media should not be removed from the filing repository until they are ready for processing, and they should be returned to the repository immediately following processing. All media and containers should be examined on entry into or removal from the filing repository. Circulation control records should be kept of every medium removed from the repository. For each transaction, such circulation control records should contain a medium identifier, a borrower identifier, the time and date the medium was removed, the purpose for which the medium was removed, the location to which the medium was taken, and the time and date when the medium is to be returned. Several vendors offer media tracking software that employs bar codes to facilitate entry of media and borrower identifiers. Such products resemble library circulation control systems that have been computerized for several decades. They will track the locations of specific media, block unauthorized removals, and generate lists of media scheduled to be returned or are past due. Media filing repositories should never be accessible when unsupervised. They should be locked when unattended.

The foregoing security procedures are most easily implemented in centralized information systems installations where media filing repositories are located within a secure computer room. Similar conditions may apply to centralized storage facilities for video or audio recordings. Where vital electronic records are maintained in user areas, security is difficult to enforce and easily compromised. Desktop computers and local area network servers may be unavoidably located in high-traffic office areas, and their media may be stored at individual workstations rather than in supervised, centralized repositories where access can be controlled. Mobile computing devices and associated media that contain vital electronic records are obviously vulnerable to theft, misplacement, or other loss when used out of the office.

Despite these complications, certain security precautions can effectively reduce the vulnerability of vital electronic records created and maintained by desktop computers and LAN servers. Desktop computers should be installed in supervised work areas. They should be locked, if possible, when not in use and the keys stored in a secure location. To avoid loss of information stored on internal hard drives, desktop computers should be attached to work surfaces. Where physical attachment of computers is impractical, the computer's system unit should be secured against the removal of hard drives. If possible, vital electronic records should be stored on network drives rather than desktop computers. Thin clients, which lack local storage capabilities, force such procedures. All computer equipment should bear ownership tags or similar identification. Program unit personnel should be instructed to challenge and report persons who attempt to remove computer equipment from work areas.

Diskettes, magnetic tapes, optical disks, and other removable media should be filed in locked drawers or cabinets until ready for processing and returned to their filing locations immediately after use. Such media should never be left unattended on work surfaces. Confidential personal data, trade secrets, or other sensitive information should not be stored in mobile computing devices. If this type of storage is unavoidable, the devices should never be left unattended.

Electronic records stored by networked computers can be accessed, and possibly damaged, by remote users. Physical security measures must consequently be supplemented by safeguards against electronic intrusion. Various software- and hardware-based access control methods are widely described in computer security publications. The following discussion delineates selected security precautions pertinent to vital records protection.

Access to computer workstations must be restricted to authorized employees. To the greatest extent practical, the installation of computer workstations should be limited to supervised areas. Employees should be instructed to challenge and report unauthorized persons who attempt to use them. Computer workstations should be turned off—and locked, if possible—when not in use. They should never be left unattended while operational. System software should automatically terminate a computer session after a predetermined period of inactivity. For organizations connected to the Internet, mission-critical applications and vital electronic records should be isolated from publicly accessible computer resources.

Access procedures for remote computers or network file servers should not be posted near computer workstations or discussed with unauthorized persons. An effective method of user authentication is critical to prevent electronic intrusion. Access to vital electronic records and their associated software should be controlled by passwords or personal identification numbers. Such identifiers typically consist of strings of alphanumeric characters that may be system-assigned or specified by individual users. Where users are allowed to construct their own passwords, they should be instructed to avoid personal names or other easily guessed character strings. Group passwords should be avoided.

Access software should blot out or otherwise suppress the display of passwords when they are entered. Passwords should not be posted near terminals or LAN workstations. They should not be printed on reports, listings, word processing documents, or other computer-generated output. If a master list of passwords is maintained in a computer file, it should be encrypted. Passwords should be changed at regular intervals and immediately invalidated on transfer, retirement, resignation, or termination of the employees to whom they were assigned. Passwords should automatically expire if not used for a specified period of time.

Passwords should be associated with specific privileges such as the ability to retrieve records (read privileges) or to add records to a file (write privileges). The ability to edit or delete vital records should be limited to those employees with a demonstrable need to perform such operations in the execution of assigned work responsibilities. Continuing need for specific access privileges should be verified at regular intervals. In applications requiring high security, two or more levels of password protection can be utilized. Alternatively, password protection may be supplemented or replaced by other user authentication and access control procedures such as hardware-based access methods that require possession of special keys or bionic verification methods. Examples of the latter include systems that recognize signatures, voiceprints, fingerprints, palm geometry, or eye retinal patterns.

Special security procedures and precautions are necessary to prevent contamination of computer programs and vital electronic records by viruses and other malicious software. Because most viruses are believed to enter computer systems through software, a centralized authority should be established to approve software procurement and installations for all computers in the organization. Software should not be purchased or installed on any computer without authorization. Software should be purchased new in sealed packages from known suppliers. Computer programs downloaded from publicly accessible information services or bulletin boards are widely suspected as sources of viral contamination and should be avoided. Newly acquired software should be processed by antiviral programs that can detect and remove viruses. Although such programs can identify and/or disable many viruses, they are not completely effective and must be combined with other preventive and protective measures outlined here.

Clues to the presence of viruses include changes in directory entries, file modification dates, volume labels, and program file sizes. Computer users should be instructed to monitor such indicators and report any suspect conditions immediately. Infected computers and all copies of potentially infected programs should be removed from service. Infected workstations should be disconnected from computer networks.

Protective Measures

Protective measures for vital electronic records are designed to support the restoration of mission-critical operations in the event of a disaster. Whether electronic or nonelectronic vital records are involved, such protective measures have historically relied on specially designed storage enclosures and purposeful duplication of records for off-site storage. These measures are most effective when combined.

Specially designed file cabinets, vaults, and other storage enclosures provide on-site protection of vital electronic records against certain threats. Vital electronic records can be protected against theft, for example, by storing them in locked file cabinets, safes, or vaults. **Underwriters' Laboratories (UL)** rates file cabinets for their resistance to tampering. Insulated storage containers offer some protection against fire by limiting records' exposure to potentially destructive heat. UL rates the fire-resistant properties of insulated storage containers in terms of the hours of protection they provide against specified temperatures and humidity conditions. For effective protection of magnetic and optical media, fire-resistant containers should bear the UL Class 125 designation. During a fire, such containers will maintain an internal temperature below 125 degrees Fahrenheit at an ambient temperature of 1,700 Fahrenheit, which is thought to be a safe level for magnetic and optical media. A cabinet, safe, or vault with a UL Class 125-1 rating will provide effective protection against damaging heat for one hour, but a UL Class 125-2 rating, which provides two hours of protection, is preferable. Insulated enclosures should also protect vital electronic records against vapor penetration and fire hose streams for the indicated periods. Because insulated file cabinets, safes, vaults, and other fire-resistant enclosures can be damaged by severe impact, the buildings in which they are installed must be able to resist structural collapse for the UL-rated exposure period. To further reduce vulnerability to damage, fire-resistant storage enclosures should be locked in areas where they will not be exposed to heavy falling objects.

Although tamperproof and fire-resistant storage containers can prove useful in certain situations, the most effective approach to vital records protection involves the purposeful preparation of back-up copies for storage at secure off-site locations. The production of back-up copies of essential files at predetermined intervals is routine operating procedures in most mainframe and minicomputer installations centers and for network servers. In desktop computer installations, where procedures are less routinized, back-up operations may be performed sporadically, if at all. For effective vital records protection, back-up responsibilities must be clearly delineated. Back-up schedules must be established and rigidly enforced.

Back-up procedures have historically been considered essential for information stored on hard drives because such devices are vulnerable to head crashes and other hardware malfunctions that imperil recorded information. Backup is also important for magnetic tapes, optical disks, and other removable media which, although not subject to head crashes, can be damaged in various ways. Back-up media selected for vital electronic records must satisfy the security and recoverability requirements of applications with which they are associated. In some computer installations, files stored on one hard drive are copied onto another. RAID arrays, as described in Chapter Two, provide redundant recording for fault-tolerant operation. For reliable vital records protection, however, back-up copies are typically made on removable media, which can be stored off-site. Historically, magnetic tapes have been the dominant media for hard drive backup in mainframe, minicomputer, and network server installations. Alternatively, optical disks can be used for that purpose. Magnetic tapes and optical disks can also be used to create back-up copies of other magnetic tapes and optical disks in computer, video, and audio applications.

A 12-media cycle method is the recommended approach for preparation and off-site storage of back-up copies. It is based on the following procedure:

- For each mainframe, minicomputer, or network server, 12 magnetic tapes or other media are labeled with the following designations:
  - Monday
  - Tuesday
  - Wednesday
  - Thursday
  - Friday 1
  - Friday 2
  - Friday 3
  - Friday 4
  - Month 1
  - Month 2
  - Month 3
  - Month 4
- Each label should also indicate the date the medium was first used, the computer installation being backed up, and the back-up software employed.
- A full backup is performed Monday through Thursday, using the media labeled for those days. The resulting back-up media are sent to or deposited in the off-site storage location at the close of each business day.
- A full backup is performed on the first, second, and third Friday of each month, using the appropriate labeled media. For months that have five Fridays, a back-up medium is prepared on the fourth Friday of the month. The back-up media are sent to or deposited in the off-site storage location.
- On the last Friday of each month, a full backup is performed on one of the monthly media, beginning with the medium labeled "Month 1."
- Back-up media for Monday through Thursday are removed from off-site storage and recycled throughout the week. The Friday media are recycled at the end of each month. The monthly media are recycled at the end of four months.

Using this method, the following back-up media will be in off-site storage on any given day:

- Media produced on the three previous business days;
- Media produced at the end of the three (or, occasionally, four) previous weeks;
- Media produced on the last Friday of the three previous months.

Off-site storage repositories for vital electronic records may be established and operated by a corporation, government agency, or other organization on its own behalf. Alternatively, a commercial storage facility designed specifically for vital electronic records may be utilized. In either case, the off-site storage facility should be located in a secure site. Some vital records repositories are located underground. They feature stringent perimeter security with bonded guards and electronic surveillance apparatus.

Back-up copies of vital electronic records should be stored at a sufficient distance from the working copies to be unaffected by the same natural disasters or destructive events. The storage facility must be close enough, however, for convenient delivery of vital electronic records as well as timely retrieval of back-up copies to support disaster recovery. For pickup and delivery of records, some in-house and commercial storage facilities offer courier services equipped with environmentally controlled trucks or vans. Some facilities also support electronic vaulting in which back-up copies of vital records are transmitted to off-site storage over high-speed telecommunications facilities.

The typical vital records repository has suitable storage facilities for magnetic and optical media. Some will also accept paper documents or microfilm, although the former—being combustible—may be excluded to minimize the danger of fire. Most storage facilities for vital electronic records are designed for computer-generated media, but they are suitable for video and audio recordings as well. Environmental specifications must be observed. Back-up electrical generators should be available to maintain environmental controls in the event of power outages.

Most storage facilities provide one or more large vaults in which the vital electronic records of different program units or, in the case of commercial repositories, different customers are stored. In some cases, safe-deposit containers or separate rooms may be provided for records requiring special security precautions. To make the best use of available storage space, back-up copies of vital electronic records should be made on the densest, most compact media compatible with application requirements. Half-inch data cartridges are preferable to nine-track magnetic tape reels, for example. Digital linear tape, eight-millimeter data cartridges, digital audio tape, and high-capacity optical disks make very effective use of available shelf space. Media compactness is particularly important for customers of commercial vital records storage facilities that base their charges on the type and amount of space consumed.

Off-site storage of vital computer records is one component in a risk control plan that includes disaster recovery provisions for computer hardware and software. Although those aspects of risk control are typically the responsibility of computer specialists, records managers should be aware of available protection options. Hardware recovery provisions are based on the availability of a back-up computer site that can be utilized to maintain computing operations if an organization's primary site is destroyed. The back-up site must provide hardware identical to or compatible with the organization's own equipment. In corporations, government agencies, or other organizations with distributed data processing operations, compatible back-up computing capabilities may exist in branch locations or field offices. In the event of a disaster, processing can be shifted to such alternate sites. Although this approach may apply to minicomputer and personal computer systems, it is rare that a large, costly mainframe computer facility will be replicated at two or more locations within the same organization.

Some organizations have established reciprocal back-up arrangements with a subsidiary, an affiliated company, or an independent organization that employs compatible computer hardware. The reciprocating parties agree to make their computing facilities available to one another in the event of an emergency. Such mutual aid agreements provide a relatively inexpensive means of obtaining back-up computing capabilities, but they are often criticized as ineffective. Reciprocal obligations must be clearly established in contracts or other formal agreements signed by responsible officials of both organizations. Terms of the agreement should be reviewed periodically and an implementation plan developed jointly by both parties. Each organization's exposure to risk is, in effect, increased because both organizations must operate with diminished computing capacity if a disaster strikes either of them. Critical processing operations must consequently be identified and prioritized in advance of an emergency. Despite the best intentions, heavy workloads at the reciprocating site may impede effective implementation. Even where reciprocal obligations are specified in writing, they may be difficult to enforce. Legal remedies are possible, but they are unlikely to provide relief in the short time frame essential to restore an organization's computing capabilities.

In most emergency scenarios, disaster recovery plans based on hot sites or cold sites will typically prove more effective than reciprocal back-up agreements. A **hot site** is a fully equipped standby computing facility designed for emergency use on short notice, typically within 24 hours of a disaster. It is an alternate facility that has the equipment and resources to recover the business functions affected by the occurrence of a disaster. Hot sites may be operated by computer manufacturers, commercial service bureaus, or other vendors who specialize in disaster recovery capabilities. They are intended for organizations that cannot tolerate an interruption of computing services. Access to hot sites is typically sold by annual membership fees or subscriptions that allow an organization to use the facility for a specified period of time following notification of an emergency. In addition to subscription fees, daily occupancy and resource usage charges may be imposed during the period of utilization. To minimize the potential for conflicts associated with simultaneous need, the number of subscriptions to a given site is limited. In most cases, use of the hot site is contractually restricted to several weeks or months. Computing equipment at the hot site must be compatible with the customer's own hardware. In some cases, the hot site also provides off-site storage facilities to which back-up copies of vital electronic records can be sent in anticipation of an emergency.

A **cold site**, sometimes described as an *empty shell*, is an unfurnished space suitable for the installation of computing and telecommunications equipment in the event of an emergency. A cold site is a computer-ready alternative facility that is void of any resources or equipment, except air-conditioning, raised flooring, utilities, and telecommunication lines. It can be used as a back-up site for disaster recovery. The occupying organization must provide the required hardware, perform installation, and make the facility operational. In an emergency, these requirements may be accomplished by purchasing new computing and telecommunications equipment for delivery to the cold site or by salvaging hardware from a damaged data processing facility. A cold site may be owned by a single organization and reserved for its own use or shared by several organizations for occupation upon notification of an emergency. In the latter case, access is sold by subscription with daily occupancy charges also imposed. Regardless of the occupancy arrangement, the implementation and activation of a cold site can require considerable advance planning to ensure timely delivery, installation, and testing following an emergency. As an interesting variant of the cold site, some vendors offer computer-ready mobile facilities and modular buildings that can be installed at a customer's own location, usually within several days.

Disaster Recovery Alternatives for Computer Installations

- Back-up arrangements with field offices, branch locations, or subsidiaries
- Mutual aid agreements with other organizations
- Hot sites
- Cold sites
- Temporary reversion to manual operations
- Temporary discontinuation of specified activities

These disaster recovery approaches were developed principally for centralized mainframe, minicomputer, and server installations. Damaged desktop computers, in standalone or networked implementations, are typically replaced by new ones. Although replacement can often be accomplished quickly, it is rarely immediate. An organization may have spare desktop computers, but installing and activating network connections and servers takes time. A period of computer downtime, however brief, is consequently inevitable. During that time, reversion to manual operations based on nonelectronic paper or microfilm records may be necessary. Temporary reversion to manual operations may also be part of a disaster recovery plan for larger computers. In such situations, records managers can make a significant contribution to disaster preparedness by determining the types and locations of paper records likely to be needed in specific applications and developing plans to make them quickly available in an emergency.

The discussion to this point has emphasized protection of vital electronic records and restoration of computer processing capabilities in the event of a disaster. To be effective, however, a disaster recovery plan for computer-processible records must also include provisions for protection of custom-developed software and documentation. As with vital records, software is typically protected through a combination of back-up and off-site storage. Magnetic tapes, diskettes, and optical disks are commonly utilized as back-up media.

Documentation can be broadly defined as the written information recorded during the development of a computer system. It is an organized set of documents explaining a system, project, etc., and the requirements needed to use and maintain the system. Its purpose is to ensure that details of a system are understood by those persons who have a need to know those details. Documentation may address both hardware and software characteristics of a given system. Vital records protection and disaster recovery plans are most concerned with software documentation, including both developmental and occupational documentation.

Developmental documentation provides narrative and graphic descriptions of computer programs. It includes, but is not necessarily limited to, a statement of purpose for a given program; a description of the hardware configuration for which the program is intended, including memory and peripheral equipment requirements; a list of required system software and support programs, including operating systems, assemblers, compilers, interpreters, and utility programs; a discussion of the algorithms employed, including flowcharts or other graphic representations of programming logic; and the program source code as written in assembler or higher-level languages. *Operational documentation* includes installation and operating instructions for a given program. User training and reference manuals are examples of operational documentation. Regardless of content, documentation may be recorded on paper, on microfilm, or in machine-readable, computer-processible form on magnetic or optical media.

Auditing for Compliance

Once vital electronic records have been identified and appropriate loss-control methods specified, the implementation of preventive and protective measures for designated records series will usually be the responsibility of personnel in the program unit that maintains the records. Periodic audits should be performed to confirm compliance. Such audits may be conducted by records management staff or delegated to another organizational unit, such as an internal audit department, that has other compliance-oriented responsibilities. In such cases, auditing for vital records compliance can be coordinated with financial or other auditing activities, thereby simplifying the scheduling of audits as well as saving both time and labor. Internal auditors can report the results of vital records compliance audits to the records manager for follow-up and corrective action where indicated. To gain the attention of top management, the internal audit reports should also be distributed to those persons who receive reports of important financial audits.

SUMMARY

A vital records program is a set of policies and procedures for the systematic, comprehensive, and economical control of losses associated with vital records. Vital records contain information essential to an organization's mission. If such records are damaged, lost, or otherwise rendered unavailable, critical business operations will be curtailed or discontinued, with a resulting adverse impact on the organization. A vital records program involves the identification of vital records, the assessment of risks to which such records are subject, and the implementation of appropriate protection methods. Although it is traditionally considered a records management responsibility, vital records protection is closely related to other loss-control and contingency-planning activities. The protection of computer-generated records, in particular, is often viewed as a facet of the broader field of computer security and disaster recovery.

In any organization, senior management has ultimate responsibility for the protection of assets, including the protection of vital records. Such responsibility is implied or explicitly stated in several laws and government regulations. In the United States, examples include the Foreign Corrupt Practices Act of 1977, the Computer Security Act of 1987, and OMB Circular A-130. Provisions against unauthorized disclosure as a facet of records security are contained in various privacy statutes.

Vital electronic records are typically identified by surveying individual program units. The end product of such a survey is a descriptive list of vital electronic records series. The list should indicate the reason each series is considered vital, the name of the program unit responsible for protecting the series, and the method of protection to be implemented. Because substantial costs are often involved, vital records protection must be limited to those records that are truly essential to mission-critical operations. Vital records must consequently be distinguished from important records. Although the latter may be very useful to a given program unit, their loss will not render the unit inoperative. For convenience, a vital records survey can be combined with an inventory of electronic records performed for purposes of preparing retention schedules.

Risk analysis begins with the identification of threats and vulnerabilities to which vital electronic records are subject. Typical risks include malicious or accidental destruction, loss of electronic storage media through theft or misplacement, corruption of electronic records through unauthorized tampering or contamination by computer viruses, and improper disclosure of electronic records through unauthorized access. Risk assessments may be based on qualitative or quantitative methodologies. In either case, assessment is based on the probability of loss for specific vital records series and the estimated damage if a given loss occurs.

A risk control program for vital electronic records includes preventive and protective measures. Preventive measures are the first line of defense against risk. Properly implemented, they minimize the probability of loss. Addressing the physical environment where vital electronic records are stored, preventive measures involve safeguards against malicious destruction, theft, corruption, or unauthorized access. Such safeguards apply to both security and working copies of vital electronic records. Protective measures, in contrast, facilitate the reconstruction of vital electronic records in the event of loss. Applying principally to security copies, they rely on specially designed media enclosures and purposeful duplication of electronic media for off-site storage. Whether prevention or protection is involved, effective risk control depends on heightened awareness of security concerns, as formalized in organizational policies and procedures communicated to all employees who work with vital electronic records.

For computer-processible information, vital records protection is one component in a risk-control plan that also includes disaster recovery provisions for computer hardware and software. Hardware recovery procedures are usually based on the availability of a back-up computer site that can be utilized in the event that an organization's primary site is damaged. Software recovery plans rely on off-site storage of back-up copies of programs and documentation.

To be effective, a vital records protection program must include compliance auditing. Rather than being performed by records management staff, audit responsibilities can be delegated to another organizational unit such as an internal audit department. In such cases, vital records compliance can be coordinated with financial or other auditing activities.

CHAPTER SEVEN

MANAGING FILES
AND MEDIA

The task of organizing information recorded on electronic media resembles its paper counterpart in certain respects. As described in Chapter Three, computer-processible electronic records pertaining to a particular business operation or activity are grouped in files created by a computer's operating system and application programs at the time the records are entered and saved. Depending on the application and the type of information being stored, a computer file may contain one or more records. A data file, for example, typically consists of multiple records, while a word processing file often contains the equivalent of a single document. An image file may similarly contain one or more graphic images. Depending on the application, files may be recorded on magnetic disks, magnetic tapes, optical disks, or other media. Although the term *file* is seldom applied to audio and video recordings, parallels can be drawn with individual audio selections or video programs recorded on magnetic tapes, optical disks, or other media. As computer-stored audio and video information becomes more commonplace, *audio file* and *video file* are likely to be more widely utilized as descriptive terms. Although the following discussion emphasizes computer files, some points are also applicable to audio and video records.

Within a given computer storage medium, files are organized into directories that are created and managed by the computer's operating system under which the files were created. A **directory** is a table of contents for a specific medium. Directory information varies with the operating system employed in a given computer configuration. File name, file size, and the date the file was last modified are typical directory data elements. Certain media, such as magnetic tapes and diskettes, usually have a single directory. The higher the storage capacity of a given medium, however, the more likely it is to contain multiple directories, each storing files of a particular type. Such multiple directories are commonly called *subdirectories*. They can be effectively utilized to group logically related files recorded on hard drives, hard disk cartridges, high-capacity floppy disks, and optical disks. Often, subdirectories are themselves subdivided, thereby creating a hierarchy of logically subordinate and superordinate directories. The permissible number and structure of such hierarchical subdivisions is determined by the operating system in use in a particular installation.

In some cases, a given magnetic or optical disk is partitioned into segments called *volumes*. Each **volume** is treated as the logical equivalent of a disk drive, even though it shares a physical drive with other volumes. Volumes are sometimes created to divide high-capacity storage devices into smaller, more manageable units. A multigigabyte hard disk drive or optical disk cartridge, for example, may be partitioned into two or more volumes, each of which will be used for a specific application. In some cases, a computer's operating system imposes limits on volume size. Where the capacity of a given storage device exceeds the permissible volume size, the device must be partitioned into multiple volumes. For example, early versions of the MS-DOS operating system required multiple partitions. Newer operating systems are designed to accommodate very high-capacity storage peripherals, and multiple partitions are unnecessary. As discussed in Chapter Two, the capacities of storage devices and media are increasing rapidly, and new computers must support the latest models.

In computer configurations, files, directories, volumes, and physical storage media are sometimes equated with cabinets, drawers, folders, and other familiar components of paper-based filing systems. The comparison, though useful, is necessarily forced. In graphical computing environments, such as Microsoft Windows or the Macintosh operating system, the information displayed when a computer is first turned on is described as a *desktop*. Storage peripherals, such as hard drives, floppy disk drives, and optical disk drives—or predefined logical volumes within those devices—are represented by labeled icons in the desktop display. If the computer's desktop is analogous to a file room, the storage peripherals and their fixed or removable recording media are the computer-based counterparts of file cabinets. Depending on the computer configuration, they may be locally installed or network resources.

When a given storage device is selected, usually through mouse operations, the computer's operating system displays a directory for the device's recording medium. A *root directory*, which is displayed first, provides an overview of the medium's contents. Although the root directory may contain files, it is typically divided into subdirectories, based on specific computing tasks or business operations. With most graphical operating systems, subdirectories are depicted as folders, but they are more properly compared to file drawers or portions of drawers. Subdirectories may contain application programs or files. The latter are represented by icons that depict their formats or associated application programs. Alternatively, subdirectories may contain folders, which represent hierarchically subordinate directories. Those folders may contain files or additional folders. With some computer operating systems, directories and subdirectories can be displayed in a tree-like structure that reflects their hierarchical relationships. Subdirectories can be nested to many levels, but complex hierarchical structures can prove difficult to understand and navigate.

LABELS AND NAMES

Effective electronic records management requires careful attention to directory organization, file grouping and naming practices, and media labeling. In centralized computing facilities, such tasks may be highly formalized. Directory structures and file names are determined by programmers, while media labels are prepared by tape librarians and others responsible for off-line storage of removable media. File names may be terse, but they usually reflect the purpose or content of the file. Many personal computer users, however, have developed their own, often idiosyncratic approaches to file and media management. Directory and file names may be cryptic, giving little indication of either purpose or content. Subdirectories may be created haphazardly, with little regard for hierarchical relationships. Unrelated files may be stored in the same subdirectory, while related information is scattered among multiple subdirectories at several hierarchical levels. Problems associated with these practices are similar to those encountered with poorly managed paper files. Information needed for a given purpose cannot be located, necessitating time-wasting searches through directories and tedious examination of individual files.

> ## Identifying Information for Removable Media
>
> - Program unit that created the medium
> - Name or type of system on which medium is to be used
> - Application software name and version number
> - File listing
> - Media capacity and recording density
> - Serial number or other unique identifier
> - Recording date(s)
> - Manufacturing date
> - Security precautions and access restrictions
> - Type of copy
> - Special attributes

To minimize or eliminate such problems, a systematic program for the management of electronic records must provide guidelines for labeling media, organizing directories, and naming files. Clear, complete labeling is essential to the identification of removable storage media such as magnetic tapes, hard disk cartridges, floppy disks, and optical disks. Descriptive information about computer, video, and audio media should include, but will not necessarily be limited to, the following:

- The name of the program unit that created the removable storage medium or on whose behalf it was created.

- The name or type of computer, video, or audio system on which the medium is to be used, unless it can easily be determined by physical examination of the medium itself (as is the case, for example, with certain video and audio tapes).

- For computer media, the name and version number of the application software with which the recorded information is to be used.

- A list of files, applications, video programs, audio recordings, or other information the medium contains. For computer media, file locations are automatically recorded in directory listings generated by the computer's operating system. The directory is recorded on the medium itself. In graphical operating environments, distinctive icons typically identify the computer programs used to create specific files. For video and audio tapes containing more than one program, media labels should indicate the physical locations where particular programs begin. The location may be expressed as an odometer reading that represents the distance from the beginning of a tape. Alternatively, some video and audio tape recorders generate electronic codes that mark the starting locations of individual programs. In either case, a list of odometer settings or program numbers must be manually prepared.

- Media capacity and/or recording density, if not indicated on the medium itself.

- A serial number or other unique identifier.

- The date or span of dates during which information was recorded onto the medium.

- The date the medium was manufactured. The life spans of magnetic and optical media begin with their manufacturing dates rather than the date that information was recorded. To estimate the remaining life span of a given medium, its manufacturing date must be known. Unfortunately, manufacturing dates of magnetic tapes, floppy disks, and optical disks are rarely printed on the media themselves or in accompanying product documentation. When the manufacturing date cannot be determined, the purchase date may be an acceptable substitute. Users assume that media were recently manufactured when purchased.

- Special storage and handling instructions, security requirements, or access restrictions, if any.

- The medium's status as a working copy, back-up copy, storage copy, etc.

- Special recording procedures that can affect the way in which a given medium will be played back or otherwise utilized. Examples include the use of Dolby noise reduction with audio tapes, stereo mode recording of VHS video tapes, or compressed recording of files on computer media.

As a practical consideration, these data elements will not fit onto the relatively small labels provided with most computer, video, and audio media. In such cases, label contents can be limited to a serial number or other brief identifiers, with more complete information recorded in a separate logbook or other human-readable documentation. Various vendors offer color-coded adhesive labels to identify magnetic tapes, optical disk cartridges, and other media by serial number. Where the shelf-type filing cabinets described later in this chapter are utilized, such color-coded labels can facilitate detection of misfiled media in large collections. Internal volume labels should be assigned to removable computer media to permit identification if their physical labels become detached or defaced. Volume labels can consist of serial numbers or other unique identifiers. In addition to maintaining descriptive information about an electronic medium in human-readable form, it can be stored as a word processing document or other text file on the medium itself.

Low-capacity computer media, such as conventional diskettes, usually contain a single directory. Unrelated files should not be intermixed within such media. Low-capacity diskettes should be dedicated to specific applications or business operations. A given diskette might be reserved for files created by a specific word processing program, for example. More restrictively, a diskette might be limited to files created with a specific word processing program and pertaining to a particular business activity such as a specific project. If voluminous information is involved, additional restrictions may be appropriate. Separate diskettes may be maintained for specific types of word processing documents such as project correspondence or project reports. Alternatively, files produced by different computer programs may be combined on a single medium, provided they are logically related. A diskette may contain word processing files and spreadsheet files pertaining to a specific business activity, such as budget preparation, or a specific project. Storage of interrelated files on a given medium is made practical by the availability of office suites and other integrated software packages that can exchange files created by different application programs.

With higher-capacity media, such as hard drives and optical disks, similar restrictions should be applied to directories and subdirectories. Computer users should not mix unrelated files within directories. Separate directories should be created for specific programs or business operations. Such directories can be divided into subdirectories that reflect the logical interrelationships of file types associated with specific computer applications or business activities. As an example, a separate directory might be established for each computer program installed on a personal computer. In a graphical operating environment, each directory would be pictorially represented as a folder labeled with the name of the computer application, such as Word, WordPerfect, or Excel. Each directory might be organized into subdirectories, which are pictorially represented as labeled folders within directory folders. One subdirectory might contain the application program, such as Microsoft Word for Windows and its related files (help files, spelling dictionaries, thesauri, grammar checkers, and so on). Additional subdirectories might be established for specific types of word processing documents such as correspondence, memoranda, and reports, created and processed by the program. These subdirectories might be further divided topically, chronologically, or in some other way.

Some personal computer users prefer to group application programs in a single directory, with separate subdirectories for each program and its supporting files. Data, text, or other files created and processed by those application programs can be logically organized in other directories by business activity. As another example, an engineer who works on four projects simultaneously might create a single directory for application programs and separate directories for each project. The application directory might be divided into subdirectories for individual programs, such as Microsoft Word for Windows, Excel, and AutoCAD, that support project-related tasks. In a graphical operating environment, the four project directories would be represented by folders labeled with the project name or other identifier. Subdirectories might be created for specific project-related information such as word processing files, spreadsheet files, and CAD files.

Regardless of organization, meaningful, informative directory and file names are critical for convenient, accurate identification of desired electronic records stored on a given medium. Some operating systems display the contents of directories and subdirectories in a tree-like structure that reflects their hierarchical interrelationships. Alternatively, directories, subdirectories, and files may be listed alphabetically, by name, or chronologically, by the date they were created or last modified. In any case, the folder labels or other names assigned to media directories and subdirectories should clearly indicate their scope, enabling users to determine the likely directory and subdirectory locations of desired files. File names should likewise indicate the contents and/or purpose of programs, documents, databases, images, or other information the files contain.

With commercially available software packages, directory and file names are assigned automatically when a given package is installed onto a hard drive or other storage medium. Default names, determined by the software's developer, can be modified by computer users, but it is seldom done. Other directories and subdirectories must be named by computer users when they are created. Files created by specific programs are similarly named when they are initially saved. Rules for naming directories and files are defined by computer operating systems. Older operating systems, some of which remain in use, impose significant restrictions on file names. With MS-DOS, for example, file names are divided into two parts: the file name proper and an optional **extension**. File names can be one to eight characters in length. They may contain alphabetic characters, numeric digits, selected punctuation marks, and certain other symbols. The optional extension usually describes the type of information an MS-DOS file contains. It consists of one to three characters and is separated from the file name by a period (or dot). Widely encountered MS-DOS extensions include "exe," "com," and "bat" for program files; "doc" for word processing files; "txt" for ASCII text files; "wks" for spreadsheet files; "dat" and "dbf" for databases; and "bak" for backup files. Image files are often identified by extensions, such as "tif" or "pcx," that indicate the graphic format utilized for image recording. These MS-DOS extensions are so widely recognized that they are sometimes employed for files created by other computer operating systems, including those that do not specify rules for file extensions.

Given the eight-character limit on MS-DOS file names, constructing mnemonic names that adequately reflect file contents and are readily comprehensible can be difficult but not impossible. A name such as Q1PROG01.RPT might be assigned to a word processing file that contains the first quarterly progress report of 2001 for a particular project. Word processing files that contain subsequent quarterly reports for that year could be named Q2PROG01.RPT, Q3PROG01.RPT, and Q4PROG01.RPT. Similarly, spreadsheet files that contain quarterly budget estimates might be named Q1BDGT01.WKS, Q2BDGT01.WKS, and so on.

Other computer operating systems impose fewer restrictions on the length and character content of file names. As their principal advantage, long file names permit the construction of informative labels that meaningfully reflect file contents. With the VMS and OpenVMS operating systems, which are used by Compaq's

Alpha and VAX computers, file names can contain up to 39 characters, but they are limited to letters of the alphabet, numeric digits, and the dollar sign. Case distinctions are ignored. Unix file names can contain up to 256 characters, including letters of the alphabet, numeric digits, and many other symbols. Certain symbols, reserved by the Unix operating system for other purposes, are excluded. Unix file names are case sensitive. With the Macintosh operating system, file names can contain up to 31 characters, including any character except the colon. Macintosh file names are case sensitive. With new versions of Windows, file names can contain up to 255 characters, including letters of the alphabet, numeric digits, spaces, and many other symbols. Windows file names are displayed as typed, but uppercase and lowercase characters are considered identical when selecting file names.

Formalized guidelines for media and volume labeling, directory structures, and file names can simplify and routinize the organization of information recorded onto computer media; often, however, a given file, known to be recorded on a given medium, cannot be found. The file name may have been forgotten or misunderstood, for example, or the file may have been renamed or moved to another subdirectory. Similar problems, typically attributable to misfiling, can arise in well-organized paper filing installations. When they do, users must manually search through all or part of a file drawer or group of drawers to locate a desired document. With computer storage media, such manual searches—which necessitate the sequential inspection of individual files—can prove prohibitively time-consuming and logistically impractical. Although the number of files stored on a given diskette is limited by media capacity, hard drives, hard disk cartridges, and optical disks may contain thousands or tens of thousands of files.

The lost-file problem is addressed by utility programs that can locate specified files recorded on a given magnetic or optical medium. Such utility programs are often bundled with computer operating systems. The user specifies a file name to be matched and the storage medium to be searched. Depending on the program, the user may specify an exact match of the file name or a substring match, the latter including left or right truncation as well as embedded character strings. Some utility programs can also perform or limit searches by file type, date created or last modified, size, or other attributes. Certain utility programs will search the complete contents of files, rather than file labels, for specified words, phrases, or other character strings. Such programs display segments of files that contain the specified character string and its surrounding context for operator examination.

These utility programs typically perform sequential searches of a specified medium. As a result, search time will vary with the capacity of the medium being searched, the speed of the computer, media access times, and other factors. To speed up retrieval operations, searches can be limited to specified subdirectories or to types of files.

RECORDS MANAGEMENT APPLICATION (RMA) SOFTWARE

As an alternative to directory and subdirectory schemes based on computer operating systems' file management capabilities, several software companies offer computer programs to categorize, store, and control electronic records throughout their life cycles. Designed specifically for electronic recordkeeping, such programs are collectively described as *records management application (RMA) software*. Their characteristics are described in the U.S. Department of Defense 5015.2-STD, *Design Criteria Standard for Electronic Records Management Software Applications*, which defines baseline functional requirements for conformity with records management objectives specified in 44 U.S.C. 2902. The functional requirements are used by the Defense Information Systems Agency when evaluating commercial RMA software. Published in 1997, the 5015.2 standard has since been endorsed by the National Archives and Records Administration and adopted as a standard by other U.S. government agencies. Though developed specifically for the U.S. government, the approach and content of the 5015.2 standard are useful for local governments and for nongovernmental organizations.

RMA software is best suited to electronic documents, as opposed to multi-record databases. Although individual RMA products differ in details, they all accommodate electronic records in a variety of formats, including word processing documents, electronic messages (with attachments), spreadsheet files, desktop publishing files, computer-generated reports, document images, photographic images generated by digital cameras, and computer-aided design files. RMA software transfers electronic records from their originating applications into a separate repository for retrieval when needed. Depending on the installation, the transferred records may be stored on hard drives, optical disks, or other media. Records transferred into RMA software from their originating applications are considered the official copies for reference and retention purposes. Once transferred into RMA software, electronic records cannot be modified. They may be supplanted or supplemented by newer versions generated by external applications, but these records are treated as new ones.

RMA software provides a common interface to all electronic records, regardless of their originating applications. Based on privileges defined by the system administrator, authorized persons can retrieve, display, print, or copy records in the RMA repository. The records can be indexed by customer-defined categories. The 5015.2 standard specifies a number of indexing parameters (metadata), including the date created, date filed, author, originating organization, recipients, subjects, and format. RMA software can also employ user-defined file plans and classification schemes for subject categorization, retention designations, vital records identification, and other purposes.

Most RMA products offer extensive retrieval capabilities including exact or partial matches of designated index elements, relational operators, Boolean searches, wild card characters in search strings, proximity commands, full-text searching, and relevance ranking of search results. Some RMA programs include a thesaurus that links synonymous search terms. Electronic records are retrieved in their original formats. Among their most important features, RMA products provide effective version control for electronic records subject to occasional or periodic revisions. All versions of a record are linked to one another. Authorized users can retrieve the latest version of a record or any earlier version. If desired, retrieved records can be exported to their originating applications or to compatible programs. RMA software maintains audit trails indicating the user, date, time, record identifiers, type of transaction, and other information for all retrieval operations, including failed attempts by unauthorized users.

Among their most important features, RMA products will automatically delete electronic records when their designated retention periods have elapsed. Disposition instruction codes can be assigned to electronic records when they are transferred to RMA products. The assigned retention periods may be based on elapsed time and/or specific events. RMA software also presents notices of impending destruction of records for confirmation by authorized persons. However, destruction can be overridden by authorized persons for litigation holds or other reasons. Some RMA software can also index and track nonelectronic records in active file rooms, off-site storage, or other locations.

MEDIA FILING EQUIPMENT

Removable electronic recording media are stored off-line when not in use. The selection of appropriate filing equipment for removable electronic media is an important component of any program for the systematic management of active electronic records. As with paper documents, records managers may be expected to advise and assist individual program units in planning filing installations for electronic media, identifying procurement sources, and evaluating specific filing products for computer, video, and audio media. Media filing installations were once exclusively encountered in centralized computer, video, and audio facilities, but they are now commonplace in office areas. As desktop computers, network servers, camcorders, and other electronic recording devices proliferate, storage equipment is required for the removable media they generate.

In some organizations, records managers may develop written specifications and lists of approved products and suppliers to guide program units. Such an approach is usually acceptable in straightforward installations that involve the selection of a few cabinets for a relatively small quantity of media. In large, complex installations, however, media filing requirements must be carefully studied and various products analyzed on an application-by-application basis.

Regardless of the selection methodology employed, the purpose of filing equipment is to make electronic media accessible when required for reference and to provide an appropriate repository for such media when not in use. The size and type of filing equipment selected for a given situation must be well suited to and compatible with various installation and application characteristics, including the number and types of electronic media to be stored, the amount of available floor space and its floor-loading characteristics, the users' reference requirements, and the surrounding decor. To knowledgeably advise program units, records managers must be familiar with the available types of media filing products and understand the situations in which they can be most effectively utilized.

Where high-storage capacity is required, media filing installations have historically relied on shelf- or rack-type cabinets. Such products have been used for decades by centralized magnetic tape libraries in mainframe and minicomputer installations. As their name suggests, shelf-type filing cabinets resemble bookcases. Depending on cabinet design, magnetic tape reels may rest on shelves separated by wire racks that maintain the reels in an upright position; alternatively, tape reels may be suspended from clips inserted into a specially designed hanger bar. Tape reels measuring 10.5 inches or less in diameter can be accommodated. In most cases, reels of different sizes can be intermixed within shelves.

Shelf-type filing cabinets are particularly well suited to large, active filing areas where they cost less than drawer-type equipment. They provide faster, more convenient access to electronic media and make more efficient use of available floor space. Compared with drawer-type equipment, shelf-type filing cabinets require considerably narrower aisles, an important consideration in climate-controlled vaults and other expensive storage areas where space is often limited. In very active filing areas, shelf-type cabinets permit convenient, simultaneous access to magnetic tapes by multiple workers. Because drawers need not be opened and closed, media filing and refiling time and labor are reduced.

Shelf widths range from two feet to more than four feet. A three-foot shelf can hold about 35 reels of magnetic tape wrapped in tape-seal belts and suspended from clips. Shelf capacities are reduced when wire racks are used. A typical cabinet contains five or six shelves, the latter configuration approaching a height of seven feet. Most shelf-type cabinets for magnetic tapes are available in single- or double-sided models. When configured with six 50-inch shelves, a double-sided unit can store up to 600 magnetic tape reels in less than 10 square feet of floor space. Individual cabinets can be fastened together side-by-side, front-to-back, or—if ceiling height permits—on top of one another. Although the simplest and least expensive models are open-faced units, some shelf-type cabinets are equipped with retractable front panels or lockable tambour-style doors that can be closed over the shelves. Closed doors offer improved appearance, protection against dust, and greater security, although shelf-type cabinets can only be considered truly secure when installed in a vault area. As a potential limitation, retractable front panels consume some interior space and may be incompatible with adjustable shelves. With some units, shelves may slide forward in the manner of lateral-style, drawer-type filing cabinets.

Similar high-capacity, shelf-type cabinets are available for half-inch data cartridges, which have replaced magnetic tape reels in many mainframe and minicomputer installations. A two-foot shelf can hold about 25 cartridges stored in compartments that are demarcated by metal or plastic dividers. When compared with magnetic tape reels, half-inch data cartridges offer more compact storage, both in terms of media recording capacity and physical cartridge dimensions. A double-sided cabinet with 50-inch shelves can store about 1,200 3490E-type data cartridges—the equivalent of about 5,400 reels of magnetic tape—in less than eight square feet of floor space. When stored in shelf-type filing cabinets, 5,400 reels of magnetic tape would occupy over 90 square feet of floor space. A shelving unit for magnetic tape cartridges is shown in Figure 7-1.

Multiple shelving units can be connected in side-to-side or front-to-back configurations. To maximize storage density, several companies offer sliding shelving units that are mounted onto tracks. To access a given shelving unit, the adjacent units are moved aside, manually or by the use of motorized controls. Some cabinet manufacturers offer kits to convert conventional magnetic tape shelving for half-inch data cartridges.

For maximum versatility, several manufacturers offer mixed-media storage units that use interchangeable shelves and racks to accommodate different sizes and types of electronic media within the same cabinet. Such a cabinet might, for example, contain one or more hanging bars for magnetic tape reels, several racks for half-inch data cartridges, and additional shelves for hard disk cartridges or optical disks. If desired, shelves and hanging frames can be included for binders, computer print-outs, file folders, microfilm, and microfiche trays, thereby permitting storage of electronic media and related human-readable documentation in the same cabinet. A mixed-media storage unit is shown in Figure 7-2.

Figure 7-1:
High-capacity shelving unit for magnetic tape cartridges. (Courtesy: IBM)

Figure 7-2:
Mixed media storage unit with interchangeable shelves and rack. (Courtesy: TAB Products)

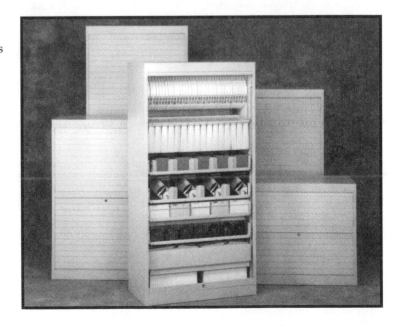

Drawer-type vertical and lateral filing cabinets, the historical mainstays of paper document storage in office installations, are poorly suited to magnetic tape reels. However, drawer-type cabinets are available for smaller media, including half-inch, quarter-inch, and eight-millimeter data cartridges; digital audio tapes; video cassettes; audio cassettes; hard disk cartridges; diskettes; and optical disks. A typical 10-drawer unit measures approximately 26 inches wide by 30 inches deep by 60 inches high. Using dividers to partition drawers into multiple rows for media filing, such a cabinet can store approximately 1,250 half-inch data cartridges, 1,300 quarter-inch data cartridges, 2,300 quarter-inch minicartridges, 650 video cassettes, 2,700 audio cassettes, or 12,000 diskettes.

Regardless of the media for which they are intended, drawer-type cabinets are typically manufactured of steel with selected aluminum and plastic parts. Key-controlled locks may be included, but they are seldom adequate for electronic records that require special security. Safe-type files, with drawers controlled by combination locks, are available for installations that require them. Insulated, fire-resistant models are also available. As with paper files, guides and dividers can be used to separate media into categories. Out guides are also available to mark the locations of media removed from files.

As a group, drawer-type filing cabinets are poorly suited to very active, high-volume records management applications. Time and effort are required to pull out and replace drawers each time media are retrieved, and only one person at a time can conveniently access a given cabinet. In addition, drawer-type cabinets make inefficient use of available floor space. In particular, limitations on cabinet height result in a significant amount of wasted space between the top of the cabinet and the ceiling of the room where the cabinets are installed. Often, the tops of cabinets contain piles of media or documentation to be filed or that the cabinet cannot conveniently accommodate. A variant, sometimes convenient approach to drawer-type filing consists of a computer workstation with one or two drawers for media storage.

Other media filing equipment is intended for applications where accessibility is more important than high-storage capacity. Diskettes, compact disks, and DVDs, for example, may be stored in vinyl sleeves that are edge-punched for enclosure in ring binders. The binders may be stored on shelves, in drawer-type filing cabinets, or on work surfaces. Wheeled carts and desktop storage racks for magnetic tape reels and half-inch data cartridges are principally intended for centralized computing facilities. Such devices make the most active media conveniently available. They also provide a staging area for tapes awaiting processing or reshelving.

A wide variety of computer storage products, ranging from racks to covered trays, are commonly utilized to store diskettes, magnetic tape cartridges, optical disks, and other media encountered in desktop computer and LAN server installations. Similar products are available for video and audio recording media. Such storage units are usually constructed of plastic or metal. They are typically positioned near the computers on which the filed media will be processed. Capacities range from less than a dozen to more than a hundred pieces of media.

Tub files house frequently referenced media in an open cabinet that is accessed from the top. Often mounted on casters, tub files can store diskettes, optical disks, hard disk cartridges, magnetic tape cartridges, video cassettes, and audio cassettes. A tub desk, as its name suggests, combines a tub file with a work surface. Carousel files consist of storage racks or bins mounted onto turntables that can be manually rotated. They are available for magnetic tape cartridges, audio and video cassettes, diskettes, optical disks, and other removable media.

Motorized filing devices employ mechanical components to deliver electronic media to users, thereby saving labor and speeding retrieval in very active installations. Vertical motorized shelf files, the most common variety, were introduced in the early 1960s. They consist of shelves mounted onto a revolving transport mechanism inside a large cabinet. Although vertical motorized shelf files are most commonly utilized for paper records, they can be configured with shelves or trays for electronic media. To retrieve a given medium, the operator determines its shelf number, typically by consulting an index that may be manually prepared or computer-generated. The operator enters the shelf number into a calculator-style keypad, causing a revolving transport mechanism to position the indicated shelf at an opening. The operator then searches the shelf for the desired medium. Among their advantages, vertical motorized files provide rapid retrieval, effective security against unauthorized access, and good storage density. On the negative side, they cost substantially more than manual filing cabinets of comparable capacity. As a further complication with cost implications, vertical motorized files are very heavy. Floor reinforcement or other expensive side modifications may be necessary.

AUTOCHANGERS AND HIERARCHICAL STORAGE MANAGEMENT (HSM)

Whether manual or motorized, filing devices discussed to this point are designed for off-line storage of electronic records. They require operator handling of removable media. When a given tape or disk is required for reference purposes, it must be located, removed from its cabinet or other container, and mounted into an appropriate drive for processing. When work is completed, the medium must be returned to its off-line storage location.

As their name suggests, autochangers automate this process. Also known as *jukeboxes* or *library units*, **autochangers** are mass storage peripherals that provide unattended access to large quantities of computer-processible information. Available for most optical disks and many magnetic tape formats, autochangers store electronic media in stacks, bins, or other receptacles. Acting on instructions from an external computer, an autochanger selects a specified optical disk drive or magnetic tape and mounts it into a drive for recording or playback of information. Depending on the device, an autochanger may incorporate one or more optical disk drives or magnetic tape units. When processing is completed, the autochanger removes the medium from its drive and returns it to the appropriate stack or bin.

Although autochangers operate as on-line peripherals, specific optical disks or magnetic tapes are not brought on-line until they are requested and mounted. Consequently, autochangers are said to provide "near-line" access to the media they contain. Media loading times range from less than 15 seconds to more than one minute, depending on the device. A full interchange cycle, however, includes the time required to locate desired information once an optical disk or magnetic tape is mounted and to unload and reshelve any previously mounted media.

Optical disk autochangers have been used in electronic document imaging and data storage implementations since the mid-1980s. Multifunctional models can accommodate 5.25-inch magneto-optical disks in write-once and rewritable formats. Compact disk autochangers can accommodate CD-ROM and recordable CD media. DVD autochangers are also available. Some models can co-mingle CDs and DVDs. Magnetic tape autochangers are available for digital linear tape, digital audio tape, eight-millimeter data cartridges, and very high-capacity magnetic tape formats. They permit unattended backup in mainframe, minicomputer, and network server implementations.

Optical disk and magnetic tape autochangers can also be incorporated into **hierarchical storage management (HSM)** configurations. Few, if any, computer systems employ a single storage technology for electronic records. Minicomputer and mainframe installations invariably include hard drives and magnetic tape peripherals. Most desktop and notebook computers are configured with hard drives, floppy disk drives, and CD or DVD drives. Hierarchical storage management concepts categorize and rank computer storage devices and media by their responsiveness, capacities, and costs. A typical computer storage hierarchy can be depicted as a four-level pyramid:

1. At the apex of the pyramid, a computer's main memory encompasses random-access memory (RAM) and read-only memory (ROM) circuits. Composed of semiconductor materials, main memory is fast but expensive and limited in capacity. It is reserved for computer programs and recorded information under immediate execution by a central processor. Because random-access memory requires an uninterrupted power supply to retain its contents, it is unsuitable for long-term storage. RAM circuits provide working storage. To prevent loss of information, the contents of random-access memory should be saved to nonvolatile media at frequent intervals. Read-only memory circuits, which have prerecorded contents, do not permit direct recording of information by computer users.

2. Hard drives are the principal on-line storage peripherals in most computer installations. They are used for information that must be immediately and continuously available for display, editing, printing, or other purposes. Hard drives are the storage devices of choice for frequently referenced electronic records.

3. Autochangers for optical disks and magnetic tapes provide high-capacity near-line storage for information that may be referenced at any time but that is less likely to be retrieved than information recorded on hard drives. Such information must be available conveniently, but a delay of several seconds or even several minutes is tolerable. Optical disk and magnetic tape autochangers sacrifice some responsiveness to obtain higher storage capacity than most hard drive configurations can provide. In some cases, autochangers offer lower storage costs than hard drives for very large quantities of information.

4. Removable computer media, stored off-line until needed, form the base of the hierarchical storage pyramid. Such media are used for back-up operations and archiving of inactive electronic records. Those applications are characterized by infrequent reference. In the fourth level of the storage hierarchy, rapid access is less important than high capacity and low cost. Removable media may be stored in office areas or computer rooms. Back-up copies are often stored off-site for vital records protection. Information retrieval is subject to significant, but anticipated and presumably tolerable, delays. Access times for information recorded on off-line media may range from one hour to one day or longer, depending on the storage location.

Hierarchical storage concepts are implicitly implemented in any computer configuration that incorporates two or more storage technologies. When different magnetic and optical devices are combined in a computer configuration, a system manager or authorized users can employ operating system commands or utility programs to transfer electronic records from one level of the storage hierarchy to another as reference activity or other considerations warrant. In mainframe, minicomputer, and network server installations, for example, inactive data files are routinely transferred from hard drives to magnetic tapes for off-line storage. Similarly, electronic document images may reside on hard drives for a relatively brief period of intense reference activity, then be transferred to an optical disk autochanger for additional months or years; ultimately, the optical disks may be removed from the autochanger for off-line storage.

These operations require manual intervention, however; the system manager or user must determine when the transfer of electronic records should occur, keep track of the storage locations of particular information, and initiate retrieval operations if the transferred records must be restored to higher hierarchical levels for reference or other purposes. As a fully automated alternative, HSM software is available for mainframes, minicomputers, and network servers. It migrates computer files between storage components based on reference activity. Files are stored on hard drives, near the top of the storage hierarchy, when they are frequently referenced. As they become less active, they are moved to lower levels in the hierarchy: from on-line to near-line storage, where present, and eventually to off-line storage when reference activity falls below a predetermined level. From the user's perspective, however, all information appears to reside on hard drives. When previously migrated files are requested, hierarchical storage management software automatically restores them to hard drives from lower hierarchical levels. Migration is typically based on a file's reference history, but additional factors, such as the need to free hard disk space for other purposes, may also be considered. Alternatively, file migration patterns may be based on the ages of electronic records, which are typically related to frequency of reference; as previously discussed, reference activity for most electronic records decreases with age.

MEDIA MANAGEMENT

Computer, video, and audio records stored on magnetic and optical media are vulnerable to damage from inherent media instabilities, as well as from various external conditions and events such as inappropriate storage environments, careless handling, and improperly adjusted equipment. To protect their electronic records, organizations must develop formal guidelines for the storage, care, and handling of magnetic and optical media. When systematically implemented, such guidelines will minimize the potential for media damage, thereby increasing the likelihood that electronic records will remain useful for their intended purposes.

The following discussion presents recommendations for the management of magnetic and optical media in the following areas:

- Selecting blank media for electronic records
- Maintaining appropriate environments for media storage
- Utilizing handling procedures and precautions to minimize the potential for physical damage to magnetic and optical media.

The discussion is limited to removable electronic media—floppy disks, magnetic tapes, and optical media—suitable for off-line storage of electronic records. Hard disks, as previously defined, are fixed storage media. Hard disk cartridges, although removable, are subject to damage from head crashes and other equipment malfunctions; they are designed for actively referenced information rather than off-line storage. As a cautionary note, systematic care and handling guidelines will not lengthen the limited life spans of electronic media relative to paper and microfilm; those life spans are defined by scientific facts not business practices. However, the procedures and precautions discussed next will increase the likelihood that a given magnetic or optical medium will remain useful throughout its anticipated life span, whatever that may be.

Selecting Blank Media

A systematic approach to managing magnetic and optical media for computer, video, or audio recording begins with the selection of appropriate blank media. Certain characteristics of magnetic and optical recording media can have a significant impact on their suitability for specific applications. Corporations, government agencies, and other organizations should purchase high-quality computer, video, and audio recording media from known manufacturers. Media of uncertain origin and potentially marginal quality should be avoided. Brand-name magnetic and optical media are preferable to off-brand products. Brand-name media are typically subjected to tightly controlled manufacturing processes and strict quality control procedures. Produced from high-quality materials, they are thoroughly tested prior to sale and have low error rates. Although off-brand magnetic tapes and diskettes are often attractively priced, they may be poorly constructed. Off-brand magnetic media are particularly vulnerable to particle shedding, which can lead to equipment damage as well as loss of recorded information.

Similar procurement practices are advisable for optical disks. Through the late 1980s, optical disk users had little choice but to purchase blank media from manufacturers of optical disk drives. At that time, many optical disks were proprietary products, and drive manufacturers were the sole sources of compatible media. With the adoption of standards for certain optical disk formats, however, alternative procurement sources have become available. Recordable CDs, recordable DVDs, and 5.25-inch magneto-optical disks, in particular, are sold by multiple suppliers, including mail-order companies that offer substantial discounts. For best results, optical recording media, like their magnetic counterparts, must be selected for quality rather than price.

Where applicable, blank magnetic and optical media should conform to specifications published by national and international standard-setting organizations such as the American National Standards Institute (ANSI), British Standards Institution (BSI), Deutsche Industrie Normen (DIN), European Computer Manufacturers Association (ECMA), Japanese Standards Association (JSA), and the International Organization for Standardization (ISO). Further, magnetic and optical media should comply fully with specifications established by the manufacturer of the equipment on which the media will be recorded or read. Type II or Type IV audio cassettes, for example, should not be used in tape recorders that are limited to Type I media. Fully compliant media are sometimes described as *qualified* or *certified* for use in a given drive. Blank media should be used only for its intended purpose. Conventional VHS video cassettes should not be used for Super-VHS recording. Single-sided floppy disks should never be formatted for double-sided recording.

Magnetic and optical media intended for long-term storage of electronic records should be recently manufactured and used as soon as possible after purchase. Lifetime estimates for magnetic and optical media begin with their manufacturing dates, not the date on which information was recorded. Large quantities of magnetic or optical media should not be purchased far in advance of their anticipated recording dates; a portion of their estimated life spans will have elapsed before they are used. New media should be used for storage copies of important information. Recycled media—magnetic tapes, diskettes, or rewritable optical disks previously used for data, video, or audio recording—are unacceptable for that purpose.

Prior to use, magnetic and optical media should be stored in environmental conditions specified by their manufacturers. Such specifications are rarely restrictive. Typically, the temperature in the storage area should range from 40 to 120 degrees Fahrenheit (5 to 48 degrees Celsius), with a relative humidity of 20 to 80 percent and a maximum wet bulb temperature of 80 degrees Fahrenheit (26 degrees Celsius). In some geographic locations, humidity limits may pose problems if blank media are kept in warehouses or other storage areas that lack air-conditioning. If possible, records managers should determine whether unrecorded magnetic media were previously stored under conditions of high temperature or high humidity. Such conditions promote media degradation through hydrolysis, a process in which absorbed moisture interacts with and damages magnetic storage media. If hydrolysis is suspected, a period of low-humidity storage is recommended to reverse media degradation. In any case, new electronic media should be acclimated to their environments for a period of at least 24 hours prior to recording.

For very important electronic records intended for long-term retention, two or more storage copies should be created. To provide the greatest protection against the possibility of defective media, magnetic tapes, diskettes, or optical disks of the same type but from different manufacturing lots should be utilized for each storage copy.

Some manufacturers offer several grades of magnetic or optical media with varying performance and price characteristics. Standard-grade magnetic tapes, diskettes, and optical disks—the least expensive variety—are often acceptable for routine information processing. Media of the highest available quality are preferred, however, for storage copies of important information. A manufacturer's most expensive recording media are sometimes describes as *super premium* products. Compared with standard-grade media, they provide greater protection against signal dropouts that cause permanent read/write errors. Super premium magnetic tapes and diskettes are more likely to produce error-free recordings and preserve high signal levels in storage. They are manufactured to higher tolerances than most equipment requires.

Similar gradations of product quality are encountered with video and audio recording media. Super premium video tapes feature very small magnetic particles for superior image quality, while super premium audio tapes can record a broader range of frequencies than their conventional counterparts. Among optical disks, gold CD-R media, also described as *gold and gold* disks, offer superior longevity and performance when compared to green CD-R media, which is described as *green and gold*. Super premium magnetic and optical media often carry a lifetime warranty against manufacturing defects. Less-expensive media, by contrast, are warranted for specific time periods, usually one to three years. However, manufacturers' warranties customarily provide replacement media as the sole remedy for defective products. Liability for damage to recorded information is specifically disavowed.

Super premium magnetic and optical media often incorporate additional features their conventional counterparts lack. As an example, some manufacturers apply a proprietary coating to the reverse side of super premium magnetic tapes. Such backcoating reduces tape slippage and friction, improves scratch resistance, and minimizes the generation of debris that can produce signal dropouts. Some manufacturers combine backcoating with a conductive substrate to reduce static electricity, which can attract airborne debris. As an additional advantage, super premium tapes and disks typically have high-precision housings that minimize vibrations and otherwise enhance recording and playback. Although too often ignored in product selection, properly designed housings can have a significant impact on media performance and reliability. Over time, poorly constructed reels, cartridges, and cassettes can experience dimensional changes that may impede media loading, increase friction, and promote tape stretching. Poorly constructed housings can also damage read/write heads and drive mechanisms.

Although the stability of magnetic and optical media is not defined by published national or international standards, accelerated aging tests conducted by media manufacturers and independent researchers provide lifetime estimates for some magnetic and optical recording materials. These tests suggest that certain media, such as metal particle tapes and gold compact disks, enjoy stability advantages over other types. Manufacturers of metal particle tapes claim life spans of at least 30 years for their products, and some research studies suggest that longer lifetimes are likely. Magnetic tape formats that employ metal particle recording materials include digital linear tape, eight-millimeter data cartridges and video cassettes, and digital audio tape. With CDs, gold resists oxidation, thereby enhancing stability. Where media longevity is more important than storage capacity or fast retrieval responsiveness, records managers may prefer CD-R to magneto-optical disks. CD-R drives are slower and provide less on-line capacity than magneto-optical products, but CD-R media have longer life spans than magneto-optical disks. Based on manufacturers' claims, lifetime estimates for CD-R range from 75 to 200 years, as compared with 30 years for magneto-optical disks. In the past, some 5.25-inch magneto-optical disk manufacturers offered a choice of glass or plastic substrates. Glass substrates are typically more stable than their plastic counterparts, which tend to absorb moisture. The newest magneto-optical drives, however, support plastic media exclusively.

Because it is closely packed, information recorded at high densities is particularly vulnerable to losses associated with debris. Submicron particles that pose no significant threat at lower recording densities can eradicate information from media recorded at higher densities. Lower recording densities may consequently prove safer for magnetic media containing important information destined for long-term storage. This recommendation is most meaningful for video recording media. Video tapes intended for long-term storage should be recorded at the fastest speed, which equates to the lowest recording density; as an added advantage, the fastest recording speed also provides the highest image quality. In computer applications, high recording densities—which are associated with the newest products—may be required to satisfy capacity requirements. Further, the highest-density computer media have different chemical compositions and longer lifetime estimates than older, low-density formats.

To decrease the likelihood of print-through in magnetic recording, thin tapes should be avoided. Examples of thin tapes include C-120 audio cassettes, which provide two hours of recording time at 60 minutes per side; T-160 and T-180 VHS-type video cassettes, which can provide more than eight hours of recording time in the EP mode; and extra-length computer tapes. Several manufacturers offer low-print audio tapes specifically designed to minimize print-through.

Storage Copies

For effective management of magnetic and optical media, storage copies must be differentiated from working copies. The latter, as their name suggests, are intended for ongoing information processing and reference requirements; storage copies, in contrast, are created to satisfy retention requirements or for back-up protection. Storage copies are invariably recorded on removable magnetic or optical media. They often contain inactive records transferred from hard drives. Regardless of content, storage copies are seldom referenced. Their use is typically restricted to the creation of additional working copies if existing working copies are damaged. They also permit recovery of information in the event of a system failure or other disaster.

Storage conditions can have a significant impact on the life spans of magnetic and optical media. The following discussion presents recommendations for facilities and procedures for storage copies of magnetic and optical media that contain important electronic records. Such storage copies are sometimes described as master copies to distinguish them from working copies. The recommended storage environment combines temperature and humidity controls with minimization of contaminants. It is designed to preserve the utility of information recorded on magnetic and optical media for their estimated life spans. To the extent that an organization's storage conditions deviate from those presented here, media life will be shortened.

High temperatures and high relative humidity accelerate the deteriorative aging of magnetic tapes and diskettes. In particular, a hot, humid storage environment promotes hydrolytic degradation of binder materials, which can have a devastating impact on the chemical composition and longevity of magnetic media. These effects are well documented in scientific literature. Prevention of binder hydrolysis is consequently the principal purpose of temperature and humidity control.

All publications on this subject affirm the advantages of a cool, dry storage environment for recorded magnetic media. Since the 1960s, however, journal articles, conference papers, and manufacturers' product literature have presented different, sometimes conflicting, temperature and humidity recommendations. Intended as an authoritative source, ANSI/NAPM IT9.23, *American National Standard for Imaging Materials—Polyester Base Magnetic Tape—Storage*, was published in 1996 as the first American national standard for storage of computer media. (Similar standards for storage of photographic media, including microfilm, have been available for decades and are well known to records managers.) As its title indicates, the IT9.23 standard pertains to storage copies of magnetic tapes with polyester base materials only; it does not cover diskettes or older magnetic tapes with acetate base materials. The IT9.23 standard specifies medium-term storage conditions, which are suitable for the preservation of recorded information for a minimum of 10 years, and extended-term storage conditions, which are suitable for the preservation of recorded information of permanent value. The standard does not state or imply, however, that magnetic tapes have permanent keeping properties.

For medium-term storage of magnetic tapes, the IT9.23 standard specifies a maximum temperature of 73 degrees Fahrenheit (23 degrees Celsius) with a relative humidity of 20 to 50 percent. Temperature variations in the storage area must not exceed 4 degrees Fahrenheit (2 degrees Celsius) over a 24-hour period. Humidity variations must not exceed 10 percent over a 24-hour period. Rapid cycling of temperature and humidity can damage binder materials and media substrates.

For extended-term storage of magnetic tapes, the IT9.23 standard specifies three combinations of temperature and relative humidity:

1. A maximum temperature of 68 degrees Fahrenheit (20 degrees Celsius) with relative humidity ranging from 20 to 30 percent;

2. A maximum temperature of 59 degrees Fahrenheit (15 degrees Celsius) with relative humidity ranging from 20 to 40 percent; or

3. A maximum temperature of 50 degrees Fahrenheit (10 degrees Celsius) with relative humidity ranging from 20 to 50 percent.

As the temperature in the storage area rises, relative humidity must be more tightly controlled. The IT9.23 standard notes that protection against environmental damage is enhanced when magnetic tapes are stored at a low temperature and low relative humidity, but it warns that very low temperatures can lead to separation of tape lubricants from binder materials. The minimum acceptable storage temperature is 46 degrees Fahrenheit (8 degrees Celsius). Temperature variations in the storage area must not exceed 4 degrees Fahrenheit (2 degrees Celsius) over a 24-hour period. Humidity variations for extended-term storage must not exceed 5 percent over a 24-hour period. These temperature and humidity recommendations are similar to specifications for microfilm storage presented in ANSI/NAPM IT9.11, *Processed Safety Photographic Films—Storage.*

For medium-term and extended-term storage, the IT9.23 standard notes that an air-conditioned facility is usually necessary to maintain temperature and humidity within approved limits. Specialized air-conditioning equipment may be necessary to maintain low temperatures within the specified humidity ranges. Where air-conditioning is not practical or required, as in underground storage areas with naturally low temperatures, dehumidification will usually be necessary.

Temperature and humidity ranges specified in the IT9.23 standard differ from storage recommendations previously presented by other authorities. Based on a survey of published scientific studies and manufacturers' specifications for extended storage of computer tapes, the first edition of this book recommended an air-conditioned facility with a temperature of 63 to 68 degrees Fahrenheit (17 to 20 degrees Celsius) with relative humidity ranging from 35 to 45 percent. A 1990 recommendation from the National Archives and Records Administration similarly specified a temperature of 62 to 68 degrees Fahrenheit (16 to 20 degrees Celsius) with relative humidity of 35 to 45 percent. Those recommendations do not conform to specifications presented in the IT9.23 standard; at 62 to 68 degrees Fahrenheit, relative humidity in the tape storage area should not exceed 30 percent. SMPTE RP-103, *Recommended Practice,* published by the Society of Motion Picture and Television Engineers in 1982, specified a temperature of 67 to 74 degrees Fahrenheit (19 to 23 degrees Celsius) with a relative humidity of 30 to 70 percent as an acceptable range that minimizes the risk of media degradation while still permitting some flexibility in facility design. That specification is clearly out of compliance with the IT9.23 standard. Storage recommendations by manufacturers of magnetic media are often less restrictive than those presented in the IT9.23 standard and other published authorities.

The IT9.23 standard is limited to magnetic tape. At the time this chapter was written, no comparable national or international standards existed for optical disk storage. The preparation of all-encompassing storage specifications for optical disks is complicated by the many combinations of recording technologies and media employed by write-once, rewritable, and read-only optical disk systems. Manufacturers' product specifications typically indicate the environmental conditions under which their optical disk drives and media will operate reliably, without regard to the specified environment's impact on the stability of recorded information. With few exceptions, optical disk systems are engineered for use in ordinary office environments. Acceptable operating temperatures cited in product literature for read/write optical disk drives range from 50 to 140 degrees Fahrenheit (10 to 60 degrees Celsius), with a maximum gradient of 50 to 68 degrees Fahrenheit (10 to 20 degrees Celsius) per hour. Relative humidity can range from 10 to 80 percent, with a maximum gradient of 10 to 20 percent per hour. A broader range of environmental conditions is specified for media storage—16 to 122 degrees Fahrenheit (minus 10 degrees to plus 50 degrees Celsius) with a relative humidity of 10 to 90 percent.

These recommendations are obviously less stringent than the extended-term storage specifications presented in the preceding discussion of magnetic tapes. If they are correct, optical storage media require minimal climate controls to attain life spans comparable to or greater than those of magnetic tapes stored in very tightly controlled environments. Stability tests conducted on CD-R media estimate their life spans at 75 to 200 years when stored at 77 degrees Fahrenheit (25 degrees Celsius) with 40 percent relative humidity. Lifetime estimates for other optical disks, though much shorter than those for CD-R, are based on accelerated aging tests that are based on an office environment. Published reports and manufacturers' product literature do not indicate whether the life spans of such media can be extended by comparably tight environmental controls. Given that high temperature and high humidity promote oxidation, the cool, dry storage environment recommended in the ANSI/NAPM IT9.23 standard for storage of magnetic tapes cannot be harmful to optical disks, but whether it is helpful is uncertain. Given their moisture-absorbing tendencies, optical disks with plastic substrates should not be stored or used in humid areas.

Extreme temperatures must likewise be avoided. Optical and magnetic media should never be stored in direct sunlight, placed near radiators, or otherwise exposed to intense heat sources. CD-R media, which are not housed in protective cartridges, may be damaged by exposure to light. Their dye layers can fade, with a resulting reduction of contrast that will impede retrieval of recorded information. CD-R media should be stored in jewel boxes or other containers when not in use, and the containers should be kept in closed cabinets. Light stability is not an issue with other optical disks.

For additional protection against the adverse effects of high humidity, magnetic and optical media can be stored in foil-lined corrugated cartons, together with a bag of desiccant materials such as calcium chloride or silica gel. To prevent loss of lubricants during long-term storage, magnetic media should be enclosed in polyethylene bags. This procedure will also preserve cleanliness and protect the media against contaminants. Although some magnetic and optical media are encapsulated in protective cartridges, they are not hermetically sealed. Dust and other contaminants can infiltrate media housings, rendering portions of recorded information unreadable. As previously discussed, very small dust particles can damage information recorded on high-density media.

Cleaning equipment and supplies are available for specific media; however, a clean, dust-free storage environment affords the best protection against contaminants. Air-conditioning is usually necessary, both for temperature and humidity control and to remove pollutants. Although most air-conditioner filters will capture dust particles measuring 10 microns or larger, smaller particles can damage high-density magnetic recordings. Electronic air filters are typically necessary to trap such particles. The IT9.23 standard cautions against gaseous impurities such as ammonia, chlorine, peroxides, smoke, sulfides, and oxides of nitrogen.

Media storage areas must be cleaned regularly. To minimize scattering of dust particles and other potentially harmful contaminants, proper housekeeping habits must be observed. Some authorities recommend double-bagged or water-filtered vacuum cleaners as the preferred cleaning instruments. The IT9.23 standard specifies a vacuum system with an exhaust pipe that evacuates dust from the storage area. Static-free, chemically inert wipes are recommended for cleaning shelves and media containers. Ordinary dust rags, steel wool, abrasive cleaning materials, or chemical cleaning solutions should not be used. Floors should be dry-mopped or cleaned with a minimum amount of water followed by dry mopping. Floor wax and buffing machines can generate debris from abrasions caused by foot traffic.

To minimize the likelihood of cinching, magnetic tapes should undergo a slow unwind/rewind cycle to obtain a smooth, evenly tensioned pack prior to storage. Until recently, many experts assumed that magnetic tapes in storage had to be unwound and rewound at regular intervals to alleviate accumulated stress or to tighten loose tapes. Such rewinding is described as *exercising* or *retensioning* a tape. Some published sources recommend annual rewinding of magnetic tapes, which creates an enormous burden of time and labor costs in large media collections. Others report that rewind intervals as long as 3.5 years are acceptable for tapes stored in a controlled environment. Current thinking suggests, however, that periodic rewinding of magnetic tapes is not necessary. The IT9.23 standard is notably silent on this issue; periodic rewinding is not mentioned in its discussion of tape tensioning. Some media manufacturers advise against periodic rewinding of magnetic tapes, although they do recommend a full unwinding and rewinding to exercise stored tapes just prior to use.

For early detection of dangers to recorded information, storage copies of magnetic and optical media should be inspected regularly. The IT9.23 standard recommends inspection of magnetic tapes at five-year intervals, with more frequent inspections if temperature and humidity deviations have occurred. Earlier publications recommended annual inspection of stored media. Frequency aside, inspection should involve a visual examination of the medium and its housing, followed by the retrieval or playback of recorded information. In a large collection of magnetic or optical media, individual examination of magnetic tapes, diskettes, or optical disks can prove prohibitively time-consuming. In such situations, a portion of the collection should be sampled. Alternatively, one or more control media containing test signals can be created for inspection purposes. Such control media should be created on the same system, with the same recording materials, and with the same recording characteristics as media that contain data, video images, or audio signals. The control media should be inspected on a regular basis for recording errors and physical damage. If permanent errors are detected in the control media, the entire media collection must be examined.

To provide additional protection against permanent error conditions that can render information unretrievable, the contents of magnetic tapes, diskettes, and optical disks can be copied onto new media at regular intervals. Such periodic copying is described as *renewing* magnetic or optical media. If new media are used, periodic copying can extend the life of recorded information indefinitely, thereby effectively overcoming problems associated with the nonarchival nature of electronic media.

Copying can also be used to transfer information from deteriorating or obsolete media. Digitally coded information can be copied an indefinite number of times without degradation. In the case of video and audio recording based on analog signals, however, an inevitable loss of image and/or sound quality will occur from one generation of copy to the next. This loss imposes limits on the number of times such information transfers can be performed. The extent of generation loss will vary with the quality of the original recording and the characteristics of equipment and media utilized for copy production. To minimize the adverse effects of temperature and humidity variations, media copying should be performed in the long-term storage environment itself.

Magnetic and optical media removed from an environmentally controlled storage facility and taken to a work area with different environmental characteristics should be acclimated to the new environment before use to prevent moisture condensation. Such acclimatization is especially important for densely recorded digital media with narrow track widths. According to the IT9.23 standard, temperature acclimatization for magnetic tapes can take 30 minutes to 4 hours, depending on the type of medium. Humidity acclimatization is a slower process, requiring one day to several weeks or longer. Wider tapes require longer acclimatization times than their thinner counterparts. The acclimatization process can be accelerated by unwinding and rewinding a magnetic tape several times, thereby exposing more of the tape surface to the new environment. Exposed media will achieve thermal equilibrium in seconds and moisture equilibrium in minutes. Magnetic media intended for long-term storage should be returned to an environmentally controlled facility immediately after use.

Computer tape cartridges, video cassettes, audio cassettes, diskettes, and optical disks should be stored in containers when not in use. To prevent the accumulation of dust and other contaminants, containers should be closed at all times, even when they are empty. To prevent accidental overwriting of information intended for long-term storage, write-enable rings should be removed from magnetic tape reels. With diskettes, magnetic tape cartridges and cassettes, and rewritable optical disks, write-protect tabs or other recording inhibitors should be activated.

To prevent accidental erasure of electronic records, permanent magnets and any other objects that generate magnetic fields are prohibited in storage areas for magnetic media. Most optical media are unaffected by magnetic fields, but magneto-optical disks are a notable exception. Their contents are subject to accidental erasure through inadvertent exposure to magnetic fields of sufficient strength. Combustible materials are likewise forbidden in media storage areas. Carbon dioxide or other dry fire-protection methods should be employed. The method selected must not produce potentially harmful residues.

For magnetic and optical media that contain vital electronic records, as defined in Chapter Six, additional copies should be created for storage at a secondary site. The environmental controls and storage precautions outlined previously should be implemented at the duplicate site.

Media Handling

All information storage media are imperiled by use; improper handling is a common cause of physical damage to information recorded on magnetic and optical media. Certain magnetic tapes, diskettes, and optical disks are encapsulated in protective cartridges; however, they are not impervious to harm. Computer room personnel, administrative workers, or other employees may handle media in a careless manner. Magnetic tapes, diskettes, or optical disks may be damaged in transit or by improperly adjusted equipment. Media surfaces can be scratched or otherwise defaced, with resulting eradication of recorded information.

The potential for media damage can be minimized or eliminated by strict adherence to proper handling procedures and precautions. The following discussion is based on recommendations presented in various published sources and in manufacturers' product literature. The recommendations presented here apply equally to working copies and storage copies, although the latter should be handled as little as possible. If frequent reference to storage copies is anticipated, one or more working copies should be made.

Magnetic media must be handled gently at all times. Nine-track reels, for example, should be carried by their hubs to avoid damage to protruding tape edges. Magnetic tape cartridges and cassettes, diskettes, and optical disks should be handled by their edges. Magnetic and optical media should never be squeezed, placed under heavy objects, or otherwise subjected to pressure. Magnetic and optical media should be shelved in an upright, vertical position to prevent warping of containers. Magnetic and optical media should never be stacked horizontally; storage containers should not support the weight of other containers. All magnetic and optical media should be kept in protective containers when not in use. Storage copies of magnetic tape reels should always be enclosed in wrap-arounds, which should not be removed until a given tape is about to be used. Wrap-arounds should be replaced immediately after the tape is used.

Adhesive labels should be used to identify media contents. To avoid applying pressure to media, the contents of labels should be written before attaching them to magnetic or optical media. Because erasers exert pressure and generate potentially troublesome debris, they should not be used to modify media labels. Outdated or otherwise incorrect labels should be removed and replaced with correct ones. Graphite pencils can likewise generate debris. They should not be used for label preparation. Adhesive labels should never be attached to the unrecorded sides of CDs. Such labels may contain solvents that can damage a disk's protective coating and reflective metal layer. For the same reason, permanent markers should not be used to label CDs. Markers with water-soluble ink are acceptable, however. Some CD-Rs are designed for use with ink jet or thermal transfer labels, but an improperly aligned label can put a CD out of balance when it is spinning at high speed. Removal of an adhesive label can damage the protective coating on a CD, as can ballpoint pens or other writing instruments with sharp points.

Contact with magnetic and optical media should be limited to protective housings. To guard against the damaging effects of skin oils and fingerprints, recording surfaces should never be touched. Portions of magnetic media that are routinely exposed require special handling precautions. With 5.25-inch diskettes, for example, recording surfaces are exposed in both the oval slot and hub ring. Magnetic tapes are likewise exposed along one edge of audio cassettes and data cassettes. When handling such media, care must be taken to avoid contact with the exposed recording surfaces. Cartridge shutters, which expose certain magnetic and optical media when mounted into appropriate drives, should never be retracted manually.

Environmental conditions for working copies are less restrictive than those required for storage copies. For magnetic media, published sources and manufacturers' recommendations specify temperatures of 60 to 90 degrees Fahrenheit (16 to 32 degrees Celsius) with a relative humidity of 20 to 80 percent. Manufacturers' recommendations for optical disks, as previously noted, are even less stringent. High humidity is the leading cause of chemical damage to magnetic and optical media. When combined with high temperature, it can also promote the evaporation of lubricants and growth of fungus on magnetic tapes and diskettes. Very low humidity, on the other hand, increases static electricity, which attracts airborne debris and creates head/media interface problems. With magnetic tapes, low temperatures encourage loose tape windings, promote loss of lubricants, and increase the likelihood of cinching. A work area characterized by both high temperature and high humidity poses the greatest threat to magnetic and optical media. Combinations of low temperature and low humidity, though still potentially troublesome, pose fewer risks. For magnetic media, the minimum temperature specified in the IT9.23 standard should be observed.

Work areas must be cleaned regularly. Dust should be cleared from containers prior to removing magnetic or optical media. Dust should be cleared from nine-track reels prior to removing wraparounds. Eating, drinking, and smoking should be prohibited in all areas where magnetic and optical media are used or stored. Food and beverages may be accidentally spilled onto media. Smoke particles are potentially destructive contaminants that can infiltrate media housings and storage devices. Because they increase the relative humidity in localized areas, coffee makers and other devices that create water vapors should not be operated in close proximity to magnetic and optical media. Media should not be exposed to radiators, direct sunlight, or other sources of heat. Placing magnetic and optical media on top of tape or disk drives exposes them to both heat and dust. Some computer peripherals, such as printers, generate debris. Media and their associated storage equipment should be located as far away from such devices as is practical.

Although the dangers of accidental erasure are less significant than other threats to media stability, magnets must be prohibited in all offices or other work areas where magnetic or magneto-optical media are utilized. To avoid inadvertent exposure to magnetic fields in transit, a distance of three inches should be maintained between magnetic or magneto-optical recording media and the sides of transport containers. Specially designed transit cases are available for that purpose.

Magnetic and optical media should not be loaded into recording or playback equipment until the information they contain is ready to be processed. Media should be removed from equipment immediately after use and should never remain in equipment when not in use. Equipment operators and others responsible for the care and handling of magnetic media should visually inspect a given medium each time it is used. Unusual conditions should be reported for corrective action. Examples of such conditions include scratches, cracks, or other damage to media or protective casings; tape rubbing against the side flanges of a reel or cartridge; folded tape layers; buckling or cinching; excessive accumulations of dust or other contaminants on media or containers; and particle shedding. Suspect media should be tested immediately for usability. A new copy should be made of any medium that appears to be physically or chemically damaged.

Readability problems can often be resolved by cleaning CDs and video disks prior to use. Dust can be removed from such media with a soft, lint-free cloth by wiping them in a circular motion from the center to the outer edges. Conventional household cleaners should never be used with read-only optical disks; they contain solvents that can damage the protective overcoat on a disk. With magnetic tape and optical disks, temporary errors can usually be corrected by cleaning the media in a manner specified by the manufacturer. Several manufacturers offer cleaning devices and supplies for magnetic and optical media. Such kits should always be used in strict conformity with their manufacturers' directions. Repeated occurrences of temporary errors indicate media deterioration. Such tapes should be recopied as soon as possible.

Magnetic and optical media are affected by the storage peripherals in which they are read or recorded. Increased operating speeds and recording densities make the condition of storage equipment an important consideration in a systematic program for care and handling of magnetic media. All storage peripherals must be in proper operating condition. Defective devices can damage magnetic and optical media. They should be taken out of service and not used until repaired. Preventive maintenance procedures recommended by equipment manufacturers should be enforced. Because dust, oxide particles, and other contaminants can affect recording and playback, machine components that come into contact with magnetic and optical media should be cleaned regularly in a manner specified by the equipment manufacturer. Examples of such components include read/write heads, guides, and rollers. In minicomputer and mainframe installations, tape drives should be cleaned once per shift and whenever permanent errors are encountered. Read/write heads and tape cleaner blades should be cleaned twice per shift and immediately before any critical operation. Tape-drive guides must be properly adjusted to prevent edge damage.

SUMMARY

Within computer storage media, electronic records are organized into files that are grouped into directories and, in the case of high-capacity media, subdirectories. These entities are sometimes equated with the familiar components of paper-based filing systems. Although such comparisons are somewhat forced, electronic storage media can be viewed as the computer-based counterparts of file cabinets, while directories and subdirectories are compared to drawers or portions of drawers. In graphical computing environments, directories and subdirectories are typically represented by folders, while files are represented by icons. The term *file* is seldom applied to audio and video recordings, but parallels can be drawn with individual audio selections and video programs contained on a given tape or disk.

Systematic file grouping and labeling practices are prerequisites for effective management of electronic records. Clear, informative labeling is essential for identification of removable computer, audio, and video media. In computer applications, internal volume labels should also be assigned. Unrelated files should not be intermixed within media, directories, or subdirectories. Meaningful file and directory names are critical for accurate identification. Such names should reflect the purpose and contents of specific directories and files. Increasingly, computer operating systems permit long file and directory names. Even where constraints are imposed by the operating system, mnemonic names that reflect file content can usually be devised, and file extensions can be effectively utilized to designate particular file types. Despite proper naming practices, files may become "lost" within high-capacity storage media. Addressing this problem, utility programs are available that will search all or part of a designated medium for files containing specified character strings.

Records management application (RMA) software is designed to categorize, store, and control electronic records throughout their life cycles. Available products can import electronic records in various formats from their originating applications and index them for retrieval when needed. Useful features include flexible retrieval capabilities, version control functionality, audit trails for reference activity, and automatic deletion of electronic records when their retention periods have elapsed.

A wide variety of filing equipment is available for removable electronic media. In large, active filing areas, shelf- or rack-type cabinets have historically been preferred for their high media capacities. Models are available for various combinations of disks and tapes. Mixed-media units can accommodate different sizes and types of media on interchangeable shelves and racks. Drawer-type cabinets are suitable for smaller electronic media, including magnetic tape cartridges, diskettes, certain optical disks, audio cassettes, and video cassettes. Other filing configurations include desktop trays, binders, and tub files. Motorized filing devices employ mechanical components to deliver electronic media to users, thereby saving labor and speeding retrieval in active records management installations.

Autochangers, also known as jukeboxes and library units, are available for optical disks and magnetic tapes. They provide unattended, near-line access to large quantities of electronic records. Optical disk autochangers are widely implemented in electronic document imaging implementations. Magnetic tape autochangers permit unattended backup of hard drives in mainframe, minicomputer, and LAN server installations. Autochangers also play an important role in hierarchical storage management (HSM) configurations.

Formalized guidelines for the storage, care, and handling of magnetic and optical media can minimize the potential for damage to electronic records, thereby increasing the likelihood that such records will remain useful for their intended purposes. Such guidelines must cover the selection of blank recording media, storage environments, and media handling procedures and precautions. Organizations should purchase high-quality blank magnetic and optical media from known manufacturers. Such media should fully comply with the requirements of the equipment in which they will be recorded or read, and they should only be used for their intended purposes. New rather than recycled media should be utilized for important electronic records intended for long-term retention. Prior to use, unrecorded media should be stored under conditions recommended by their manufacturers.

Working copies of magnetic and optical media are designed to satisfy ongoing information processing and reference requirements. Storage copies, in contrast, are created for retention or back-up purposes. Strict environmental controls, minimization of contaminants, and proper handling procedures are essential if storage copies are to remain useful for the maximum possible time. To provide the greatest protection for very important electronic records, two or more storage copies should be created. A clean storage area with tightly controlled temperature and relative humidity must be provided. Storage copies of magnetic and optical media should be inspected at regular intervals. To avoid damage from careless handling or improperly adjusted equipment, storage copies should be referenced as infrequently as possible. Careless handling is a common cause of physical damage to working copies of electronic media. Proper handling procedures must be strictly enforced. Equipment that creates and retrieves electronic records must be properly maintained.

APPENDIX A:

GLOSSARY

The following listing provides brief definitions of selected terms and acronyms pertaining to electronic records as they are used in this book. For fuller explanations of specific terms, consult relevant portions of individual chapters.

A

advanced intelligent tape (AIT)—an eight-millimeter tape cartridge format developed by Sony.

alloy—a combination of two or more metals. Many magnetic and optical recording materials consist of alloys.

American Standard Code for Information Interchange (ASCII)—a widely utilized coding scheme that specifies bit patterns for computer-processible information.

analog coding—a coding scheme in which information is represented by continuously varying signals. Electronic records created by many audio and video systems employ analog coding.

ASCII text file—a file that contains characters represented by the American Standard Code for Information Interchange. ASCII text files, which can be produced by many word processors and other computer programs, are typically devoid of formatting information.

audio interchange file compression (AIFC)—a compression method for digitized audio information.

autochanger—a robotic retrieval unit that provides unattended access to information recorded on optical disks or magnetic tapes; also known as a *jukebox*.

B

backup—the process of duplicating information, primarily for protection against damage or loss.

Beta format—a half-inch video tape cassette format introduced by Sony Corporation in 1975.

bit-mapped image file—a computer-processible file that encodes images as patterns of dots, each represented by one or more bits that define the tonal values of a given area within an image.

bits per inch (bpi)—the most common measure of linear recording density in computer systems.

C

camcorder—a video camera that incorporates a video cassette recorder.

chromium dioxide—a type of magnetic recording material employed by certain half-inch magnetic tape cartridges and by IEC Type II audio tape.

Code of Federal Regulations (CFR)—recordkeeping requirements for U.S. corporations, government agencies, and other organizations.

coercivity—the amount of force, usually measured in oersteds, required to orient magnetic particles.

cold site—an unfurnished space suitable for the installation of computer and communications equipment. An alternative facility that is void of any resources or equipment, except air-conditioning and raised flooring, that can be used as a backup site for disaster recovery.

comma separated values (CSV)—a computer file format for importing and exporting spreadsheets and databases.

compact disk (CD)—the designation for a group of optical disk products based on specifications developed jointly by Sony and Philips. Compact disk formats are available for audio signals, computer data, and other information. Each format is identified by its own acronym.

compact disk–read-only memory (CD-ROM)—a read-only optical disk format for computer-processible information.

compact disk–recordable (CD-R)—a write-once optical disk in the compact disk format.

compact disk–rewritable (CD-RW)—an erasable optical disk in the compact disk format.

computer graphics metafile (CGM) format—an image file format supported by many computer programs.

C-type cassette—a four-millimeter magnetic tape format used for audio recording and, occasionally, data storage; also known as a *Philips-type cassette*.

D

data archiving—the process of transferring electronic records from on-line storage devices, such as hard drives, to removable recording media, such as magnetic tape or optical disks, for off-line storage. In most cases, the archived data is relatively inactive and does not need to be accessible on-line.

data compression—techniques implemented through computer programs that reduce the amount of storage space required for a given quantity of information. Data compression is encountered in computer, audio, and video systems.

digital audio tape (DAT)—a four-millimeter magnetic tape format utilized for audio or data recording.

digital coding—a coding scheme that represents information by predetermined sequences of bits. Electronic records created by computer systems employ digital coding, as do certain audio and video records.

Digital Data Storage (DDS) Manufacturers Group—organization that defines specifications and data recording formats for digital audio tape.

digital linear tape (DLT)—a high-capacity recording media that uses half-inch magnetic tape enclosed in a plastic cartridge.

digital video (DV) cassette—a magnetic tape format for digital video recording.

digital videodisk (DVD)—an optical disk format intended as a successor to compact disks. DVD formats include read-only, recordable, and rewritable varieties, each identified by its own acronym.

direct-access storage device (DASD)—a hard disk drive in a large computer installation.

directory—a table of contents for an electronic storage medium.

diskette—a platter-shaped magnetic recording media with flexible substrates; also known as a *floppy disk.*

drawing interchange format (DXF)—a file format used by computer-aided (CAD) design programs.

dye-based recording—a recording process employed by certain optical storage products, including compact disk–recordable.

E

eight-millimeter tape—a magnetic tape format for data and video recording.

electronic data interchange (EDI)—a standardized method of electronically transmitting and processing data from one computer to another.

electronic record—a record that contains machine-readable, as opposed to human-readable, information.

encapsulated postscript (EPS)—a vector-based image file format based on the PostScript page description language.

extended binary coded decimal interchange code (EBCDIC)—a coding scheme that specifies bit patterns for computer-processible information.

extension—an optional addition to a file name available with certain computer operating systems. It typically indicates the type of information the file contains.

F

Federal Rules of Evidence (FRE)—rules governing the types of information acceptable as evidence in a federal court proceeding.

field—a data element within a database record.

file—a general term that denotes a collection of records. In most cases, the term is modified by one or more adjectives that indicate the type of information in a file, the applications it serves, or its relationship to other files.

fixed magnetic disk drive—a magnetic disk drive with nonremovable, rigid platters. It is the most common type of hard disk drive.

floppy disk—a platter-shaped magnetic recording medium with a flexible substrate; also known as a *diskette.*

G

gamma ferric oxide—a widely utilized material for magnetic recording. It consists of small iron particles that are dispersed in a binder compound on disk or tape substrates.

graphics image file (GIF) format—a widely utilized format for computer images in Internet, intranet, and extranet implementations.

Group 3—a file compression method employed in electronic document imaging and facsimile installations.

Group 4—a file compression method employed in electronic document imaging and facsimile installations.

H

half-inch data cartridge—a magnetic tape format developed by IBM and subsequently adopted by other manufacturers. Examples include the 3480, 3490, 3490E, and 3590 magnetic tape formats.

hard disk—a type of magnetic disk that has a rigid aluminum substrate. Hard disks are the storage media of choice in high-performance computing applications. Hard disks may be fixed or removable.

hard disk array—a group of hard drives that are treated by a computer as a single logical drive for recording and retrieval purposes.

hard disk cartridge—a rigid magnetic disk enclosed in a removable plastic cartridge.

hard drive—a magnetic disk drive with a nonremovable hard disk.

helical scan recording—a method of magnetic tape recording that uses two or more read/write heads to record data in narrow diagonal tracks.

hierarchical storage management (HSM)—a data storage management strategy in which special software is used to separate active and inactive computer data by migrating files between primary and secondary storage media.

high-definition television (HDTV)—a technology that increases the amount of detail visible in television images.

hot site—a fully equipped, standby computing facility available to subscribers for emergency use on short notice. An alternative facility that has the equipment and resources to recover the business functions affected by the occurrence of a disaster.

hypertext markup language (HTML)—a mark-up language used for formatting information on the Internet and in intranets and extranets.

I

image file—a file containing computer-processible images.

International Electrotechnical Commission (IEC)—the group that standardized designations for magnetic materials employed in audio tape recording.

J

JBIG—an image compression method developed by the Joint Bi-level Experts Group.

JPEG—an image compression method developed by the Joint Photographic Experts Group.

jukebox—a robotic retrieval unit that provides unattended access to information recorded on optical disks or magnetic tapes; also known as an *autochanger*. A storage device that holds optical disks or tapes and has one or more drives that provide automatic on-line access to the information contained therein.

K

key field—a field selected for indexing records contained in a database.

L

linear tape–open (LTO)—a magnetic tape technology for computer data.

longitudinal recording—a form of magnetic recording in which magnetizable particles are oriented horizontally within tracks on a disk or tape.

M

machine-readable information—information in a coded form suitable for processing by computers or other machines such as audio or video devices. Electronic records, by definition, contain information in machine-readable form.

magnetic card—an obsolete, rectangular medium coated with a magnetizable recording material.

magnetic disk—a platter-shaped substrate coated with a magnetizable recording material.

magnetic tape—a thin ribbon or strip of polyester coated with a magnetizable recording material; it may be wound on a reel or packaged into a cartridge or cassette.

magneto-optical disk—a rewritable optical disk that uses lasers to record information on a magnetizable material.

metafile format—a computer file format that transcends specific programs.

microcassette—an audio tape recording format utilized in voice dictation systems.

microfloppy disk—a 3.5-inch diskette.

minicassette—an obsolete audio tape recording format utilized in voice dictation systems.

mini-DV cassette—a digital videotape recording medium used in camcorders.

minifloppy disk—a 5.25-inch diskette.

MPEG-2—a compression method developed by the Motion Picture Experts Group for such applications as digitized video images and computer animation.

MP3—a compressed file format for digital audio information.

N

near-line storage—an autochanger that provides unattended access to information recorded on optical disks or magnetic tape.

nine-track tape—a magnetic tape that contains information recorded in nine parallel tracks running the length of the tape. Nine-track tape is one-half inch wide and is wound around a reel.

NTSC standard—a television standard developed by the National Television Systems Committee.

O

oersted—a measure of coercivity in magnetic recording systems.

off-line information—information stored apart from the device on which it will be retrieved or played back.

on-line information—information immediately and continuously available to a computer.

optical cards—wallet-size media coated with an optical recording material; also known as *optical memory cards.*

optical disk—a platter-shaped medium on which information is recorded by altering the light reflectance properties of selected areas.

optical tape—a ribbon or strip of polyester coated with an optical recording material.

P

paper tape—an obsolete computer format that stored digitally coded information as predetermined patterns of holes punched into a paper ribbon.

phase alternation line (PAL) format—the standard format for television images.

phase-change recording—a type of optical recording that employs materials capable of changing from a crystalline to an amorphous state, or vice versa.

Philips-type cassette—a magnetic tape format utilized for audio recording and, occasionally, data storage; also known as a *C-type cassette.*

portable document format (PDF)—a file format developed by Adobe for machine-readable documents with complex formatting characteristics.

punched card—a paper card that contains characters represented by predetermined patterns of holes punched in designated columns.

Q

QIC formats—a group of standard recording formats for quarter-inch magnetic tape cartridges.

quadraplex recorder—an older type of video recorder that utilized two-inch tape.

R

read-only optical disk—a type of optical disk that contains prerecorded information. Produced by a mastering and replication process, such disks have no recordable properties.

redundant array of inexpensive disks/redundant array of independent disks (RAID)—these devices are hard drive arrays with fault-tolerant attributes.

remanence—the magnetism that remains in magnetic recording material when an external magnetic field is removed.

removable disk systems—magnetic or optical disk systems that permit removal of platter-shaped media from drives on which they are recorded or read. The removable disks may feature rigid or plastic substrates. They are often encapsulated in protective cartridges to facilitate handling.

rewritable optical disk—a type of optical disk that permits erasing and overwriting of previously recorded information.

S

SECAM—the Sequential Couleur a Memoire format for television images.

serpentine recording—a recording format that features two or more groups of parallel tracks that run from the beginning to the end of a magnetic tape and back again.

source documents—paper documents that contain information to be converted to electronic records. A record—hard copy or original—on which an original transaction was captured.

standard generalized markup language (SGML)—a markup language adopted by the U.S. Department of Defense for its Computer-aided Acquisitions and Logistic Support (CALS) initiative.

substrate—the base material on which a recording layer is coated, as applied to electronic storage media. Substrates may be rigid or flexible. They are usually platter-shaped or ribbon-shaped.

SuperDisk—a high-capacity floppy disk format, also known as *LS-120*.

super-VHS (S-VHS)—a variant of the VHS videotape recording format that yields high-quality images.

SYLK—a file format developed by Microsoft for the interchange of information among computer programs.

T

tag image file (TIF) format—an industry standard format supported by many computer-generated imaging programs.

tellurium—a recording material employed by some optical disks.

text file—a computer file that contains character-coded representations of letters of the alphabet, numeric digits, punctuation marks, and other symbols encountered in typewritten documents. Text files may be created by word processing programs, electronic mail programs, or other computer software.

Type I magnetic tape—audio recording tape coated with gamma ferric oxide.

Type II magnetic tape—audio recording tape coated with chromium dioxide.

Type IV magnetic tape—audio recording tape coated with iron particles.

U

U-matic—an obsolete video recording format that utilized three-quarter-inch tape enclosed in cassettes.

Underwriters Laboratories (UL)—a testing laboratory that rates file cabinets for resistance to tampering and rates fire-resistant properties of insulated storage containers. UL also tests various consumer products.

unicode—a computer coding scheme that can represent many different characters in multiple alphabets.

Uniform Rules of Evidence (URE)—a set of rules governing items admissible into evidence in U.S. courts.

V

vector-based image format—a method of defining computer-processible images as geometric shapes; also known as *object-oriented* or *shape-defined images.*

VHS—a half-inch video tape cassette format.

VHS–Compact (VHS-C)—a variation of the VHS format designed for use with camcorders.

video disk—a platter-shaped medium that stores video images accompanied by audio signals. Most video disks are read-only media.

virus—a computer program that replicates itself into other programs that are shared among systems with the intention of causing damage.

vital record—a record that is essential to an organization's mission. A record identified as essential for the continuation or survival of the organization if a disaster strikes. Such records are necessary to re-create the organization's legal and financial status and to determine the rights and obligations of employees, customers, stockholders, and citizens.

volume—a logical subdivision created when a physical storage medium, such as a magnetic disk, is partitioned into segments.

W

waveform audio file (WAV) format—a format for digital audio information.

write-once optical disk—a nonerasable type of read/write optical disk; also known as a *WORM disk*. A digital optical disk on which data is recorded once and can be read as often as necessary.

APPENDIX B:

SUGGESTIONS FOR FURTHER STUDY AND RESEARCH

Since the early 1980s, electronic records have been discussed in a large and rapidly growing body of books, articles, conference papers, and other publications containing more detailed or otherwise different treatments of topics covered in this book. Library databases, which are widely searchable at library Web sites, are the best resources for citations to books and monographs about electronic records. Large national and academic libraries are likely to have the most complete holdings. The Library of Congress catalog (www.loc.gov) is a good starting point. "Electronic Records" is a Library of Congress subject heading, as are "Computer Storage Devices," "Data Recovery (Computer Science)," "File Organization (Computer Science)," "Magnetic Recorders and Recording," "Magnetic Disks," "Magnetic Tapes," "Optical Disks," and "Optical Storage Devices."

Various business indexes and databases contain citations to articles about electronic records in professional journals, popular periodicals, and newspapers. Examples of on-line databases likely to be available in many medium-size and larger academic and public libraries include ABI-Inform, Business and Management Practices (BaMP), Business and Industry Database, Business Dateline, General Businessfile, Globalbase, Management Contents, Newsletter Database, PROMT, Trade and Industry Database, and Wilson Business Abstracts. Articles indexed in these databases range from brief overviews of electronic recordkeeping issues and concerns to detailed case studies that describe records management practices in specific companies or government agencies.

Scientific and technical databases index articles, reports, conference papers, and other publications that deal with trends and innovations in information storage. They also index the capacities, performance attributes, life spans, and other characteristics of specific magnetic and optical media. Examples of such databases include Abstracts in New Technology and Engineering (ANTE), Computer Database, Ei COMPENDEX (Engineering Index), Information Science Abstracts,

INSPEC, SciSearch (Science Citation Index), and Wilson Applied Science and Technology Abstracts.

The legal status of electronic records, particularly their role in evidence, is examined in hundreds of articles in law reviews and other legal publications. The well-known Lexis and Westlaw on-line services provide the most comprehensive indexing of these legal information sources. Other useful legal databases include the Legal Resource Index and the Wilson Index to Legal Periodicals and Books.

Many Web pages contain information about issues and concerns relating to systematic management of electronic records. The best single reference source is the Records and Information Management Resource List (www.infomgmt.home-stead.com), which can also be reached through links at the Web pages of ARMA International (www.arma.org), PRISM International (www.prismintl.com), and other organizations. It categorizes and provides links to hundreds of sites about electronic records in addition to many other topics. Search engines, such as Google or Alta Vista, are obvious starting points to locate pertinent Web sites, but the voluminous results they deliver can require time-consuming browsing. At the time of this writing, for example, a Google search for Web pages containing the phrase "electronic records" retrieved over 144,000 items covering policies, procedures, practices, projects, and problems in varying levels of detail and with varying degrees of reliability and usefulness. When searches are narrowed to focus on specific topics, fewer items are retrieved, but the results are still unwieldy. For example, a Google search for "electronic records" and "vital records" retrieved over 2,600 items, and a search for "electronic records" and "file formats" retrieved over 1,300.

The Web sites of national, state, and provincial archival agencies contain much useful information about electronic records, including policies, procedures, and position papers. Examples include the Web sites of the U.S. National Archives (www.archives.gov), National Archives of Canada (www.archives.ca), National Archives of Australia (www.naa.gov.au), and British Public Records Office (www.pro.gov.uk). Readers are cautioned that Web addresses and site contents are subject to change.

INDEX

A

accelerated aging tests, 117, 168
access software, 138
acclimatization, 170
adhesive labels, 171
administrative (operational) retention criteria, 95
Administrative Procedures Act, 109
administrative retention requirements, 112
admissibility into evidence, 103
advanced intelligent tape (AIT), 35
American National Standards, 12
American National Standards Institute (ANSI), 163
American Standard Code for Information Interchange (ASCII), 54, 59
analog coding, 1
annualized loss expectancy (ALE), 133
ANSI character set, 55
application directory, 151
archival media, 116
archival records, 93
areal density, 22, 43
ARMA International, 187
arrangement, 82
ASCII character sets, 59
ASCII text files, 59
AU file format, 69
audio cassettes, 158, 170
audio file, 53, 147
audio file formats, 68
audio interchange file compression (AIFC), 67, 70
audio interchange file format (AIFF), 67, 70
audio tape cassettes, 84
audio tapes, 37
auditing for compliance, 144
Australian Archives Act, 14
Australian Electronic Transaction Act, 111
Australian Securities and Investment Commission, 99

authentication, 104, 106, 119
autochangers, 43, 159
autochangers and hierarchical storage management (HSM), 159
automated information system, 8, 75
automated recordkeeping systems, 8

B

backup, 21, 26
back-up file, 53
back-up procedures, 140
back-up protection, 165
back-up schedules, 140
back-up site, 142
Baudot code, 56
Bernoulli Box, 27
best evidence rule, 106, 108
Beta format, 39, 40
Betacam format, 40
binary coded decimal (BCD) code, 55
binder hydrolysis, 166
binder, 20, 158
bionic verification methods, 138
bit-mapped image files, 62, 65
bits per inch (bpi), 28
British Public Records Office, 188
British Standards Institution (BSI), 163
business indexes and databases, 187
business records exceptions, 107

C

California Corporations Code, 100
camcorder, 40
Canadian Personal Information Protection and Electronic Document Act, 125
Canadian Privacy Act, 125
Canadian Uniform Electronic Evidence Act, 105
carousel files, 159
C-format recorders, 39

checklist for inventorying electronic records
    series, 80
chromium dioxide, 21, 29
circulation control records, 136
Code of Federal Regulations (CFR), 97
coding schemes, 54
coercivity, 36
cold site, 142
color-coded adhesive labels, 150
comma separated values (CSV), 61
Commerce, Department of, 98
compact disk (CD), 38, 43, 45, 46, 68, 84
compact disk audio (CDA) format, 68
compact disk autochangers, 160
compact disk-digital audio (CD-DA), 46
compact disk-read-only memory (CD-ROM),
    46, 68
compact disk-recordable (CD-R), 46, 117, 162
compact disk-rewritable (CD-RW), 46
compression algorithms, 86
computer-aided acquisitions and logistic sup-
    port (CALS), 58, 62
computer-aided design (CAD), 24, 62, 75
computer graphics metafile (CGM) format, 64
computer-output microfilm (COM), 1, 10, 75
Computer Security Act, 123, 126
computer security committees, 122
concepts and issues, 1
consultation method, 78
copy type(s), 81
crystallographic information file (CIF) format, 65
C-type cassettes, 38, 68

D
data archiving, 21, 24, 26, 29, 93, 116
data backup, 13
databases, 3, 60, 113
data compression, 29, 30
data distribution, 21
data elements, 150
data interchange format (DIF), 60
data migration, 13, 118
data warehousing, 113
dates covered, 82
DDS-DC format, 36
Delaware Code, 100
desktop storage racks, 158
Deutsche Industrie Normen (DIN), 163
digital audio tape (DAT), 35, 36, 38, 84, 141
digital coding, 1
digital data storage (DDS) format, 36

Digital Data Storage (DDS) Manufacturers
    Group, 36
digital line graph (DLG) format, 65
digital linear tape (DLT), 31, 84, 141
Digital S media, 41
digital signature, 110
digital video (DV) cassette, 40
digital video / versatile disk (DVD), 43, 46, 84
direct-access storage devices (DASD), 21
directory, 147
disaster recovery plans, 142
disk array, 22
disk file, 53
diskettes, 25, 84, 117, 137, 172
disposition instruction codes, 155
document content architecture (DCA) format, 57
documentation, 144
domains, 20
drawer-type filing cabinets, 158
drawing (DWG) format, 64
drawing interchange format (DXF), 64
Drug Enforcement Administration, 99
DVD-Audio disks, 69
DVD formats, 43
DVD media, 46
DVD-ROM, 47, 68
D-VHS, 41
DXF CAD, 65
dye-based recording, 46

E
eight-millimeter data cartridges, 34, 84, 141, 158
eight-millimeter tape, 40
electronic commerce, 3, 8
Electronic Communications Privacy Act, 125
electronic data interchange (EDI), 8, 98, 100
electronic document imaging systems, 9, 62, 101
electronic mail, 112
electronic recordkeeping systems, 7
electronic records, 8, 11, 14
electronic records as official copies, 95
electronic signature, 110
Electronic Signatures in Global and National
    Commerce Act, 110
electronic source records, 95
encapsulated PostScript (EPS), 64
erasable optical disk formats, 47
E-Sign bill, 110
establishing the program (vital records), 123
estimated growth, 83
estimated life spans, 163

evidence, 103, 188
exercising (magnetic tape), 169
extended binary coded decimal interchange code (EBCDIC), 55
extensible markup language (XML), 58
extension(s), 65, 152

F
Federal Acquisitions Regulations, 99, 103
Federal Food, Drug, and Cosmetic Act, 99
Federal Rules of Evidence (FRE), 105, 107, 108, 109
field, 60
file, 53, 147
file compression, 65
file formats for electronic records, 53
file names, 149
file type, 81
fixed magnetic disk drive, 21
flat files, 61
flexible image transport system (FTTS), 65
floppy disks, 21, 25, 27, 149
Food and Drug Administration (FDA), 99
formats for compound documents, 57

G
gamma ferric oxide, 21, 25
General Accounting Office, 116
general concerns, 13
general retention schedule, 91
general support systems, 124
geographical information systems (GIS), 62, 64
graphical interchange file format, 63
graphics image file (GIF) format, 63
Group 3 compression algorithm, 63, 66
Group 4 compression algorithm, 63, 66
growth of electronic records, 3

H
half-inch data cartridges, 29, 141
half-inch magnetic tape cartridges, 84
half-inch magnetic tapes, 28
half-inch reel tape drive, 28
hard disks, 21
hard disk array, 22
hard disk cartridges, 24, 86, 149
hard drive, 5, 10, 12, 21, 22, 23
hardware environment, 86
hearsay, 106
helical scan recording, 35
hierarchical storage management (HSM), 160

high bias cassettes, 38
high-definition television (HDTV) format, 68
Hollerith code, 56
hot site, 142
human-induced events, 130
hydrolysis, 163
hypertext markup language (HTML), 55
hypertext telecommunications protocol (HTTP), 55

I
identifying risks, 130
identifying vital records, 127
image files, 61, 147
importance of electronic records, 7
important records, 128
inadequate controls, 9
information life cycle, 14, 16, 113
information redundancy, 10
initial graphics exchange specifications (IGES), 64
integrated retention schedules, 92
Internal Revenue Code, 100
International Electrotechnical Commission (IEC), 38
International Organization for Standardization (ISO), 68, 163
inventory follow-up, 89
inventory methodology, 77
inventory scope, 72
inventory strategy, 72
inventorying electronic records, 71
IRS Revenue Procedure 98-25, 100
issues and concerns, 8
IT9.23 standard, 166

J
Japanese Standards Association (JSA), 163
JBIG compression algorithm, 66
Joint Photographic Experts Group, 64
JPEG, 64
JPEG-LS, 66
jukebox, 43, 159

K
key field, 61

L
labels and names, 148
legal criteria, 94
Legal Resource Index, 188

legal retention requirements, 112
legal status of document images, 101
legal status of electronic records, 188
legal status of electronic signatures, 110
legally mandated retention periods, 96
Lempel-Ziv-Welch (LZW) compression
        algorithm, 63, 66
Lexis, 188
library unit, 159
light stability, 168
limitations of assessment periods, 109
linear tape-open technology, 31
longitudinal recording, 34
lossless compression algorithms, 66, 102
lossy compression algorithms, 66
LTO Accelis, 32
LTO Ultrium, 32

M

machine-readable information, 8, 19
magnetic cards, 42
magnetic disk, 2, 12, 21, 147
magnetic disk drives, 21
magnetic media, 20, 172
magnetic tape, 11, 15, 21, 28, 32, 93, 117, 137,
        140, 147, 149
magnetic tape autochangers, 159
magnetic tape cassettes, 56
magnetic tape drive, 5, 11, 28
magnetic tape libraries, 136
magnetism, 19
magneto-optical cartridges, 45
magneto-optical (MO) disks, 43, 44, 117
magneto-optical drives, 45
managing files and media, 147
managing vital electronic records, 121
markup codes, 58
markup formats, 58
markup languages, 58
mass storage peripherals, 159
master copies, 165
master file, 53
master retention schedule, 91
media capacity, 19, 150
media characteristics, 85
media compactness, 141
media filing equipment, 155
media filing repositories, 136
media handling, 14, 171
media management, 161
media manufacturing date, 85

media stability, 12
media stability and system dependence, 115
metadata, 154
metafile formats, 62
microcassette, 38
microfiche, 10, 157
microfilm, 2, 11, 12, 98, 157
microfloppy disks, 26
migration, 161
minicassette, 38
mini-DV cassettes, 41
MiniDisc, 45
minifloppy disks, 25
mission-critical applications, 7, 15, 22, 128
mission-critical electronic information, 4
mixed-media storage units, 157
Model Law on Electronic Commerce, 99, 111
motorized filing devices, 159
MP3 format, 67, 69
MPEG-2 standard, 68

N

National Aeronautics and Space Administration,
        116
National Archives and Records Administration
        (NARA), 30, 97, 101, 154
National Archives of Australia, 188
National Archives of Canada, 14, 188
National Information Infrastructure Protection
        Act, 125
National Institute of Standards and
        Technology (NIST), 124
native formats, 53
natural disasters, 130
near-line access, 159
near-line information, 87
New York Electronic Signatures and Records
        Act (NYESRA), 111
nine-track computer tapes, 28
nine-track magnetic tapes, 28, 30, 84, 117, 141
nine-track tape drive, 28
nonproprietary file formats, 153
normal bias cassettes, 38
NTSC standard, 67
Nuclear Regulatory Commission, 103

O

obsolete magnetic media, 42
obsolete optical disk formats, 48
Occupational Safety and Health Administration
        (OSHA), 99, 100

oersteds, 36
official copy(ies), 96, 119, 154
off-line information, 87
off-site storage repositories, 87, 141
OMB Circular A-130, 124
on-line information, 87
on-line peripherals, 159
operational retention parameters, 112
operational retention periods, 113
optical cards and tape, 49
optical cards, 49
optical character recognition (OCR), 54
optical disk, 12, 19, 43, 93, 137, 147
optical disk autochanger, 160
optical disk cartridge, 15, 43, 84
optical disk drives, 9
optical disk libraries, 43
optical disks for computer recordkeeping, 48
optical media, 2, 19, 172
optical memory cards, 19, 49
optical tape, 19, 49, 50
other computer tape formats, 37

P

paper-based electronic media, 50
phase alternation line (PAL) format, 68
phase change recording, 46, 47
Philips-type cassettes, 38
physical storage requirements, 84
planetary data system (PDS) format, 65
playback stability, 115
portable document format (PDF), 58, 63
portable network graphics (PNG) format, 64
preventive measures, 135, 145
PRISM International, 188
privacy statutes, 125
probability estimates, 133
program components, 13
program-specific retention schedule, 91
proprietary file formats, 53
protective measures, 135, 139
Public Health Services Act, 99
punched card, 2, 50
punched paper tape, 2, 51, 56

Q

QIC formats, 32
QIC-Extra cartridge, 34
QIC-Wide format, 34
quadraplex recorders, 39
qualitative risk assessment, 131

quantitative risk assessment, 132
quantitative risk assessment, formula for, 133
quantity, 83
quarter-inch magnetic tape cartridges, 32, 84, 158
questionnaire method, 78

R

raster-based image files, 62
read-only optical disks, 44
read privileges, 138
read/write head, 20, 27
real audio (RA) format, 69
reciprocal back-up arrangements, 142
recordable optical disks, 44
recording density, 25, 28, 150, 165
recording stability, 115
records, defined, 14
records and information management resource
     list, 188
records inventory, 71, 91
records management application (RMA) soft-
     ware, 153
records series, 74, 79
redundancy, 11, 16
redundant array of inexpensive/independent
     disks (RAID), 23, 140
reel-to-reel tape drive, 28
reference activity, 87
relationship to human-readable records, 88
remanence, 21
remote access, 12
removable hard disks, 21, 23, 24, 115
removable media, 93, 115, 137, 149, 161
renewing, 169
research criteria, 95
retensioning, 169
retention concepts, 93
retention criteria, 94
retention requirements, 88
retention schedule, 15, 91
retention schedules for electronic records, 91
Revenue Canada, 101
rewritable optical disks, 44
rich text format (RTF), 57
risk analysis, 123, 129
risk assessment, 129
risk control, 134

S

scientific and technical databases, 187
search engines, 188

Securities Exchange Commission, 103
security copy, 81, 135
selecting blank media, 162
Sequential Couleur a Memoire (SECAM), 68
series title, 80
serpentine recording, 29
shelf-type filing cabinets, 156
Singapore Electronic Transaction Act, 111
Society of Motion Picture and Television
     Engineers, 167
software distribution, 26, 29
software environment, 86
sort field, 61
sort key, 61
source documents, 8, 72, 104
spatial archive and interchange format (SAIF), 65
spatial data transfer standard (SDTS), 65
spreadsheet files, 59
stability, 15, 115
standard generalized markup language
     (SGML), 58
statutes of limitations, 110
storage copy(ies), 15, 81, 138, 163, 165, 171
storage location(s), 85
storage media for electronic recordkeeping, 19
storage peripherals, 148
subdirectories, 147
substrate, 20, 44, 164
suggestions for further study and research, 187
summary description, 81
Super Digital Linear Tape (SDLT), 31
super premium products, 164
SuperDisk, 26, 27
Super-VHS (S-VHS), 40, 86, 163
supporting files, 88
survey instrument, the, 79, 94
Swiss Federal Law on Data Protection, 125
SYLK format, 60
system dependence, 11

T
tag image file (TIF) format, 63
tagged image file (TIFF) format, 63
tags, 58
tape file, 53
temporary file, 53
text files, 54
timesharing, 9
transaction-oriented records, 114
transparent arrangement, 12
Transportation, Department of, 99

Travan technology, 34
Trojan horse, 131
tub files, 158
Type I magnetic tape cassettes, 38
Type II magnetic tape cassettes, 38
Type IV magnetic tape cassettes, 38, 86

U
U-Matic cassettes, 39
U-Matic systems, 39
U-Matic tape, 39
U-Matic videocassette players, 86
Underwriters' Laboratories (UL), 139
Unicode, 55
Uniform Business Records as Evidence Act
     (UBREA), 107
Uniform Commercial Code, 110
Uniform Electronic Transactions Act (UETA), 111
Uniform Photographic Copies Act (UPA), 101
Uniform Photographic Copies of Business and
     Public Records as Evidence Act, 101,
     108, 109
Uniform Preservation of Business Records Act,
     97
Uniform Rules of Evidence (URE), 105, 107,
     108, 109
United Kingdom Data Protection Act, 125
United Kingdom Electronic Communications
     Act, 111
United Kingdom Public Records Act, 14
United Nations Commission on International
     Trade Law (UNCITRAL), 99
update file, 53
user retention parameters, 112
U.S. National Archives and Records
     Administration (NARA), 30, 97, 154, 188

V
vector-based images, 62, 64
Vermont, State of, Insurance Division, 100
VHS-Compact (VHS-C), 40
VHS format, 39
VHS video cassettes, 163
video cassettes, 84, 158, 170
video disks, 3, 49, 173
video file, 53, 147
video image communication and retrieval
     (VICAR) format, 65
video recording standards, 67
video tape libraries, 136
video tapes, 39, 98

virus, 130
vital electronic records, 13, 16
vital electronic records program, 15
vital record status, 88, 127
vital records, 15, 121
vital records program, 121
vital records protection, 15, 16, 121, 127
vital records repository, 141
vital records survey, 127
volume, 148
volume labels, 150

W

waveform audio file (WAV) format, 69
Westlaw, 188

wheeled carts, 158
Wilson Index to Legal Periodicals and Books, 188
word processing files, 56
working copy(ies), 15, 81, 135, 165, 171
World Wide Web Consortium (W3C), 63
WORM media, 44
worm, 131
write privileges, 138
write-once optical disk drives, 86
write-once optical disks, 44

Z

Zip drive, 27

ABOUT THE AUTHOR

William Saffady, Ph.D., is a Professor at the Palmer School of Library and Information Science, Long Island University, where he teaches courses on information management topics. He previously held similar faculty positions at the State University of New York at Albany, Vanderbilt University, and Pratt Institute.

Dr. Saffady is the author of over three dozen books and many articles on records management, document imaging, information storage technologies, office automation, and library automation. Recent books published by ARMA International include *Micrographics: Technology for the 21st Century*; *Cost Analysis Concepts and Methods for Records Management Projects*; *Electronic Document Imaging: Technologies, Applications, Implementations*; *Computer Storage Technologies: A Guide for Electronic Recordkeeping*; *Knowledge Management: A Manager's Briefing*; *The Value of Records Management: A Manager's Briefing*; *The Business Case for Systematic Control of Recorded Information*; and *Records and Information Management: A Benchmarking Study of Large U.S. Industrial Companies*.

In addition to teaching and writing, Dr. Saffady serves as an information management consultant, providing training and analytical services to corporations, government agencies, and other organizations.

ABOUT
ARMA INTERNATIONAL

ARMA International is the leading professional organization for persons in the expanding field of records and information management.

As of September 2002, ARMA has about 10,000 members in the United States, Canada, and 37 other countries around the world. Within the United States, Canada, New Zealand, Japan, Jamaica, and Singapore, ARMA has nearly 150 local chapters that provide networking and leadership opportunities through monthly meetings and special seminars.

ARMA's mission is to provide education, research, and networking opportunities to information professionals, to enable them to use their skills and experience to leverage the value of records, information, and knowledge as corporate assets and as contributors to organizational success.

The ARMA International headquarters office is located in Lenexa, Kansas, in the Kansas City metropolitan area. Office hours are 8:30 A.M. to 5:00 P.M., Central Time, Monday through Friday.

ARMA International
13725 W. 109th St., Ste. 101
Lenexa, Kansas 66215
800.422.2762 – 913.341.3808
Fax: 913.341.3742
hq@arma.org
www.arma.org